CRITICAL ACCLA   THE SLOW FOOD MOVEMENT

'Slow Food stands for sanity   world.   stands for civility, diversity and
dignity, for the right of people **Leal**   n food ltures. It stands against
commercial imperialism, gastr ꟼ ꟼ   ogenis   on and the diminution of human
pleasures. Aside from that, it's a rather splendid organisation.'

Matthew Fort, Food Editor, *The Guardian*

'Through Slow Food I met the most generous, thoughtful, and passionate young
people driven to change everything vile, corrupt and wrong in the harvest of food for
our table – a loud voice of angry revolution that is so great and reassuring now.'

Dan Lepard, Artisan Baker

'Poetry, proof of multiple wild habitats, exquisite nutrition, and the welfare of coastal
micro socio-economies all intertwine when we consider the noble wild salmon.
Threatened in Europe and Atlantic North America, she departs and takes her magic
with her. In Ireland we see the Slow Food "eco-gastronomic intervention" making a
critical contribution to the wider efforts to conserve salmon for her own sake.'

Mark Boyden, Stream Scapes Director and Coordinator
of the Irish Smoked Wild Atlantic Salmon Presidia

'The first time I heard about Slow Food, over a decade ago, these two small words
made perfect, revolutionary sense. They still do.'

Clarissa Hyman, Glenfiddich Food Writer of the Year, 2002

'It not just about the food, it is about the way we must live.'

Oliver Peyton, Restaurateur

'Slow Food reinforces the links between passionate producers and consumers who
care.'

Randolph Hodgson, Neal's Yard Dairy

'Slow Food encompasses so much that I feel strongly about – sustainability by
diversity – the right to choice in the food we eat.'

Darina Allen, Ballymaloe, Cork, Ireland

'For producers, Slow Food is both a benchmark and an umbrella under which to
shelter against growing red tape – it offers us small producers an incentive to not be
dragged down the commercial route.'

Peter Gott, Sillfield Farm, Cumbria

slow food

Collected Writings on
Taste, Tradition and
the Honest Pleasures
of Food

FOREWORD BY CARLO PETRINI

GRUB STREET · LONDON

This edition published in 2003 by
Grub Street
The Basement
10 Chivalry Road
London
SW11 1HT
Email: food@grubstreet.co.uk
www.grubstreet.co.uk

Text copyright © Slow Food Arcigola Editore srl – Bra (Cn) 2003
Copyright this edition © Grub Street 2003

British Library Cataloguing in Publication Data
   Slow food: collected thoughts on taste, tradition and the
   honest pleasures of food
   1. Food 2. Food – Philosophy
   641.3'001

ISBN 1 904010 23 7

Cover design by Hugh Adams, AB3 Design
Typeset by Pearl Graphics, Hemel Hempstead
Printed and bound in Great Britain by Biddles Ltd, King's Lynn

CONTENTS

FOREWORD • Carlo Petrini 7

INTRODUCTION
Slow Food UK • Wendy Fogarty 9
Slow Food Ireland • Clodagh McKenna 11
Slow Food Australia • Sophie Herron 12

ONE: SOUR POWER
Balsamic Vinegar • Giorgio Triani 14
Pickles • Elisabeth Clift 18
Chutneys • Radha Kapoor-Sharma 21
Vinegar and Provence • Misette Godard 25

TWO: PIQUANCY
Kindling the Japanese Flame • Sylvie Guichard-Anguis 30
Chilli Pepper • Vito Teti 33
Spices and Aromas • Françoise Aubaile-Sallenave 38

THREE: CORKS AND BUBBLES
Nursery Slopes • Michel Smith 42
Sherry • Julian Jeffs 45
The Enviable Profession • Stephen Brook 48
The French Selection • Roger Feuilly 50
The Queen Bee • Hugh Johnson 54
Vermouth • Piero Sardo 60
The Origins of Champagne • François Bonal 63
The Revival Route • Michel Smith 67

FOUR: STREET FOOD AND MARKETS
Shopkeepers and Peddlers • Nelly Krowolski 73
Sunday Morning in Limogne • Annie Hubert 76
Falafel • Philip Sinsheimer 80
Khao Soy and other Noodles • Annie Hubert 84

FIVE: BEER AND FAR
5000 Varieties • Manfred Kreiner 87
Ale Movement • Lesley Chamberlain 90
Holland, Pilsner and the Others • Grazia Solazzi 93

Bar-Restaurant-Bazaar • Lesley Chamberlain 95
Belgian Paradise • Davide Faggioli 98
The Post-Industrial Pint • Michael Jackson 101

SIX: ANOTHER WORLD
The Devil's Avocado • Daniel Chavarria 106
Frozen Fast Food • Pier Lorenzo Tasselli 113
Mapping What We Eat • Marco Riva 120
More from Less • Vic Cherikoff 125
The Banquet •Raymond Buren 128

SEVEN: TAPAS
En Sevilla • Enrique Bellver 132
Remember Spain • Carlos Delgado 134
Without a Tablecloth • Carlos Delgado 138
A Lifestyle • Manuel Vázquez Montalbán 140

EIGHT: HOT POT
The Convict's Diet • Annie Hubert 143
Either Milk or Fish • Hocine Benkheira 149
Herring Countries • Jørgen Mønster Pedersen 153
A Latter-Day Religion • Lesley Chamberlain 157
Paul's Lunch • Laurence Ossipow 160
The Rigours of Snacking • Sylvie Guichard-Anguis 167
Venus in the Supermarket • Lesley Chamberlain 170

NINE: HOME ON THE RANGE
What a State • John Irving 173
The Great British Trifle • Sarah Freeman 176
The Poets' Lakes • Laura Mason 179
The New Ireland • Roz Crowley 183
Salt, Fat and Smoke • Regina Sexton 187

Contributors' List 190

FOREWORD
Carlo Petrini

$\mathcal{T}$he cultural goals of the international Slow Food movement are: to defeat all forms of chauvinism, to re-appropriate diversity and to indulge in a healthy dose of cultural relativism.

Slow, the international herald of taste and culture, our quarterly review, first saw the light in April 1996 when it was published in three editions: Italian, English and German. The eleventh number (September 1998) was also published in Spanish and French editions, and *Slow* thus began to speak five languages. It is now published ten times a year in Italian under three different titles – *Slow*, *SloWine* and *SlowArk* – and several numbers are also available in English, German, French and Spanish.

Slow focuses on the geography of food and consumption and trends in taste, *SloWine* speaks about wine, beer, spirits and travel, and *SlowArk* addresses biodiversity, the Slow Food Presidia and traditional local food and beverages. Edited by Alberto Capatti – an intellectual who has played a fundamental role in the study of the history and trends of European gastronomic culture – *Slow* is now in its seventh year, and the volume you have in your hands provides an opportunity to reflect upon its importance for the development of our movement.

Browsing through the titles chosen to group together the excerpts from the review, you have an overview of the topics it has addressed over the years, and reading the articles you will note crossovers of significant ideas. Biodiversity, defence of local cultures, the Ark project, a firm stand on biotechnologies, animal well-being – these are just some of the themes that have characterized Slow Food's activities over the last few years.

From the Ark idea, for example, we have developed the Presidia, concrete initiatives to reactivate economies tied to products on the verge of extinction. Wherever it has been applied, the Presidia project has always worked very well indeed, and we are now striving to promote it planet-wide.

The Slow Food Award for the Defence of Biodiversity is presented every year to people whose research, production, marketing, popularisation or documentation activities benefit biodiversity in the agro-industrial field. It is closely linked to the Presidia project in so far as many of the winners produce or safeguard products or produce worthy of support and protection. Recently the Slow Food Foundation for Biodiversity has been formed to collect donations from every corner of the world to fund the project.

To supplement and enhance all this, Slow Food recognises the need for education in the fields of taste, food and agriculture. It thus brings consumers, experts and producers together in initiatives such as Taste Workshops, 'Master of Food' courses, the University of Gastronomic Sciences (to be inaugurated in 2004), collaborations with primary schools, and the publications of its publishing house, Slow Food Editore.

Down the years, *Slow* has accompanied all the movement's manifold activities, stressing how it has developed from being a purely food and wine – eno-gastronomic – association into an *eco*-gastronomic champion of vegetable, animal and cultural diversity. Not that we have ever forgotten our origins as lovers of the pleasure of food, wine and conviviality and as revivers of a passion for slowness, such an indispensable instrument for improving the quality of our lives. In its pages, *Slow* relates the Slow Food adventure and describes the prospects for the movement's future developments.

Slow Food now boasts more than 70,000 members all round the world, a vast global network of men and women capable of generating ideas and programmes to defend taste and the right to a responsible, knowing form of pleasure; one that is respectful of cultural and material diversity, and one in which all can share. Distinctive in style, *Slow* is the *fil rouge* which sews this network together, representing it as it evolves. Born with the Internet, but printed on paper, written by collaborators from many, many countries and produced in the small market town of Bra in Piedmont, *Slow* is not only the organ but also the cultural pulse of Slow Food.

SLOW FOOD UK

Wendy Fogarty

Slow Food began in the United Kingdom in 1997 with the creation of the first convivia (local chapters) in the rural Cotswolds and in metropolitan London. Since this time, the culinary landscape of England, Scotland, Northern Ireland and Wales has undergone somewhat of a cultural revolution as a succession of food scares and increased concern for sustainability have given rise to heightened consumer awareness and a renewed passion for all that is local, regional, traditional and new. Suddenly, regional diversity is being celebrated and our small producers are the heroes of the British table.

This change in sensibility has been in no small way precipitated by the vigorous growth of food and farmers' markets in rural and urban areas and at the time of writing, there are over 390 farmers' markets alone and the calendar year is once again filled with local food festivals, agricultural shows, weekly and monthly fresh produce markets. In London, Borough Market has returned to its roots as 'London's Larder', drawing in producers from around the country and becoming such a centre for culinary excellence that it is winning praise nationally and internationally from everyday folk and opinion leaders.

The renewed passion for all that is regional, seasonal and artisanal, has also spurred the growth of Slow Food in Britain where there are now over seventeen convivia located in villages, towns and cities – from Aberdeen in the north, to York in the east, to Carmarthenshire in the west, Frome in the south west and the village of Rushden in the south east. The convivia are characterised by an incredible diversity that reflects the local distinctiveness of their regions, but in common and through their programme of events (producer visits, taste workshops, seminars and dinners) they are helping local communities to rediscover their landscapes and culinary treasures and are giving voice to producers.

Slowly but surely, a new era has dawned from Britain's culinary heritage, but our small producers remain under threat from super-hygienist legislation which can stifle artisanal production and which add incredible costs to production and stress to farmers and producers. Not least of all, they have the potential to denude the British table of taste, tradition and diversity. The challenge for Slow Food in the United Kingdom is to continue to celebrate our regional diversity, and to offer small farmers and artisans whatever protection we can – by helping to raise their visibility and accessibility and by giving consumers as many reasons as possible to support them.

Through Slow Food's unique taste workshops, the development of the British Ark of Taste and Presidia, the proposed children's taste education programme, our participation in Slow Food's key international events, (Cheese and the Salone del Gusto), and the creation of national events, we will work towards achieving these aims and towards the development of a vibrant food culture in Britain. In this regard, some milestones have already been achieved: in 2001 Trade Partners UK (a division of the Department for Trade and Industry) provided vital financial support to enable many of our cheeses to be showcased in the Great Hall of Cheese and in 2002, 45 producers from as far afield as the Highlands and Islands of Scotland, to the Isle of Man, the Cumbrian fells and the Cornish coast, participated at the Salone del Gusto, thanks to the invaluable support of Food from Britain and the government's Foot and Mouth Recovery programme – collaborations that will continue. Publications like *Slow* also give us freedom of speech and an opportunity to encourage a wider appreciation of the products, producers and people that we celebrate. For Slow Food in the UK, our work has only just begun! To the many members, like-minded associations and organisations who have worked with us, we thank you for your energy and support and look forward to future collaborations.

SLOW FOOD IRELAND

Clodagh McKenna

Suddenly it seems that everyone in Ireland is talking about Slow Food. At a macro level government is starting to take notice, the media is giving us coverage and we are attracting the support and interest of important decision makers. At a micro level membership is rising, events are overbooked and – most importantly of all – the movement is capturing the imagination of consumers.

What is making Slow Food so successful?
For anyone with even a passing interest in food, Ireland has become an extremely exciting place to live or visit. Of all the many developments, two are particularly thrilling. The first is the emergence of the producer as hero. After a long period of being ignored farmers, fishermen, growers and artisans are being recognised – and rewarded – for the skill and care they devote to their chosen work. The second is the rapid expansion of farmers' markets and specialist food shops. Over a relatively short period high quality, often locally produced food has become widely available. Crucially, the sense of connection between producer and consumer – which was under threat – is growing stronger. As a result everyone is benefiting. Producers are enjoying increased demand for their goods. Consumers are being offered a previously inconceivable range of produce.

The last year has brought many Slow Food triumphs. Ireland's first Presidia, to celebrate wild smoked salmon, has just been convened and further Presidia are being discussed including Raw Milk Cheese and the Kerry Cow. There are already five very active convivia and more are being planned. We have produced our first Slow Food Guide containing details of over 50 producers. We have also organised our first major national event – a Slow Food Weekend – which attracted over five hundred participants.

SLOW FOOD AUSTRALIA

Sophie Herron

*W*ith our diverse, buzzing and multicultural food culture, Slow Food has found a ready home in Australia, where the movement has been active for almost a decade. Slow Food Australia's sixteen convivia are establishing themselves in all parts of the country, memberships are ever-growing, and new groups are steadily popping up all over the place. From Sydney's slick eateries to the beaches of Byron Bay and just around the corner from Coffs Harbor's Big Banana, Slow Food is catching on in Australia.

One of the most significant events recently held by Slow Food Australia was the 2nd National Congress, held at Mildura, Victoria. Here, on local chef Stefano Di Pieri's historic riverboat *The Avoca*, around 150 delegates assembled to review the structure of the movement and launched three major new projects: the Australian Ark of Taste, the Slow Rivers Initiative and a project to host a Southern Hemisphere focused version of the Salone del Gusto in Melbourne, 2005.

Outgrowing its early days as a fledgling gastronomic group, Slow Food Australia is now enthusiastically adopting a clear educational and eco-gastronomic agenda. The Ark of Taste and Slow River projects alone are working towards promoting, protecting and doing all they can to support Australians working for sustainability and to define and protect our food culture and excellent culinary standards.

As with Slow Food in any country in the world, it's the people behind the movement that give dynamism and a future to the movement. Australia is lucky to have a group of wildly passionate eco-gastronomists driving the movement, from Slow Food Australia Governor James Broadway to campaigners for food quality, diversity and education such as Stefano Di Pieri, Stephanie Alexander, Maggie Beer, Margaret Alcock and Joanna Savill.

And an ever growing group of passionate convivia leaders and Slow Food contributors around Australia are working harder than ever to infuse their diverse regions with Slow Food ideals and philosophies. Farmers' markets for example, are a burgeoning phenomenon in Australia, supported and often driven forward by Slow convivia leaders and members and Slow Food Brisbane is soon to inaugurate the world's first Slow Food Library in conjunction with the State Library of Queensland.

There is a great sensibility to Slow Food in Australia and its story is just about ready to take off, with one of the Southern Hemisphere's biggest food festivals planned for 2005, under the umbrella of Slow Food Australia. The future looks bright and very slow.

BALSAMIC VINEGAR
Giorgio Triani

*T*he genesis of typical products – by which I mean 'real' typical products – is always cloaked in mystery. Maybe that's what makes them typical! The products at the top of any scale of typicality are unrepeatable because the factors and processes that have combined to make them possible are not entirely clear. The balsamic vinegar of Modena (like its neighbour, the *culatello* of Zibello) is one such product. For a start, the environmental, climatic and cultural characteristics of the limited area in which it is produced are not all that different from those of the broader surrounding area. The fact is that throughout the Emilian plain, from Piacenza to Bologna and along the lower Po Valley, the natural and human environment is more or less the same. Yet *culatelli* and balsamic vinegar are only made in the provinces of Parma and Modena (and to a lesser extent in that of Reggio). True, 'more or less' may mark the imperceptible distance that makes the difference between a good cured meat and a good vinegar and an extraordinary delicacy and an extraordinary condiment. Yet it is also true that no historical, scientifically valid reason exists to explain why, how and when balsamic vinegar – the fruit of a very complex technique and manufacturing process – began to be produced. As a result, comparative analysis simply cannot tell us why such a refined, special 'culture of vinegar' grew up and developed in Modena and in no other province of Emilia.

The authoritative work on the subject is *L'aceto balsamico tradizionale di Modena*, edited by Gianni Salvaterra for the producers' consortium and published by Calderini. This study explains that 'the story of how balsamic vinegar came into being is too old to be told with absolute certainty. Some reckon that its birth was a chance event: a certain amount of boiled wine "must" (the *saba* used in Modenese cooking) must have been forgotten in a jar somewhere, then found later in an advanced state of acetification.' But surely similar phenomena must have taken place on countless occasions in other areas of Italy without giving rise to a special way of producing vinegar. So it certainly wasn't only a question of chance. For example, the *Vita Mathildis* written by the

Benedictine monk Donizone recounts that Matilde's father Bonifacio was producing a fine vinegar in the castle of Canossa in 1046, yet the term 'balsamic' was only associated with vinegar for the first time in 1747, when it featured in the *Register of grape harvests and wine sales on behalf of the Private Ducal Cellar* of the Duke of Modena.

A gastronomic glory

The exceptional nature of the balsamic vinegar of Modena is also implicit in the obvious historical observation that vinegar was used by the earliest civilizations. The Egyptians, Chinese, Greeks and Romans knew how to produce it and use it accordingly as a condiment, a drink and medication. In the Middle Ages, the alchemist physician Basilius Valentinus wrote that 'in medicine and alchemy, it is impossible to do anything useful without the help of vinegar'. Later, during the cholera epidemics of the late-nineteenth century, vinegar was officially recommended for washing fruit and vegetables. Vinegar, in fact, can be used not only as a disinfectant but also as a preservative. Indeed, until recent years it played a predominant role in the tradition of marinating food. Today the tendency is to consider it an almost residual ingredient in the fine art of *haute cuisine*, though in the classic 'oil and vinegar' formulation of everyday salads and greens, its presence is perceptible as a contrast to the food thus dressed.

Until a few decades ago, the renown and use of Modena balsamic vinegar was exclusively confined to the area in which it is produced. Pellegrino Artusi failed to mention it in his classic *La scienza in cucina e l'arte di mangiar bene*, while Luigi Carnacina, the chef who left his mark on cooking in the Fifties and Sixties, was unaware of its existence. It was not until the Eighties that the balsamic vinegar of Modena rose to gastronomic glory, and this was entirely thanks to *La cucina regionale italiana*, a collection of recipes by that great innovator of national cuisine, Gualtiero Marchesi. Once Marchesi had set the trend, the product lost no time in achieving international recognition and making its appearance on the tables and menus of international *haute cuisine*. This speedy elevation of status actually coincided with the passage from essentially domestic production largely for home consumption to market-oriented production. It is a change of profile that is very recent. Not until 1965 did a ministerial decree establish precise 'Characteristics of composition and methods of preparing the balsamic vinegar of Modena'. The Ministry of Agriculture and Forestry finally granted the DOC designation in 1983, while the producers' consortium came into being in 1979.

Though official recognition of a typical product may respond to a particular demand, the actual development of the market for this product obviously depends on a number of social and cultural factors that can influence scale of production and the reach of the product, both nationally and internationally. What counts is clearly the values and perceptions of individuals and groups as they go about the business of eating both in their own homes and elsewhere. Diet and hunger, the two extremes of gastronomy, appear to converge in the case of balsamic vinegar. Indeed, this actually explains balsamic vinegar's rise to cult product status, a must on any table. Without overly stretching the point, it could be said that the success of Swatch watches is a textbook case of the same phenomenon. Swatches possess the same capacity to evoke and satisfy a very widespread social feeling, which goes under the name of 'mass elitism'. This is a deceptive but effective way to meet the general public's need for 'designer' products. For the fact is that 'true' balsamic vinegar remains a product accessible only to the happy few: those who can count on cultural and gastronomic as well as financial capital. Let me explain. Balsamic vinegar can be found both cheaply on supermarket shelves and in specialized food shops and delicatessens in phials that are as tiny as they are expensive. There is obviously an abyss between the two products, the first being a normal wine vinegar with added caramelized sugar, the second the result of 12 years' ageing, 25 in the case of a refined extra-old variety. For the moment, however, the image of the product counts more than the product itself.

Global and local

The reasons for this are many and various. The first is that the name 'balsamic vinegar' sounds good, while the product itself has a very characteristic colour and flavour, plus that touch of eccentricity that never goes amiss. As a 'balsam' it conjures up images redolent with heady nature and its gifts, the healthy ones that are bound to be 'good for you'. With its pronounced but delicate flavour, it heightens the taste of meats, sauces and especially the vegetables and salads that are no longer necessarily a side dish in these days of fashionable diets. In fact the increased consumption of vegetables with the advent of the most wild and wonderful dressed and mixed salads is the main cause for the growing balsamic vinegar craze.

There is no doubt that it is a remarkably versatile product, able to satisfy both the palates of people on low-calorie diets and those of connoisseurs attracted by the significant variations in taste it can create. Balsamic vinegar should be used neither too abundantly nor too parsimoniously. As the producers' guides and manuals prescribe, 'balsamic vinegar is versatile, but also tricky. If you don't know how to use it properly, you risk ruining everything. Oddly enough, it is impossible to establish how much to use and when. In short, balsamic vinegar is a solo player; so it's best to savour it first on the tip of a tablespoon and gradually assimilate its rotundity or its tart acidity (. . .). For special uses, deciding on the right amount is up to the sensitivity of the user.'

To cut a long story short, balsamic vinegar is literally the acid test of gastronomic skill, though its internationalization is more a matter of savour than savvy. It owes much of its success in English-speaking countries (especially the States), the rest of Europe (especially Germany) and Japan to the appeal of refined Italian-made niche products in general. It manages to be 'glocal', at once global and local, exotic and national, typical of its place of origin and adaptable to the tastes of consumers the world over. Crossing the classic geographical and gastronomic borders, it has become a part of the most various national and traditional cuisines. In oriental cuisine, for example, it is a perfect replacement for soy sauce, while in the USA it is ideal as a barbecue sauce. Likewise, it goes well with northern European dishes and supplements wine vinegar in meat and fish marinades.

In conclusion, what better image than that of balsamic vinegar ice-cream to sum up the success of this strongly typified product in the modern cuisine? A bittersweet image blending history and modernity, mixing classicism and extravagance and bringing together high and low, far and near. An image that stands for the strength and independence implicit in the belief that anyone anywhere can 'invent themselves a tradition' on the basis of the conviction that balsamic vinegar of Modena is the mother of all vinegars.

PICKLES
Elizabeth Clift

*P*ickles must surely qualify as the poor relation in the context of the history of food. They suffer from such a lack of documentation that it is difficult to place them in a historical context. Though they have always been a way of preserving vegetables and fruit (and thus valuable vitamins) through winter periods and storing gluts of valuable crops, unlike other forms of preservation, they do not seem to have enjoyed any great periods of particular fashion and popularity. In fact pickles seem never to have benefited from imaginative treatment in general; except perhaps in America where the word 'pickle' refers to a pickled cucumber of which there are now some fifty or more variations, depending on type of processing, flavouring and cut of the 'pickle'. Indeed in America the 'pickle' has found its way into some incredible concoctions: pickle loaf luncheon meat for example! A staggering 5 million pounds of pickles are consumed daily in America, and Pickle Packers International Inc. even defines the perfect 'pickle' as having no less than seven warts per square inch.

It is generally agreed that the Egyptians and Sumerians discovered fermentation about 2000 BC and with it the ability to preserve fruit and vegetables, particularly the cucumber, a plant introduced to the Tigris valley from the Indian continent. Some 1500 years later Roman civilization had mastered the art of preserving by salting, and the combined techniques led to what we know today as pickling . . . a vegetable first steeped in brine or dry salt and then preserved in acetic acid.

Pickles are rarely mentioned in early historical manuscripts, though cucumbers feature here and there in the Old Testament. 'We remember the fish which we did eat in Egypt freely; the cucumbers, and the melons, and the leeks, and the onions, and the garlick,' wail the people of Israel when faced with a diet of manna. Among the ancients, Aristotle, Cleopatra and Tiberius are all thought to have appreciated the qualities of the 'spiced and preserved cucumbers' mentioned in Pliny's writings. Julius Caesar included them in his legionaries' rations, and the quartermasters for the early merchant seamen were later to follow suit, since such provisions were a guard against scurvy during the long sea voyages. Pickles turned up again in French army rations during the Napoleonic wars, and I was curious to discover that they also featured in the American troop rations of the Second World War. But then given that nation's 'pickle' consumption, perhaps it's no wonder.

It was during the thirteenth century that pickles gained a place in the diet of the English aristocracy. Indeed, they became a dish in their own right at feasts at the court of King John. For pickles were more than a way of preserving food, although this was obviously important. They also gave piquancy to a diet that must often have been very bland. By the time Gervase Markham came to write *The English Housewife* in 1615, the range of pickles had increased to encompass samphire, asparagus, onions as well as cucumbers and a 'world of others too tedious to mention'. Most were consumed as 'sallats', and Markham goes on to describe a very elaborate one suitable for a great feast fit for princes. It contained almonds, raisins, capers, olives, currants, red sage and spinach, all mixed together with sugar and then placed in a dish with vinegar, oil and more sugar. Thin slices of orange and lemon were laid over this, followed by a layer of well pickled cucumbers, a layer of shredded cabbage lettuce and a further layer of oranges and lemons. This leaves out the other prized ingredient for sallats, the pickled flowers that Markham advises the prudent housewife to preserve in distilled vinegar to keep their colour.

It is worth considering the main preserving ingredients involved in this process, given that salt was an expensive commodity with great hierarchical traditions and grape vinegar was a luxury certainly not available to the ordinary households of northern Europe, where strong traditions of pickling were evolving. The salt used by all these busy housewives laying down their winter stores was not the expensively refined table salt, which was in any case too fine. For in England at least, the home-produced salt was augmented by Bay salt, a coarse dark salt full of impurities derived from the bay of Bourgeneuf and later from all down the French Atlantic coast. The coarseness was especially suited to preserving of all kinds, although one presumes that the clarity of some of the pickles may have been compromised a little. As for vinegar, for those without access to the grape verjus it would either have been made from strong ale fermented in the sun or from crab apples left to rot and then pulped by hand using wooden hammers and strained into barrels to be kept together with a dozen handfuls of damask rose leaves for every hogshead of verjus.

But what exactly is a pickle? I believe the British must be held responsible for any confusion in terminology between pickles, chutneys and relishes. The dreaded Branston pickle, the scourge of many a poor ploughman, is not a pickle at all but a chutney, and chutneys are a much later introduction into the European diet. A pickle is usually a vegetable first steeped in brine or dry salt and then preserved in liquid with a minimum acetic acid ratio of 5%. Refinements over the last centuries have been few and far between. Commercialism has crept in, but with little imagination, and the outcome has been a mouth-puckeringly sharp acid pickle.

The heartland of good pickles is still in the home though, with that band of dedicated store cupboardists who are often the backbone of the Women's Institute. A well-stocked store cupboard is something both to envy and to marvel at. I take great pleasure in viewing someone else's neatly stacked jars labelled and dated in neat little writing; even more fascinating is viewing a store cupboard in another culture to see the staple pickles of another country and of course to steal a few ideas to take home. There can be no one more smug than the prudent housewife on a cold damp winter evening reflecting on the contents of her store cupboard and deciding what crunch and flavour to eat with that evening's supper, particularly in the presence of unexpected guests.

For myself, I run a traditional country Inn with my sister in the depths of rural Worcestershire and for us our pickled store cupboard is an essential part of our menus throughout the year. Radishes, rocket pods and nasturtium seeds garnish cooked lamb dishes; carrot and celeriac sallat accompany dishes of cured pork; the strong little tree onions are served with bread and cheeses; sweet pickled damsons with rich vanilla ice-cream; pickled cherries go perfectly with cold spiced meats and smoked duck breast; autumn field mushrooms are a treat with smoked eels; and green walnuts and horseradish are a must for cold beef. Moreover pickled octopus and sepia fish (which almost fall over the fence into the chutney bracket, but I refuse to see them go) form part of a mixed hors d'oeuvres, and baby beetroots, both red and yellow, and red cabbage find their way onto the inevitable ploughman's plate.

Then of course there is the list of the pickles yet to be tried, given the availability of ingredients and time. This year I may travel with the big pan to be in the right place at the right time to try the central European plum and pepper pickles, the American bread and butter pickle that was taken from Europe by the early settlers, water melon rind, garlic – the possibilities are endless. Yet for most Europeans nowadays pickles imply little more than gherkins, onions and cucumber. If I have my way, the list will soon be expanding and pickles will again enjoy fortunes long lost.

CHUTNEYS

Radha Kapoor-Sharma

*T*he camera moves slowly around the rustic kitchen stopping an instant on the gleaming brass pots and pans before settling on the frame of a slim young woman in a simple cotton sari, her hair in an untidy knot at the back of her head. She delves deep into a large jar containing what appears to be mango pickle, leans back on her haunches and sucks noisily on a piece. An expression of pure contentment crosses her face. The subtle message of the scene is not lost on the Indian viewer: the young woman is evidently expecting a child.

This cinematic euphemism for pregnancy derives from the Indian woman's relish of all things sour, particularly pickles. Pregnancy of course only heightens this desire. Strangely in India, though men and women seem equally fond of salt and sweet dishes, the sour is largely the preserve of the woman. The taste for pickles and chutneys crystallizes early in childhood when young children are often fed from their mother's plate, but it is the girl child who, by virtue of hanging around the kitchen a great deal in traditional households, is unconsciously much more influenced. However, the initiation into the realm of the sour perhaps takes place when village children raid trees of the neighbourhood in search of tamarind or green mangoes. The prized fruit is dipped into salt (sometimes salt mixed with red chilli powder) and is immediately devoured with great zest. For city children the only readily available comparable substitute today is a wedge of lime covered with salt.

However, for urban and rural households alike, no meal is really complete without a judicious mix of the salt, the sweet and the sour. The sour takes several forms ranging from cooling drinks made from either lime juice or green mango pulp to a thin tomato-based sauce (*rasam*) that accompanies certain South Indian dishes and is either drunk from small bowls or is poured over steamed rice; from lentil dishes that are cooked with tamarind juice to vinegar blended meat preparations; from pickles that are made to last a full year to chutneys that can last a few days at most. Variety is definitely the life of Indian cuisine and it is the vast palette of pickles and chutneys made to tickle the palate that add spice to the meal.

21

Homemade

Pickles and chutneys form a vital part of an Indian meal and all self-respecting housewives ensure that their table boasts, if not of an array, then at least of one or two pickles or chutneys. Meant to be eaten in small quantities, both pickles and chutneys are accompaniments to the main meal and serve to perk up the fare offered. Sluggish summer appetites are revived with the addition of these relishes to the table. They are believed to aid digestion as well. In fact in South India the best way to end a meal is inevitably curd and rice with pickle. And astonishing though it may seem, in the South, a combination of *rasam*, pickle and rice is advocated in cases of nausea and retching.

Pickles and chutneys have been made in India for centuries and the recipes passed down zealously from generation to generation. English, French and other languages have borrowed the word 'chutney' and *achar*, the Indian word for pickle, has been incorporated into Portuguese and been adopted by English through the Portuguese. *Achar* carries the same meaning as pickle in English. To the popular mind pickle seems to be an innovation of the British that has spread its roots all over the world. This culinary 'imperialization' of a basic part of an Indian meal has only furthered the cause of pickles and the pickle industry.

Yet in India, though bottles and tins of pickles are sold in stores all over the country, each family prides itself on the homemade ones it can offer family members and guests. Pickles are basically made from seasonal fruits or vegetables (though meat and fish pickles also exist) and so 'pickling' time must carefully be set aside during the season of that particular fruit or vegetable when it is in abundance and therefore cheap. The summer months are the mango pickling months. Large jars, crocks and bottles are brought out in preparation. They are washed and dried very carefully, for one undetected droplet of water could cause the full year's supply of mango pickle to mildew. The fruit is washed and dried thoroughly before being cut into small pieces or strips according to the requirements of the recipe. Children happily join in the work as it is vacation time. The mango is then pickled with a host of spices and one or more preserving agent. Pickles are preserved with salt, oil (generally mustard oil), vinegar or lemon juice. Some are cooked while others are left to mature in the sun. The wait for sun-dried pickles to become ready for eating can seem painfully long for the young and even the not so young. Some condiments must be consumed within a few days whereas others can last years. The popular favourites are mango, lime, chilli, garlic, mixed pickle and in North India, a sweet and sour pickle made of winter vegetables like turnip, cauliflower and carrots. Pickles are adapted to family tastes. They vary from hot and sour to sweet and sour to tangy and spicy.

Two differences

Similarly, chutneys cover the full gamut of tastes but also include sweet and mild flavours. They are made from standard or seasonal fruits and vegetables, herbs and dried fruit or nuts. Chutneys differ from pickles on two counts essentially. The first is the consistency. Chutney is of a reasonably smooth consistency with the fruit or herb having been either ground to a paste or cooked to a mashed pulp. The grinding is usually done on a special flat stone called a *sil* with a small round stone called a *batta*, though electric grinders are now beginning to be used as substitutes. A mortar and pestle can also be used to pound the spices and other ingredients to a pulp-like texture. The requisite consistency is obtained by the judicious addition of water, vinegar, lime or tamarind juice. The second difference is that chutneys are made to be eaten fresh or within a few days at most. They generally contain no preservatives. Like pickles they add a new dimension to the meal, add colour to the table and revive dull appetites. What is more, they are particularly rich in vitamins. Coconut chutney is virtually an omnipresent feature of South Indian meals, whereas in the North, in Muslim and Hindu households alike, a hot favourite is mint chutney. This cooling relish goes well with both vegetarian and non-vegetarian dishes and can be put together in a jiffy. Mint chutney sandwiches are a very popular snack with children of today who love to take them to school for their mid-morning break; and they are equally popular with working mothers who are perpetually short of time. In India, chutneys are a daily affair, and therefore quick to make. They have nothing in common with their bottled counterparts in the West that are the end result of a fairly long cooking process, are sweeter, more elaborate and contain preservatives.

Still, for Indians living abroad the bottled varieties of pickles and chutneys remain a very welcome way of enlivening bland meals. However, since nothing can really compare with the homemade ones from back home, the earnest request of Indians abroad when asked what they'd like from India is inevitably some homemade pickle. A request that it is better to turn down heartlessly, unless you particularly like the look and smell of pickle oil in your suitcase!

Recipe for Mint Chutney
Ingredients
1 medium sized onion
a few cloves of garlic
1 sprig of mint leaves
2-3 sprigs of coriander leaves
1-2 green chillies
juice of 1 lime (*or* lemon)
salt to taste
1 small green mango (optional)

Method

Grind the onion, garlic, mint and coriander leaves coarsely in an electric mixer with one green chilli. Add some salt and the juice of half a lime and grind to a finer texture. Add more lime juice, salt and another green chilli if necessary after tasting. Mix a little water if you prefer a thinner consistency. Serve chilled.

All ingredients can be varied to suit personal tastes. The only important thing to remember is that the quantity of coriander should be double or more the quantity of mint. The inverse would result in a very bitter taste.

VINEGAR AND PROVENCE
Misette Godard

*V*inegar is wine that has gone acid, wine that has taken on a sour taste. While we appreciate smoothness in wine, it is pungency that we are looking for in vinegar, a taste that contrasts with the range of savours familiar to us. The search for diversity of flavour would appear to be universal, and people in the north of Europe who cannot count on vineyards compensate for this lack by making cabbage go acid and using its juice to replace vinegar.

In Mediterranean countries, people stopped preparing *sauerkraut* at the start of the last century. Their taste for wine fostered the cultivation of the vine, and wine and vinegar thus became easily available. Researching his major study of eating habits in Provence in the late Middle Ages[1], Louis Stouff unearthed no written recipes but only accounting records, contracts signed with fruit and vegetable growers and notaries' archives. From these documents it is possible to deduce what the eating standards were, but we have no evidence of ways of cooking and combining flavours.

It is not until the end of the nineteenth century that we find publications that include the typical recipes of Provençal cuisine. These are generally mixed in with other recipes of classic French cuisine, to which the Provençals turned for special meals such as weddings and christenings, which took place in private homes until relatively recently. Recipes using raw ingredients seem to have been reserved for different sorts of celebration, relating to work: a grand *ailloli* for the end of the harvest, for example, or a *bouillabaisse* for informal get-togethers down by the sea.

All late manuscript and published sources of the nineteenth century present the same association of two cuisines, classic and regional. Jean-Baptiste Reboul's well-known *La cuisinière provençale* is no exception. In the first edition, published in 1897 – lost without trace by the publisher and unfindable in libraries – the author explains that he has decided to confine himself to a 'well-defined context embracing only Provençal cuisine and little more . . .'. The warm reception reserved for the book and 'for each reprint, which was supplemented by appendices of some importance, though most of them did not refer to Provence

. . .' encouraged Reboul to 'carry on in the same direction'[2].

The book's sensational success pushed the *Manuel complet de la cuisinière provençale* by Marius Morard, a near contemporary of Reboul's, published in 1886, almost entirely into the shade. Morard's decision to publish more recipes reflecting Provençal habits[3], while highlighting differences between them[4], failed to pay off. Reboul was thus right when he argued that the public liked recipe collections that encompassed different contexts.

The principle was well grasped by the eponymous publisher of *Le cuisinier Durand* (1830). After noting that 'in France there are two cuisines, one in the north, another in the south', he goes on to point out that 'far from limiting itself to local necessities', his book also intended to take those of other countries into consideration, concluding that 'this creates a huge advantage; it makes the book a European work'[5]. Now Durand was the first chef to address the problem of Provençal cuisine in print. It is thus fair to say that once written recipes did appear in manuscript form and in books, readers have had to distinguish genuinely regional from more heterogeneous material.

Revolution and recipes

The name of a recipe may be explicit, as in the case of *'bouillabaisse'*, or misleading (*'moutarde de Provence'*, for example turns out to be a synonym of *ailloli*).

Over the years, the advent of 'American' vegetables turned every reference on its head. The tomato, initially a discreet presence, became the emblem of Provençal cuisine. Numerous waves of immigration also made their influence felt: *soupe au pistou*, for example, may have been of Genoese origin.

It is probably easier to understand the question if we consider the general context in which written recipes spread. They actually appeared in the decades that followed serious crises: the French Revolution, first of all, which provoked the downfall of the great households that were the depositories of tradition; the reorganization of the national administration, which was seen as a threat to everyone's cultural references; the continental blockade that marked the decline of the port of Marseilles; a cholera epidemic . . . and so on and so forth.

This situation is described in a manuscript in my possession. It was written by a cultivated woman, a reader of J. J. Rousseau and Grimod de la Reynière: 'Events were truly disastrous; many people accustomed to keeping domestic staff were reduced to having only one person, and a poor one at that. For the same reason, where once they ate the most delicate fare, they now have to make do with the plainest and grossest foods, which have to be cooked well and cheaply if they are to be decent.'

A few years later, in the preface to his book, Durand gives the impression that he has got the message: 'The haste shown by our fellow citizens in their insistence on seeing this long promised book published may account for some imperfections in the presentation . . .'[6]. He then goes on to say: 'economy, real economy, is the prime asset of our day . . .'[7].

Later authors show that they share the same concerns. In 1965, Louis Giniès observes that 'Provençal cuisine always has the advantage of being economical'[8]. This then is a well-established characteristic and one worth taking into account.

Vinegar is a condiment to be used as it is. It is produced in abundance and is thus cheap. In the eighteenth century, Dutch ships loaded barrels of vinegar at the port of Marseilles to sell in Russia, where it replaced the acid juice of *sauerkraut* in *borsch*. Our invaluable manuscripts confirm that a similar use was made of vinegar in Provence at the start of the nineteenth century. After all, it is a well-known fact that in times of penury there is a tendency to return to old habits. The Provençal version of the soup – made of barley, peas and potatoes, dressed with salt and vinegar and served with slices of farmhouse bread – is as poor as they come. One author, fond of the habits of the past, speaks admiringly of thick peasant soups, but none of them is dressed as roughly as the one I have described[9].

As such soups were abandoned, so the use of vinegar changed. Since it was always available in large quantities, its direct consumption decreased and was replaced by the pickled chopped vegetables brought by Dutch ships from India. Prepared in France with raw vegetables, such fare was known as *variantes* and was used to accompany cold meats. *Variantes* were always available at markets, where they were displayed to the public in large coloured buckets.

Vinegar production was largely absorbed by the caper industry. In the eighteenth century, Provence was already supplying the whole of Europe with capers[10]. At the time of Villeneuve, the business increased so much that, with cucumbers and mixed pickles, it used up two thirds of total vinegar production[11]. It was thanks to the use of pickled cucumbers and especially capers, both of them local products, that a hint of sourness was added to culinary preparations.

Marinades

Different types of marinades are prepared in Provence, together with all the classic vinegar-based sauces. *Anchoïade* and, above all, *ailloli* are typical. *Ailloli* long remained true to Pliny's recipe[12], before being transformed into a garlic mayonnaise in the course of the last century.

The use of pickled capers to add a sour flavour is extremely widespread. Capers are to be found in the sauce of the same name used to accompany fish, hollandaise sauce, beurre noire, and in mixed diced vegetables. *Raïte*, a sauce of olive oil, red wine and capers in abundance is typically Provençal. Recipe books recommend it with fried cod, but in families it is often served with cold cuts. Capers are also used in omelettes and to stuff olives.

Vinaigrette also plays a fundamental role, and the tradition of serving it with hot sweetbreads dates from the Middle Ages. Salads dressed with a vinaigrette are served as a starter to exalt the importance of the condiment. Provençals tend to regard lettuce as insipid for salad, preferring wild leaves. In the eighteenth century, Garidel[13] cites dozens of such leaves, and I have counted 40 in the manuscripts in my possession. *Mesclun*, a mixture of wild and cultivated leaves, is very much in vogue today, though not as much as *salade niçoise*, which would take a separate chapter to describe.

In this article, I have sought to fit Provençal cuisine into a precise time frame to save it from the usual clichés. From the time in which vinegar was used as a condiment for the soups of the poor to the vinaigrette used today to dress *salade niçoise*, Provence has evidently experienced a multiplicity of processes of evolution to which its cuisine has gradually adapted. In fact every wave of novelty has brought with it a batch of 'true' Provençal cuisine: from the infatuation of the European aristocracy and the leisured classes for the Côte d'Azur in the winter to the development of the port of Marseilles and nineteenth-century cruises; from the hordes of the first beneficiaries of paid summer holidays in 1936 to the fashion for holiday homes in the Luberon after 1960. Yet the lemon is still no match for vinegar in the art of 'tasty dressing'.

Notes

1 Louis Stouff, *Ravitaillement et alimentation en Provence aux XIVème et XVème siècles*, 1970.

2 Citations from the preface written by the author for the most recent editions.

3 It is certainly misleading to speak of 'the' *cuisinière provençale*, since more than one cook was involved. The one who cooks on the coast is of course different from the one you meet inland.

4 Morard, for example, lists as many as seven recipes for *bouillabaisse*. No doubt a record.

5 *Le cuisinier Durand*, preface, p. VI.

6 Durand, op. cit., preface, p. VIII.

7 Ibid, p. IX.

8 Louis Giniès, *La cuisine provençale*, 1965, p. 10.

9 René Jouveau, *La cuisine provençale de tradition populaire*, 1976, pp. 31-43.

10 Savary, *Dictionnaire universel de commerce, d'histoire naturelle et des arts et métiers*, 1762.

11 Villeneuve, op. cit., T. III, pp. 112-113

12 Pliny, *Natural History*, 19, 112.

13 Pierre-Joseph de Garidel, *Histoire des plantes qui naissent aux environs d'Aix et dans plusieurs autres endroits de la Provence*, 1718.

KINDLING THE JAPANESE FLAME
Sylvie Guichard-Anguis

One of the key expressions of gastronomic appreciation in Japan is a very precise statement uttered in a knowing tone: 'Assari shite iru', words that long left me utterly perplexed. As a compliment it is actually practically untranslatable. 'It is simple, light, pure' is about as close as you can get. The positive essence of the expression means that the natural flavours are simply heightened. To the churlish, on the other hand, it might seem a subtle way of saying that the food is insipid and tasteless.

Many Japanese like to boast of such 'delicate' palates that they can taste flavours that are not noticed by those whose taste buds have been ruined by an excess of food whose true savours are masked by all kinds of additives. I will always remember the student of Indian origin who made fried bread the night before leaving on a package tour because she deemed Japanese food to be 'utterly tasteless'.

Japanese cuisine, like French cooking, essentially relies on salt and herbs to bring out tastes. The meticulous Japanese student, asking a crucial question about salt during a cooking lesson, gives an inkling of the true importance of this ingredient, the use of which is taken for granted in other cuisines. Japanese *haute cuisine*, to which all the elegant *ryôtei* restaurants aspire, does not in practice make use of spices. It is in these restaurants, like the tea houses where the tea ceremony is performed, that the menus are almost sublimated in their pursuit of *assari* (simple) tastes. This cuisine is based on flavours that are free of artificiality, there is a strong link with the seasons, and great attention is paid to the appearance of the food, the arrangement of the ingredients and the choice of crockery.

Ingredients with strong flavours are not, however, entirely absent from Japanese culinary preparations. *Zanthoxylumsanshô*, the small seeds of which are used to decorate vegetable dishes or grilled meat, is surprising in the midst of a menu that focuses on much more subtle flavours. The same ingredient is sold as *tsukudani* (a preparation for preserving food, based on soya sauce, crystallized sugar and sake), which is used to flavour plain rice. Hot green peppers, or *shishitogarashi*, either toasted, fried or cooked slowly, provide a strong note in menus whose other flavours pale in the pursuit of natural tastes.

Marinated or fermented vegetables, *tsukemono*, such as *daikon*, a large white radish, turnips, eggplants and cucumbers are prepared with large quantities of hot red peppers. Since they are considered preserves, they are only put on the table at the end of the meal to accompany plain rice whose 'natural' flavour is the maximum expression of the concept of *assari*.

While respecting the traditional precepts, the cuisine of the Nagasaki region uses quantities of these red hot peppers in a sauce called *namban tsuke*, or 'Southern Barbarians' (the reference is to the Portuguese). Chicken pieces or fried sardines are marinated (*tsuke*) in a mixture of vinegar, sake, sugar and salt to which chopped red hot peppers, Japanese leeks and ginger are added.

Curries, Gratins and Spaghetti

Dishes of this kind, like the *tsukemono* with hot red peppers, suggest that spicy cooking was brought to Japan from other countries, particularly from neighbouring or distant Asian regions. For such appear to be the origins of some of the basic components of today's informal Japanese cuisine, which is both popular and economical. Far from using certain traditional Japanese ingredients, which have now become prohibitive for daily consumption, today's most widespread dish is simply curried rice, which is found throughout the Japanese archipelago. A deep plate is two-thirds filled with white rice onto which a ladleful of a thick yellowish sauce is spooned. The two-coloured effect is enlivened by a few slices of red candied ginger. Eaten with a soup spoon, this dish has an infinite series of variations: with minced or diced meat, vegetables, etc. It also features in a big way among the Japanese culinary innovations designed to save time: it can be bought ready-made in sealed packages or bags and then heated up. Indian restaurants that began popping up in major Japanese cities several decades ago testify to the integration of curry in Japanese eating habits.

Curried rice in Japan is considered a western dish, as are French gratins and Bolognese. In Japanese recipe books, authentically Japanese cuisine is distinguished from Chinese cooking. The latter is largely responsible for the first contacts with spices, due to the popularity of Sichuan cuisine. For most Japanese, the first encounter with spicy tastes is usually the tofu based dish, *mabodoiû*: cubes of tofu are heated in a very hot thick sauce enriched with minced beef.

Mutton is another ingredient that is not traditional to Japanese cooking, but which is now extremely widespread. It is grilled over a slab, which is placed on the table, cut into fine strips and dipped in sauces flavoured with hot red peppers.

This dish, which is perhaps a nomadic Mongol speciality, is duly referred to as *Gingisukan*, Genghis Khan!

The colonization of Korea and the Korean minority numbering several hundred thousand account for the fact that certain Korean dishes have been introduced into the everyday Japanese diet. There are many restaurants specializing in Korean grilled food. These restaurants are generally inexpensive and besides fillet steak they serve chitterlings (heart, tongue, tripe) marinated before being cooked in fairly strong sauces and accompanied by plain rice and *kimuchi*, hot pickled vegetables. The most common vegetables prepared in this way are *daikon*, or white cabbage, and cucumber, which are ever present at Korean meals, whether simple or grand. They are now so widely eaten that all large Japanese supermarkets stock them. In recent years interest in the cuisine of the Korean peninsula has widened beyond the basic dishes to include soups, and rice- and pasta-based dishes.

The most recent wave of spicy food to make its mark on Japanese eating habits dates back to the 1980s, with the arrival of a type of cuisine that was defined at the time as 'ethnic'. In fact it was Thai, Vietnamese and Indonesian food, which immediately became a hit. These dishes were said to stimulate the appetite even during the summer heat, which causes many problems in the Japanese archipelago. The use of fresh herbs and the different combinations of seafood, vegetables and meat, which the Japanese adore, were hugely successful among large sectors of the population. New gastronomic traditions along with the ability and desire to expand the traditional range of Japanese flavours are proof of great culinary curiosity. Japanese cuisine has been considerably enriched and will probably continue to be so in the future.

CHILLI PEPPER
Vito Teti

*O*ne of the earliest and most important descriptions of the use of chilli pepper in the cuisine and medicinal remedies of southern Italy was set down by Tommaso Campanella. In his *Medicinalium iuxta propria principia* (Lyons, 1635), a compendium of philosophical, botanical, dietary and anthropological interest, he describes and prescribes its use in both food and medicine. Campanella dwells on *piper rubrum indicum* when explaining how the aroma of certain plants is linked to the malefic influence of Mars (in those days the planets, plants, animals, men and disease were all held to be interrelated). The chilli pepper, is as hot as onions and strong vinegar, he claims, it causes the eyes to burn, and has a sharp, irritating flavour, like rhubarb and hellebore.

Many sources bear witness to the fact that from the end of the sixteenth century chilli pepper was increasingly used alongside the older aromatic plants, such as garlic and onions, in the popular cuisines of many Italian regions. It conferred a new taste to the monotonous, mainly vegetarian diet, just as meat was starting to become scarce for Mediterranean peoples, as Sereni and Braudel have pointed out. The earlier passion for pepper corn (which was one of the reasons for Columbus's voyage) was supplanted by the new passion for chilli pepper. The former was mainly a prerogative of the European élite, whereas the latter was embraced by the lower classes, who readily adopted a widely available condiment well suited to a vegetarian diet in which aromatic plants played a role of primary importance.

The fact that the new 'American' vegetable has generally been viewed as strong, common and inferior is probably due to the way it has been deliberately neglected by the culinary treatises of many European countries. For years the well-to-do considered chilli pepper to belong to the realm of unsophisticated vegetarian cooking. Hardly surprisingly, the codification of national Italian cuisine achieved by Pellegrino Artusi in his *La scienza in cucina* (1891), pays practically no attention to the food of the lower classes in southern regions (Calabria, Basilicata), and does not mention chilli pepper or other condiments. Indeed, chilli pepper does not appear to have been mentioned in cultivated spheres until 1931, when Marinetti's first Futurist dinner at the Taverna Santopalato in Turin included an entrée of green chilli peppers, salami, butter, pickled mushrooms and anchovies.

Despite the omissions of authors and recipe books that reflected middle-class tastes in central and northern Italy, chilli pepper had achieved due recognition among a number of Neapolitan gastronomists in the late eighteenth and early nineteenth centuries. In his *Il cuoco galante* (Naples, 1773), Vincenzo Corrado included a sauce of tomatoes, peppers or chilli pepper to flavour fried pork entrails, macaroni and fried salt cod. He also used chilli pepper in a 'garnish', or sauce made from various ingredients (cooked ham, finely sliced chicken breast, capers, pine nuts, pistachios, parsley, spices, beaten eggs, white wine, bay, coriander, cinnamon, salt, and what he terms 'American' peppers) and used for stuffing goats' heads.

Ippolito Cavalcanti in his *Cucina casarinola co la lengua napoletana* (Naples, 1839), published in appendix to the second edition of *Cucina teorico-pratica* (Naples, 1837), mentions chilli pepper in a recipe for tomato sauce. Tomatoes, boiled then sieved, and simmered with lard and oil, salt and chilli pepper, were used as a sauce over fish, meat, poultry, eggs and *'ncoppa a nzò che buò'* (over anything you want). Cavalcanti also advised the use of sweet peppers as well as chillis and tomato sauce, in a *'zuppa de zuffritto'* (fried onion soup), made with pork entrails (sliced lung, heart and kidneys). Split peppers together with tomatoes and aubergine, fried with oil, lard, garlic, salt, pepper and a strong chilli pepper, made up the *'piatto d'erba stomaco'* (dish that is good for the stomach).

Dried, ground, imbibed

Until fairly recent times the folk remedies of Southern Italy included an infusion made with dried and ground chilli peppers. This shows how difficult it is to separate *haute cuisine* from the traditional cooking typical of working families in the South. In fact both approaches to food preparation owe something to each other. The renewal of 'Mediterranean cooking' has borrowed a great deal from the New World, and in so doing actually owes a great deal to those Neapolitan chefs who had an open-minded attitude both to 'foreign' *haute cuisine* and to the cooking habits of ordinary southern Italians.

Chilli pepper was preserved in various ways: dried and hung on balconies and in windows; ground to a powder in mixers or pounded in mortars; mixed with water and salt; infused in oil (holy oil); mixed with vinegar. According to *Statistica murattiana* (1811), which provides an exhaustive account of the living conditions and eating habits of the population, peppers and tomatoes were the staple vegetables in the humble Southern Italian diet, with chilli pepper widely used as a preservative in salami, particularly in Calabria, Basilicata, Abruzzo and Molise. Many writers judged the salami with chilli pepper made by the lower classes to be better than those prepared with other flavours by the well-to-do. A Calabrian folklorist at the end of the nineteenth century deplored the fact that chilli pepper had supplanted other traditional aromas.

'Salami is filled with pepper in all the Calabrian provinces; some, or rather most, make a *peperoli* (pepper) rather than a tomato preserve and use it like a *ragout* (meat sauce). Salt pork is cooked with enormous quantities of dried and powdered pepper. The flavours of sage, bay, thyme, ginger and saffron are inexorably sacrificed to the raw stimulus of pepper, which ends by somehow blunting the exquisite sensitivity of the palate, thus depriving it of taste. In folk cooking, garlic, mint, basil and parsley remain, but pepper reigns supreme.' (F. I. Pignatari, *Medicina popolare*, 'La Calabria', n. 3, 1894). In the famous *nduja* sausage (from the French *andouille*), prepared in Spilinga, more than 300 g of chilli pepper were used for each kilo of paste made from the fattiest pork cuts.

Ordinary folk were well aware of what has now been proved by science: chilli pepper prevents the decay of food, which occurs so quickly in hot climates, and capsicum appears to have anti-bacterial effects. Folklorists, travellers and people writing surveys in the second half of the nineteenth century noted how chilli pepper was the usual condiment in the thrifty daily diet. As Vincenzo Padula wrote, in the province of Cosenza, 'the poor person's lard is a provision of *peparuoli* (pepper). Labourers throw a handful onto a plate with oil and salt, and use it to flavour two loaves of bread.' Another observer noted how peasants in Abruzzo 'enjoy very hot condiments', particularly, 'chopped red pepper', pepper and cloves. In the mountainous and western regions of Basilicata the peasants made wide use of 'strong pepper' (*cerasello* or *diavolicchio*), both 'as a condiment and something to go with bread'. As observers such as Pasquale Villari noted, *Acqua sale*, the hard, black bread made with various grains, was softened in water, dressed with oil and salt, and finally was flavoured with chilli pepper, which was what made it edible. This was common fare in Apulia, Cilento and Basilicata.

The popular literature and folklore of southern Italy attest to the medicinal properties of chilli pepper (it was used to cure malaria) and make much of its (fictional) powers as an aphrodisiac. Oral poetry established an explicit link between the spiciness of hot pepper and erotic desire. Attractive women were often described as being as 'hot' as chilli pepper. Popular language established a clear relationship between chilli pepper and the male and female erogenous zones. Obviously in some regions the strong spiciness was well suited to the traditional images of the populace, who considered themselves and were considered as tough, strong and able to bear any amount of hard work.

The terms '*diavolillo*' or '*diavolicchio*' (little devil), used in many southern dialects to denote chilli pepper, bear witness to its 'stimulating', 'diabolical' character, viewed with favour and pleasure, but also with due caution. In Abruzzo, peasants used to place a plait of chilli peppers, or two chilli peppers in the shape of horns, outside the front door near a horseshoe to ward off the evil eye. It is therefore not surprising that the plastic and metal horns, still used in many southern regions for magical purposes, are made to resemble the shape and colour of some varieties of chilli pepper.

Italo-American

Past observers also underlined the abuse of chilli pepper in both cooking and remedies. Pignatari, mentioned above, noted that chilli pepper, used in Calabria to cure malarial fever, sometimes had serious consequences on health. The author of the *Inchiesta Faina-Nitti* survey (vol. II, tome I, Rome 1909) for Abruzzo and Molise noted that, 'in Vastese, peppers are in general used too much in condiments, and health workers attribute the frequent cases of gastro-enteritis catarrh, hemorrhagic enteritis, cystitis and even cirrhosis of the liver to this.'

Despite these complications, chilli pepper, along with other products with strong and specific flavours and aromas (marjoram for instance), was one of the things that the first immigrants to America looked back on with nostalgia. Immigrants' letters home are full of requests for chilli pepper seeds. Calabrians in Toronto strung up chilli peppers in bunches on the walls of their new houses, just as they would have done back home. For the immigrants it was not only a 'return' to the flavours and aromas of the country they had abandoned, but a kind of cultural passport to be presented and exhibited, sometimes ostentatiously, to others, to the 'foreigners'. It is one of history's paradoxes that southern Italian immigrants in the New World should have exhibited an 'American' product as an emblem of recognition and self-representation.

It is not unusual to find people who go about their business with chilli peppers in their pockets, ready to whip them out in restaurants to flavour convenience dishes that do not meet their approval. Thus where in the past chilli pepper was used to make an insipid diet more flavoursome, today it contributes to making dishes considered different from one's own dietary preferences tastier. 'Spiciness' has become a form of recognition, of opposition to the myth of international cuisine. In its progress from necessary ingredient to vehicle of taste, the little chilli has captured the ups and downs, the realities and myths, the successes and contradictions of the modern Mediterranean diet.

SPICES AND AROMAS

Françoise Aubaile-Sallenave

*T*he terms spicy and hot are considered by most people to be synonymous. However, a distinction should be made between spices, which are simply certain types of vegetable with very varied and complex flavours, and the relatively small sub-set of plants whose edible parts are hot to the taste (garlic, ginger, cloves, hot peppers, etc.). This hot sensation involves the sense of touch through the trigeminal nerve, and is thus not strictly speaking a flavour. Yet since in nature it is never isolated from the complex of smells and tastes of the vegetables that contain it, it actually constitutes an important part of taste and flavouring.

The term spice also deserves further explanation. Derived from the Latin *species*, it signified, in late Latinity, merchandise of all kinds including spices and medicinal drugs. In the late Middle Ages in France the word *espices* also signified scents, that is plants burned for aromatic purposes. Pietro di Eboli's poem[1] tells of the triumph of Emperor Henri VI in 1191, when *balsama* (aromatic resinous substances), *thus* (Arabian incense), *aloe* (Aloe wood), *myristica* (nutmeg), *cynnama* (cinnamon) and *nardus* (lavender) were burnt in the streets of Rome. Given their considerable commercial value, aromatic substances and spices were the drugs *par excellence*. This definition of spices still persists in Italian, a language in which a grocer is also known as a druggist. However in other Romance languages the word *specie* soon came to mean spices in a far wider sense than is current today. Spices did not only include cane sugar, cardamom (also called Paradise grain or *malaguette*), pepper, cinnamon, cloves, nutmeg (*muguette*), ginger, turmeric, rice, saffron, Brazil wood (*Caesalpinia sappan*, a large tree from India that provided a bright red dye), indigo and incense, but also figs, grapes, dates, almonds, liquorice, pomegranates, plums, oranges, lemons and olive oil. Thus first and foremost spices were valuable goods of distant origin that were sold in small quantities.

Pimento, from the Latin *pigmentum* (colouring), soon came to signify an ingredient, and thus a condiment, relating to pepper. In Medieval French the word was used in the expression *vin piment* (pimento wine), that is *vin poivré* (peppered

38

wine), and in Spanish it is retained in the word *pimienta*. When *Capsicum* (*annum* and *frutescens*) arrived from America, the plant initially took on the name of pepper in French, Italian and Spanish, and it was only in the eighteenth century that the name changed in French to *piment*, in Italian to a derivative of pepper: *peperoncino*, and in Spanish to a derivative of *pimienta: pimentón*.

In Search of Spices

Today hot (*piquant*) is synonymous with hot pepper (*pimento*). Although this association is universally recognized, it has only been the case for the last four hundred years. Yet even before the discovery of America, strong tastes were appreciated in Europe, Asia and Africa and sought in a variety of indigenous plants. In Europe these included the small fruit of water pepper (*Polygonum hydropiper*), the seeds of black and white mustard, water cress, radishes; along the Mediterranean *vitex agnus castus* fruit, rocket, pepperwort (*Lepidium sativum*), and above all garlic and onions were used by the Romans, Gauls and Germans. Mention should also be made of the Japanese *wasabi*, a close relation of the central European radish, also of the Crucifer family with its many varieties appreciated for their strength of flavour and aroma. Other important groups are the pepper family that comprises all varieties of pepper, and the Zingiberaceae, including ginger, galanga, zedoary, cardamom and turmeric, all plants from South-East Asia. The list should also include the famous *malaguette* or grain of Paradise, *Aframomum melegueta* from the Ivory Coast and Liberia, which was imported by the Arabs to Europe from as early as the twelfth century. The Rue family includes strong-smelling and -tasting plants that are somewhat differentiated: rue (Mediterranean herbs), the citrus family (small fruit trees including the citron, orange, lemon, bergamot, etc.), and also the *Zanthoxyllum piperitum* from China, whose small fruits embody both lemon and pepper flavours and aromas.

Despite these indigenous plants, people soon began searching for new flavours and aromas to enhance the pleasures of food. Some plants were so extensively used that the very species became endangered. The *Sylphium* is a case in point. A large North African umbrellifer, it was much appreciated by the Greeks and later the Romans (Apicius made considerable use of it) on account of its garlicky gum and complex aroma. From ancient times, Asian spices with their rich aromas and strong flavours were the object of far-flung trade through the Middle East to the Mediterranean area: pepper, cardamom, ginger and turmeric from India, cinnamon from Ceylon, cloves from the Moluccas, the various gums and resins from the umbrellifers of the West and central Asian deserts, *opopanax*, and assafoetida with its strong garlic taste. Such spices were used to flavour certain dishes, but above all to aromatize wine, which at the time of Assyrian, Greek and Roman banquets, was matured in enormous containers containing several hundred litres. For the Persians, southern Arabs, Greeks, Romans and also the Chinese, these spices, together with silk, spurred on travels to distant lands; spices and perfumes were sought out in southern countries: camphor in Borneo, cinnamon and aloe wood in the Indo-Chinese peninsula, sandalwood in India. From the twelfth century the Arabs were the sole intermediaries between the South-East Asian producer-countries and the European and North African consumer-countries. This was the case until Italians from Genoa, Pisa, Venice and Amalfi slowly took over. The search for spices was a constant incentive for sailors and ship-builders alike, thereby encouraging journeys of discovery that culminated in the late fifteenth century colonization of America.

In Europe
Although the taste for hot food was widespread, it was not a universal phenomenon. The southern or tropical countries which produced the spices generally had cuisines with strong flavours and intense aromas, yet strong and hot flavours and delicious aromas also characterized dishes from several North European and Slavic countries. The English, who invented ginger bread[2] in the fifteenth century, were fascinated by Indian cooking and adopted chutney and kedgeree (a derivative of Indian *khichri*, rice and lentils flavoured with pepper, ginger, cloves and cardamom) served with fish for breakfast. The Swiss spice their grison meat and in Freiburg a *brioche* known as *cuchaule* is flavoured with saffron. Cinnamon is used in the Viennese sour cherry soup. Paprika is used in Austrian and Hungarian meat dishes. Spicy bread of every shape and consistency (English Christmas pudding is a variant) are present at all Christmas dinners. Ginger, which was very popular at regal banquets during the Middle Ages, is now only used in cakes, confectionery and some drinks in England. Flavoursome preserved fish (cod, herring and trout) is typical fare in Scandinavian countries, where cooks favour the Jamaican spice *pimenta officinalis*, known for its mixed cinnamon and clove aroma, together with cinnamon, nutmeg and pepper, accompanied by indigenous aromas such as dill and mustard. In Slavic countries, grated radish, the most popular condiment for meat and vegetables, is placed on the table, often in wooden, bird-shaped dishes.

It is interesting to note that Northern Italians, Genoese, Pisans and Venetians, who were very active in the spice trade during the Middle Ages, today on the whole prefer the taste of herbs to spices, almost as if they have been put off by the scents from the canvas sacks they transported. In Southern Italy, on the other hand, spicy and hot dishes are the norm. In Basilicata hot pepper is preferred, and in Calabria it is omnipresent. In Apulia, *spaghetti alla zappatora* is served with a large quantity of chopped garlic and small red peppers, and the Abruzzo *diavoletto* (little devil) sausage owes its name to the strength of its flavouring.

Spain and Portugal, renowned for importing and spreading the popularity of hot pepper, have generally contrasting cuisines, in which the use and taste for hot food are nowadays very localized. In Spain, the Basque countries, Andalusia, Catalonia, certain regions in Aragon and South Galicia, renowned for its Padrón hot pepper, hot peppers are used in savoury hot sauces such as Catalan *romesco*, whereas in Castille the sauce for a dish like partridge stew would include only cooked garlic and peppers for flavouring. Thyme is only used to scent the house, linen and today also cars. Portuguese cuisine in Lisbon and in the Algarve features numerous varieties of hot pepper. In France on the other hand, *harissa*, a North African hot pepper paste imported by the *Pieds Noirs* following Algerian independence, has only made a timid appearance, whereas garlic is used in large quantities in the Provençal *ailloli*. However, there are meat-, fish-, crustacean- and entrail-based dishes that are served with a strong sauce called *diable*.

During the Middle Ages and the Renaissance, French cooking favoured strong tastes, whereas today it makes little use of them and even less of hot dishes. With its growing immigrant population from all over the world, present-day Europe is currently witnessing a diversification of tastes. Savoury and hot dishes from Africa, Thailand, Southern India, Indonesia and many other countries are now readily available to most people in their immediate vicinity.

Notes
1 Pietro di Eboli (1160-1200 approx.), wrote *De rebus siculis*, his poem about Sicilian events, (dated 1119) to mark the victory of Henri VI over Tancredi and Rugero of Andria.
2 Similar to the Italian *panforte* or *panpepato*.

NURSERY SLOPES

Michel Smith

*T*he nurseries supplying French viticulture no longer deserve their reputation! This is the cry often repeated by vinedressers, for whom quality has always been a major objective. 'It has become difficult to find a good nursery', concur the Cazes brothers, who farm approximately 200 hectares of vineyards in the Rivesaltes area and are among the handful of avant-garde vinedressers in the South of France. This being so, such vine growers have adopted a strategy similar to that used for barriques: they rely on three different suppliers in order to optimize the new plants and limit the chances of disappointment. For their part, nurserymen have tailored their business, offering, for example, to plant the young vines themselves in the manner prescribed by the viticulturists. The new plants are given a year-long guarantee and any plants that do not take root are replaced. In this way a kind of 'made-to-measure' supply has been established.

In France there are 1,557 nurseries producing young plants for viticulture, and the majority of these are concentrated around the large vineyards. By contrast, climate dictates that suppliers of wood should be located in the south of France. Following the renovation of Spanish vineyards and in the wake of growth in the Eastern European wine business, French nurserymen cannot afford to sit back: the high pressure of demand is the result of a European trend, which has seen an increase in the amount of land planted with vines. Moreover, the rise in the average quality and price level of wine has brought about a proportionate increase in the price of young vine plants. The small world of French nurseries has been living moments of genuine excitement in recent times: it is as if a total renewal were taking place, based on investors' demands for the sort of technical expertise that is much appreciated in the new vineyards, including those in South America. One of France's large banks, the Crédit Agricole, is engaged in the wine business through its Val d'Orbieu branch, arguably one of the most important agents in the vine-growing and wine-producing sectors in France. This institution has taken over the Pépinières Gendre (Gendre Nurseries) in Quissac in the Gard, and through this has more recently acquired 75% of the shares of another nursery, the legendary Pépinière Hyacinthe Raymond of Carpentras.

Choosing the rootstock

The Beaumajour firm run by the Laurent family in Aubignan, not far from Carpentras, is on a much smaller scale than the nurseries mentioned above. However, thanks to their land in the Muscat-de-Beaumes-de-Venise and the Côte du Rhône, the Laurents have been able to take advantage of this favourable period and their fame has spread throughout the south of France. Father and son (Yves and Sébastien respectively) have been in the business for thirty years and their nursery boasts 1,300,000 species of vine. What do they sell most? Cabernet sauvignon, merlot, chardonnay, syrah, grenache and muscat. And what's their advice to vinedressers? 'First and foremost it is important to choose the right rootstock. At the moment there are three that give good results: Richter 110 (for dry terrain), Ruggieri 140 (for wet terrain) and SO 4 (for lowland). The vinedresser must not make mistakes: for example in dry terrain the rootstock must be nurtured to encourage it to root down deep.'

Advice, however, is not enough to ward off disease, and neither does it put an end to the eternal debate over cloning. 'As soon as a clonal species appears, the vines become more productive, and thus more delicate . . . Their life expectancy diminishes and they tend to make the wine of a region uniform, thereby putting the complexity and *grands crus* at risk.' Such is the lament of traditionalist vinedressers. It must be said, however, that the majority of nurserymen market 'certified' young vine plants, produced through rigorous selection (the process starts with the 'mother' stock), and quality tested in disease-free terrain. Is a 100% guarantee possible? Experts concur that in the field of biology it is impossible to be 100% certain. Moreover they add, 'at present the best clones possible are on the market. This is the vine growers' real guarantee.'

The European Community encourages the planting of 'certified' young vine plants, to the extent that it even subsidizes French vine growers in the south of France who replant their vineyards. The ONIVIN has been waging war against the leaf-curl virus for the last five years: this is one of the main viral threats for stock-vines and grafted vines. The present committee systematically carries out a serologic test, known as Elisa, on leaves taken from stock and grafting nurseries throughout the country. Where necessary they have even gone so far as to order the extirpation of contaminated rootstock. Once the whole anti-leaf curl treatment has been completed, this may mean that as much as 10% of the cultivated area of the nursery has been uprooted.

A little ecology!

'For every technical step forward, you can be sure there'll be someone who says things were better as they were,' one disgruntled researcher has been heard to mutter. 'In the past we were simply unable to combat disease. Today there is no shortage of technical tools, and science is making great strides forward. When buying new plants, the vinedresser only needs to ask to see the certificate confirming that the necessary tests have been carried out on the stock vines. And, to be honest, even before tests became standard practice, one was always aware if the stock was of poor quality.'

The scientific lobby criticizes vine growers. And there's no denying that most vine growers are keen to do things as fast as possible: they plant vines without leaving the land to rest (at least three years) and they are not over-scrupulous about disinfection. The leaf curl virus is carried by microscopic worms which travel very slowly, but in time will move from roots near healthy vines to the vine roots themselves. A further criticism of vine growers is that they do not till the land thoroughly enough, thus causing excessive compacting which practically suffocates the vines in the earth. Furthermore, mention must also be made of the abuse of chemical products. Each of these factors probably contributes to a shortened life-span for the vineyard. Yet solutions do exist, and can be simply summed up in a few principles: greater regard for ecology, better aeration of the ground (thus encouraging roots to seek out nourishment at greater depth), and more discernment in the use of products. Alas, many of today's vine growers set out to gain as early as possible from the financial manna that wine has become. All the more reason, then, appreciating that a little ecology would do viticulture no harm. Let's not forget that vines don't thrive without human labour.

SHERRY
Julian Jeffs

$\mathcal{S}$herry is one of the greatest wines in the world – yet its sales have gone down and down. Why? The question is easy to ask, harder to answer. Apart from being one of the greatest wines in the world it is one of the oldest: a wine with a unique history. Chaucer's father was a wine merchant and when Chaucer (1340-1400) wrote about wine he knew what he was talking about. In his *Pardoner's Tale* he wrote of the white wine of Lepe:

'Of which there riseth such fumositee,

That when a man hath drunken draughtes three,

And weneth that he be at home in Chepe,

He is in Spain, right at the town of Lepe,

Not at Rochelle, nor at Bordeaux town.'

Lepe is now just outside the Sherry area, but that is recent history. The 'fumositee' is still there. Shakespeare (1565-1616) obviously loved the stuff. He spoke throught the mouth of Falstaff: 'A good sherris-sack . . . ascends me into the brain; dries me there all the foolish and dull and crudy vapours which environ it; makes it apprehensive, quick, forgetive, full of nimble fiery and delectable shapes; which deliver'd o'er to the voice, the tongue, which is the birth, becomes excellent wit . . . If I had a thousand sons, the first human principle I would teach them should be, to forswear thin potations and to addict themselves to sack[1].'

How right he was! But despite the bards it fell on hard times. In the eighteenth century sales collapsed. It was the shippers' fault. To get quick and easy profits they allowed the quality to collapse – and so did sales. It was a story to be repeated time and again. Will they never learn?

Come the nineteenth century, things started to look up. Aperitifs were then unknown, though. Sherry was taken with a slice of cake mid morning or drunk throughout the meal. A decanter was to be found on every prosperous sideboard and it was seen as the right wine with lunch. Lovers of Trollope will remember how Mr. Harding in *The Warden* during his miserable 'long day in London' suddenly felt the pangs of hunger at about four o'clock in the afternoon and made a meal of a mutton chop, potatoes, and a pint of Sherry. Those were fine drinking days! The trade reached a peak in 1875, but again the quality went down and the slump inevitably followed. By the end of the century it had no champions among the young and was drunk indiscriminately with mediocre meals by elderly ladies up for the day from the country.

A world without aperitifs must have had its awful moments: waiting half an hour for the last guest to turn up, making polite conversation with complete strangers without a glass in one's hand. Oh dear! It is not clear when the change came. No doubt like all changes it was gradual and probably began in the naughty nineties with the arrival of cocktails. By 1930 we had the first edition of *The Savoy Cocktail Book*. But Sherry is a much better drink before wine than any cocktail is and the arrival of the new-fangled bone dry Fino Sherries towards the end of the nineteenth century cleared the way, helped no end by Carl Williams of Williams & Humbert, who had shared a study at Harrow with Winston Churchill, and who invented the Sherry Party. Sherry was on the way back. Sales steadily rose. Then there was the awful chaos of war with the aftermath of post-war austerity. But good things came again and Sherry with them, reaching a peak in 1979. After that sales declined and went on remorselessly getting lower and lower until last year when they began to look up again. Why the decline? The pendulum of taste swings to and fro remorselessly, and no doubt this had a lot to do with it, but it is by no means the whole story. The United Kingdom and other countries in which wine drinking has not been traditional have taken to it in a big way but Sherry has been the last wine to benefit. The fashion has been for drinks that are supposed to be light – though by no means all of those that are light in colour are also light in alcohol. Lightness is sought, though, and many have taken to drinking white wine as an aperitif in place of Sherry or spirits. But once again it is the Sherry shippers who helped to bring disaster on their own trade. They wanted quick profits and the cash flow of a bulk trade. The concept of cash flow was one of the greatest of mischief makers and some Sherries of diabolical quality were exported. It is not surprising that a new generation of drinkers who tried them rejected them.

The future looks more positive. The pendulum is swinging back. It is still very easy to find cheap and nasty Sherries in corner shops and supermarkets, especially in The Netherlands, but it is also becoming easier to find really fine Sherries and it is these that are winning converts. Wine writers are beginning to write about them in justifiably glowing terms and lecturers are showing Sherries in tutored tastings, Sherries that their audiences never knew to exist. The message is slowly coming across, too, that of all the great wines, Sherry offers the best value. Prices have been depressed too long by over production and the fetish of cash flow. The former has now disappeared. Surplus vineyards have been torn up – and some that probably were not surplus so there may soon actually be a shortage. And shippers have at last learned that there is a market for the best and that these can command high prices.

The message is far from complete, though. Sherry is still regarded as a wine to be drunk by itself, or perhaps with soup. The fact is that even an aperitif Fino Sherry tastes best if it is accompanied with a nibble of food. It need not be much: just an olive, or a bit of cheese, or a slice of fancy sausage makes an enormous difference – those little snacks which the Spanish call *tapas*. Sherries taste really good, too, with smoked fish, can stand up to a vinegary *hors d'oeuvres*, are delicious with shellfish and are perfect with a sandwich or a light salad lunch. The Dry Oloroso and Palo Cortado styles are only just beginning to be explored: rays of Andalusian sunshine on a cold, damp day. And fine sweet sherries, which are merely cloying if drunk as aperitifs, are magnificent as dessert wines.

Let me end with another quotation. When John Galsworthy wrote *The White Monkey* in 1924 he included a conversation between the crotchety Soames Forsyte and his son-in-law Michael Mont:

'Will you have a Sherry?'

'Sherry!' repeated Soames. 'You young people think you've invented Sherry; when I was a boy no one dreamed of dining without a glass of dry Sherry with his soup, and a glass of fine old Sherry with his sweet. Sherry!'

'I quite believe you, sir. There really is nothing new . . . It's all cyclic.'

Notes

1 W. Shakespeare, *Henry IV, Part II*, Act IV, Scene III.

THE ENVIABLE PROFESSION
Stephen Brook

I have always been fascinated by what one might call the philosophical aspect of wine tasting. As a journalist specializing in wine, it is often assumed that I am a brilliant taster of wine. Although I hope I am a competent taster, my primary role is as a communicator, and this is quite unrelated to any skills I may possess as a taster. There are indeed men and women whose profession requires them to taste with sensitivity and accuracy: a cellarmaster, a buyer for a supermarket, a wine merchant assessing young Bordeaux the spring after the vintage, a sommelier. As a wine journalist, I am often obliged to taste alongside these professionals. It is not only the wine merchant who must assess the new vintage; the journalist must also arrive at an opinion. Visiting a cellar anywhere in the world, the journalist is likely to be offered, for example, samples of the same wine aged in different kinds of wood and may be asked, just out of curiosity, to elaborate on the differences between the wines and to express a preference.

The difficulty arises when one has to transcribe a sensory experience – the smell and taste of a wine – into words. Broadly speaking, it seems to me there are two schools of wine description. The first is descriptive, the second analytical. The descriptive wine assessment proceeds by analogy: it searches for similar impressions from beyond the world of wine. Thus a young Australian Cabernet Sauvignon may smell like blackcurrants, a Chambolle-Musigny like raspberries, an old Châteauneuf-du-Pape may summon up associations of tobacco or woodsmoke, a Rioja may smell of vanilla. It is easy to see the point of this style of wine analysis, as it seeks to communicate to the reader the kind of sensory experience he or she is likely to enjoy when tasting the wine for themselves.

The drawback is that the descriptive taster sometimes neglects to tell you whether the wine is any good. A commercial, unmemorable Cabernet Sauvignon may have the same aroma of blackcurrants as a great Château Latour. Other criteria than sensory impressions are required to point out that distinction.

Here the analytical taster comes into his own, by emphasizing the structure of the wine, the integration of oak if the wine has been barrel-aged, the length of flavour, the balance and harmony of the wine, its potential for further development. To be a good descriptive taster you need a good memory, an acute sense of smell, and a fine palate. To be a good analytical taster you need a good palate and a great deal of experience.

Ideally a good wine writer should be able to combine both approaches, but it does depend considerably on the audience for which one is writing. A colleague of mine writes a very successful column for a newspaper focusing exclusively on inexpensive wine. The only matters that concern him are the immediate sensory impression and whether the wine is value for money. I operate in a different sphere and have to adopt a different approach.

As a regular member of the tasting panels organized for the blind tastings conducted by *Decanter*, a magazine to which I often contribute, I have to come to a decision about the overall quality of a range of wines. It may divert the reader to discover that, in my view, wine X tastes like mango whereas wine Y tastes more like pineapple, but this kind of sensory report doesn't help me reach a conclusion on the quality of the wine. This is where analytical tasting becomes essential. All of us participating in such tastings have a responsibility to our readers. It becomes important to distinguish between the wine that is excellent to drink now and the wine that still needs cellaring for five years before it approaches its best. It becomes important to warn the reader that wine A shows very strong oak influence, while wine B, although of equal quality, does not. It becomes important to note that although wine C is just as good as wine D, it is also twice the price.

So wine tasting is not only an inexact craft, but it has to be continuously modified according to the expectations of those on the receiving end. There are a handful of men and women I have encountered who are superlative tasters in the sense that they can often identify region of production, grape variety, producer, and vintage from a single sniff and sip of a glass presented to them. I am awed by such displays of skill when I come across them, but they are feats of memory as much as of taste. At the end of the day it is the job of the wine journalist to assess as well as describe, and that calls for a multiplicity of skills.

THE FRENCH SELECTION

Roger Feuilly

$\mathcal{T}$he ambition of Champagne alchemists is to achieve the absolute. Rather than competing with each other, large wineries and small vignerons all operate according to their possibilities and history. Established 1818, Billecart-Salmon cherishes tradition with a *cuvée* dedicated to its founder, Nicolas-François Billecart. Bollinger maintains a style that derives from its deep-felt regional connections and financial independence. With its 355 acres of land, it abides by strict quality regulations and makes its wines according to *cru* and variety in oak barrels and small containers. The same process is followed for the great vintage wines, blends of *grands* and *premiers crus*, with three to eight years (the R.D. selection) of ageing on yeasts. The same rules are the watchword of Drappier, a lesser known company that has made a contribution of its own to the world of Champagne. This winery, which supplied General De Gaulle and has its offices in the presbytery of the old abbey in Clairvaux, has seven vintages in stock and is one of the few producers to place the date of dégorgement on every bottle. Its Grande Sendrée *cuvée* is one of the best in Champagne.

A house like Duval-Leroy – with its own 343 acres of land, seven of which were recently acquired in Chouilly and rate 100% in the *cru* ranking system – could easily sink into a routine. Over five million bottles are produced per year, but Carole Duval, the owner, knows the meaning of the word prestige. With its splendid Fleur de Champagne vintage *cuvée*, the Vertus-based winery stands at the top in the region, has over 14 million bottles in stock and knows that necessary progress goes hand in hand with respect for traditions. Two country gentlemen, the Chiquet brothers, offer excellent wines, too, and have brought Jacquesson back up where it belongs. In 1884, Adolphe Jacquesson invented the wire cap. Five years later the *Niantic*, a three-masted ship, entered the port of San Francisco with a cargo of their Champagne. The Chiquet are trying to live up to their history with *cuvées* that are usually the result of vertical crushing and oak-ageing. The art of blending achieves perfection here, and Perfection is the name of the *cuvée* of non-vintage brut which comes from thirty wines of different vintages, enriching the elegance and finesse of Chardonnay with the structure of Pinot Noir and the fruit of Pinot Meunier. The 1975 vintage, degorged upon request, is the best expression of their search for perfection. Excellence is also the byword at Krug, a unique winery whose style has never dwindled in six generations. It is the only house which ferments its Champagne wines exclusively in small Argonne oak barrels, and stocks its wines for six to eight years, for a yearly production of 500,000 bottles, in a series of *cuvées* of near absolute balance. The Clos du Mesnil – in the heart of Mesnil-sur-Oger – is the family jewel. 12,000 bottles of this really legendary wine are produced every year from an historical and unchanged vineyard – 4.6 acres surrounded by an enclosure since 1698. The first vintage was made in 1979 and marketed in 1985. With it, Krug broke the golden rule of its founder, Joseph Krug, who produced blended Champagne only. This is a single-vineyard Chardonnay *cuvée* from a single *cru* and and as such is almost a provocation. Henri and Rémy Krug have sacrificed less successful vintages (1984, '86, '87 and '91) and time has proved them right. Clos du Mesnil has a magnificent development for those prepared to wait for it.

After 250 years of experience, haste is not an issue at Moët et Chandon either, when it comes to presenting the pride of the house. The first one hundred cases of Dom Pérignon left Le Havre aboard the *Normandie* on 2 December 1936: since then, the success of this *cuvée* has never ended. An extremely rare and expensive rosé bearing the same name was created in 1962 and marketed in 1969, and has achieved similarly incredible results. Another legend is Mumm's Cordon Rouge, which has been touring around the world since 1875. With 830 acres of vineyards, this winery sells over 10 million bottles per year. The standard-bearer is now the *blanc de blancs* Mumm de Cramant. The Belle Epoque bottle was created by Gallé, glass-maker from the Nancy school, nearly a hundred years ago. The *cuvée* itself left the cellars in 1965 and is naturally graceful and elegant, and extraordinarily attractive.

Beyond the Vallée de la Marne, the Champagne legends and passion turn up again on the Montagne de Reims with Pommery, which owes its existence to a young, 39-year-old widow who, on 18 February 1858, took on a small family-run business that has been worshipped the world over ever since. Pommery, after many ups and downs, is now back on its feet: the *cuvée* Louise Pommery, a perfect rosé, is a guarantee. History permeates the walls of Roederer as well. Cristal, the Champagne loved by Czar Alexander of Russia, was created in 1876 and called 'the most snobbish Champagne ever made'. Since the 1917 revolution no illustrious customer has ever received it in crystal bottles. However, less aristocratic consumers appreciate a *cuvée* that has regained élan since 1924 and now belongs to the restricted circle of the most prestigious Champagne wines. Similar prestige, more discreet yet intact, is the hallmark of one of the oldest Champagne houses, Ruinart. This winery was established in 1729 by Nicolas Ruinart, who was initiated by his uncle Dom Thierry Ruinart, confidant of Dom Pérignon at Hautvillers Abbey. There in the chalk tunnels of Saint-Nicaire, listed as a national monument, the vintage *blanc de blancs* Dom Ruinart now ages for as long as necessary – nine years on average. This wine is produced in two stages: Chardonnay from the Montagne de Reims and the Côte des Blancs are fermented separately before being blended. Then, three selections undergo critical examination: only one will receive the name of this prestigious *cuvée*.

The finesse of great wines is also to be found in the Champagne produced by Jacques Sélosse. Anselme, the owner, has taken over from his father, and aims at very substantial wines, with an eye to elegance. They all come from the *grands crus* of Avize, Cramant and Oger. Fermentation takes place in the large barrels and small oak casks (some new from Vincent Leflaive). The wines are then aged on the yeasts for four years, not filtered, lightly blended and degorged at the last possible moment (the date is on the back label of the bottle). Sélosse is a craftsman who never neglects a single detail: perfection matters, and nothing else. At Veuve Cliquot, the cellars are run by Jacques Péters, one of the best 'noses' in the field. He knows how to 'listen' to vineyards, choose the best grapes from the best *crus*, and create exceptional blends. This everlasting alchemy has just found a new star, the Grande Dame rosé 1988. 'A Champagne with a capital C,' he says. Yet the Grande Dame white 1989 is supreme in its own right: blended from eight *grands crus*, it is a wonder of softness that makes a perfect aperitif. The same goes for Deutz – based in Aÿ and recently acquired by Roederer – and its *cuvée* Classic, whose prestige will be prolonged by the splendid *cuvée* William Deutz, definitely to be aged. Pol Roger's Sir Winston Churchill selection is an extremely pleasant and elegant blend, with the colour of Pinot and the brightness of Chardonnay. Gosset began under Pierre Gosset, wine-grower and mayor in Aÿ, in 1584. It is still a family concern, maintaining *poignettage*, that is *remuage* by hand, and using oak barrels for the great *cuvées* which are marketed in old-fashioned bottles, precise replicas of seventeenth-century ones. Its Celebris is a hymn to aromatic complexity against a background of finesse.

Edited by Roger Feuilly

Billecart-Salmon
Cuvée Nicolas-François 1989
This cuvée is obtained from 60% pinot noir and 40% chardonnay, all from 100% crus from the Côte des Blancs and Montagne de Reims. Golden yellow in colour, very fine nose with hints of apricot and bread, sinewy and full on the palate, with citrus notes. Pleasantly balanced, with a sharp, rich finish.

Bollinger Grande Année 1989
Mainly obtained from pinot noir (61%), this wine is golden yellow in colour with amber highlights. Pleasant aromas of dried fruits, with slight hints of jam and smokey bacon. It is creamy and rich on the palate, with gamey yet fine notes (due to the 30% of chardonnay) though the oak has not perfectly integrated yet.

Drappler Grande Sendrée 1983
An impressive cuvée, with substantial, gastronomic character of great interest. Obtained from pinot noir (55%) and chardonnay (45%), it was degorged in June 1996 (the date is on the bottle). Bright gold in colour, with aromas of grilled almond. Elegant and well-structured on the palate, with silky finish.

Duval-Leroy
Fleur de Champagne 1988
Aged for five years on the yeasts in cellars at a constant temperature of 10-11°C, this cuvée is dominated by chardonnay (75%), with the remaining 25% of pinot noir from Côte des Blancs and Montagne de Reims. Antique gold colour, fine perlage, delicate and complex nose with notes of fruit and vanilla. It is full on the palate with a background of dried fruits and grilled bread. Extremely fine, harmonious and balanced finish.

Jacquesson
Dégorgement Tardif 1975
Chardonnay 100%, harvested on 29 September, for this absolutely fantastic, 'pas dosée' cuvée, of rare complexity. Degorged upon request, this wine shows an exceptional balance between developed aromas and freshness. Golden yellow in colour, with a full nose which perfectly combines aromas of spices, rye-bread, croissants and vanilla. These notes return on the palate, against a chewy, rich background, before an utterly rounded finish.

Krug Clos du Mesnil 1985
Août fait le goût is a champénois saying which has become reality in this cuvée (100% chardonnay), one of the best in the century. After a freezing January, a dull spring, and a rainy June, summer rescued the harvest and gave quality to this extraordinary vintage. A deep golden yellow colour, with hints of flowers, dried and tropical fruit and a discreet boisé which perfectly express the various subtleties of this variety. Fresh on the palate, with elegant aromas in balance between finesse and concentration. A genuinely great wine, highly exuberant, frank and clean.

Moët et Chandon
Dom Pérignon 1988
Pale golden colour, excellent nose, with aromas of orange peel, dried fruit and jam. The entry is lively, against a background of elegance and lightness, with mineral notes and hints of citrus, and spicy and grilled bread. The top cuvée of this house (55% chardonnay and 45% pinot noir) matches its renown with perfect balance, constant finesse, impeccable freshness and unsurpassable harmony.

Mumm de Cramant Blanc de Blancs
A single-vineyard cuvée, 100% chardonnay. Pale yellow colour, fine and airy perlage, young, fresh and slightly creamy nose, with flowery and mineral overtones. Fruity and light on the palate, with a hint of lemon and a pleasant acid finish.

Perrier-Jouet Belle Epoque 1989
Chardonnay de Cramant makes this golden yellow wine characteristic and unique. Flowery and excellent nose, with a spectrum of aromas dominated by citrus and spicy notes. Full-bodied, powerful, elegant on the palate, with a fruity background which emerges dramatically on the finish.

Louise Pommery 1987
This vintage cuvée, a unique achievement by Prince Alain de Polignac, is an exception for the region of Champagne. Obtained from chardonnay (60%) and pinot noir (40%), it has a pleasant light golden colour, elegant and perfumed nose with aromas of orange and flowers. Fine and full on the palate, with an attractive richness and well-integrated acidity.

Cristal Roederer 1989
Golden colour, very mature nose, with aromas of almond, cakes and hazelnut. Naturally elegant on the palate, with buttery and cream overtones, and a fresh richness. Very fine and lingering perlage and harmonious finish. An outstanding champagne.

Dom Ruinart Blanc de Blancs 1988
This cuvée (100% chardonnay) is light golden in colour, with a powerful nose of flowerly notes and spices on mineral background. Silky and full on the palate, with mature substantial structure, balanced by an exceptional freshness which returns in its long finish on an elegant bitter note.

Jacques Sélosse Origine
A highly stylish wine, 100% chardonnay from Avize. It is a blend of various vintages (1987, '88, '89, '90) aged in new oak (80%) for one year. Golden yellow in colour, with aromas of tropical fruit and citrus, it is rich on the palate with well balanced oak notes. A splendid wine for true connoisseurs.

Veuve Clicquot Grande Dame 1989
This wine is a blend of pinot noir from the Montagne de Reims and Grande Vallée de la Marne (60%) and chardonnay Côte des Blancs (40%). Intense golden colour with green highlights, an elegant, fine and complex nose, with soft and fresh aromas of red fruits and flowery notes. Rich and harmonious on the palate, the finish is both delicate and broad.

William Deutz 1988
This subtle blend is dominated by pinot noir (50%), with chardonnay (35%) and pinot meunier (15%). Antique gold colour tinged with amber, flowery nose with almond notes, rich and fruity on the palate, with persistent mature red fruit on a finish that still reveals the dosage.

Gosset Celebris 1988
Obtained from chardonnay and pinot noir grapes exclusively from 100% grand crus of the Côte des Blancs, Montagne de Reims and Grande Vallée de la Marne, this is a pale gold cuvée, with a fine, complex nose, notes of acacia, apple, almond and fig. Dense, concentrated and elegant on the palate, while citrus overtones emerge on the finish. An exceptionally perfumed and fine wine.

Pol Roger
Cuvée Sir Winston Churchill 1986
Like Sir Winston himself, those who decided the fate of this wine claim that it has the effervescence of chardonnay and the power of pinot noir. This is the 'Churchill touch' which goes from white-fleshed fruits to butter and flowers. An almost toasty nose, rich and well-structured, yet fine on the palate. Its aromas mingle little by little before a finish which still shows the dosage yet remains fresh.

THE QUEEN BEE

Hugh Johnson

$\mathcal{H}$err H, the Kurdirektor, is the Beau Nash of Bad N. The sipping of chocolate, the munching of *Torten*, the attendance at the Opera house, the behaviour at the gaming tables are all under his surveillance.

If there were an outbreak of duelling, or someone got lost in the forest or fell in the Ader, Herr H would be told first. On his plate matters can safely be left. He is *arbiter badorum* – and merely to pass through Bad N is to be, for a while, under his arbitrating eye.

Herr H is a fat man. The walk from the Kurhaus across two hundred metres of lawn (magnolia and lime trees provide shade; the Ader light music on the way) to the coffee-house is plenty for him. However, there is no real need to go farther. Sooner or later everybody in the town passes that way, under the window of Herr H's office, and if he doesn't know who they are (and send for them or go to meet them according to their Kur-rating) he will soon find out. They must be at one of the hotels: he can even tell which one from their air, clothes, the direction in which they are walking, the degree of confidence they display. They could, it is true, have come for the day – but this kind is easiest to spot. Third possibility: they might be staying with the Margrave – but then they would not be wandering unescorted through the town. A Mercedes would be rolling softly round with rugs and succor between the Opera house and the Lindentaler Allee.

Dinner with Herr H is not easy. You have to be pleased with everything, and yet discriminating with your praise. After a false start or two you must learn to praise second, after he has pronounced. It is humiliating to be contradicted by his uncompromising summons of the maître d'hôtel and the rejection of the dish you have just begun. The easiest way is to let him choose your food (get the suggestion in first; he will do it anyway) and then eat forkful for forkful along with him until you can go no further. Keep up, the while, a flow of tales about disappointing meals in France, naming places just over the border. In Strasbourg, how you dislike the texture of the *foie gras*; in Belfort how overrated the Lion d'Or; in Besançon how there is no decent restaurant at all. Your fitness to judge thus established, compliment him on particular parts of the meal (the butter, the mayonnaise, the freshness of the fish) and above all dwell on the wine.

Ader wine is not everybody's cup of tea. It surrenders everything to its overwhelming *bodengeschmack* – its *goût de terroir*. Presumably the vintners clean their boots with it when they knock off; certainly the taste of hillside comes through with remarkable clarity. Its other quality is strength.

Modulate your praise of the wine with this in mind: if it is really effective, if, for example, you produce a new image for earthiness which captures (at whatever cost to truth) the poetry of the taste, you will be pounced upon for a visit. It will be revealed to you slowly that you have a chance of being invited into what, under the circumstances, should perhaps be described as the *badum badorum*, the Kurdirektor's own wine-growing retreat – his *Schlösschen*.

His third and fourth chins met like jaws as he talked. The high stone bank of the road, rushing past the Mercedes' window, was topped with green vines on a slatey scree of earth. Bad N had been left in proxy hands for the day: we were to see the *Schlösschen*, and see it with the *Direktor*. We had the feeling, though nothing had been said, that a bit of lunch was being laid on. On the back seat, next to Judy, was a basket of wrapped provisions, each with the elaborate wrappings of Bad N's Fortnum & Mason – Schlichter & Schreiber Gesellschaft.

The river below dwindled from snake to worm. The forest, black as its name, came and went in densely pillared patches, isolating vineyards and villages into tiny principalities of their own. We climbed for half an hour, three-quarters, and the road lost its metalled surface, became a track, still climbed. Vines on the right here, sloping giddily away down into the valley, out into the bright light; on the left the impenetrable pine-canopy of black. And in front, as we brushed the grass verge round a final corner, the *Schlösschen* silhouetted against the sky.

A rusty cross of rococo forgery stood above the archway. Below it steam issued in alternate jets and vaporous trickles from a pipe, suggesting laundry. Within the arch a great walnut tree, meagrely leafed, almost filled the courtyard with its groping. Below the tree were barrels.

'If you like', said the Kurdirektor, a little late in the day, I thought, 'I will show you my cellars. Before lunch. Already you have seen the vineyards. But you should see them at vintage time.'

I am a veteran at cellar-seeing, vineyard-gazing, bottling-line-admiring. There are certain questions.

'I suppose it is not easy to get pickers these days. Up here, I mean.' 'There is no trouble. I know plenty of people. See here is my press-house.'

We were in a white, low-vaulted hall; the refectory of a monastery, I thought. Huge round pillars squatted at the base of faintly traced curves, corner to centre, centre to corner. Here was a new daffodil-yellow Willmes-Presse, in repose like something to be wheeled out on to the apron to minister to airliners; there, now used for storing flower-pots, the old treading-press.

'How many casks is your average yield?' I said.

From the press-house we went down, past a glimpse of sculleries, by rock-roofed stairs, into the earth. It takes a time for your eyes to become accustomed. We walked past rusty iron bins, well-filled, I could see that, with brown and green bottles, label-less. He turned the porcelain light switch.

'You are under the Knight's Hall of the castle', said the Kurdirektor.

'Wine has been kept here in barrels for a thousand years, in bottles for two hundred. I have perhaps the finest wine in the world in this cave.' The dark, oval-faced *Fuders* like the yews down a church-path formed corridors, rooms, a maze. The earth floor was dry; the ceiling, criss-crossed with bare electric wires, had porcelain junctions sticking like bones from its cob-webbed surface. The sweet smell of wine and wood, of wine-darkened oak with its damp gleam and cold touch. And the silence of the tomb. I murmured admiration. Herr H was not listening to me. He was listening to the *Fuder*-music, the conversation of wine with itself. He moved, hesitantly, his chins in shadow, from barrel to barrel, row to row. Like a hound he had picked up a scent – that was it, it was a scent, not a song, he was following. He hovered; he paused; he stopped.

'Here', he said to himself. His breathing was short. 'Here', he said to me. 'I will make you taste young wine first. Always young before old. This is a baby, an infant; so fresh, so fair. Not every year – not by any means every year – perhaps once since the war have we made wine like this. And then once, perhaps two or three times, I taste it perfect. Last week it was that *Fuder*' (he pointed down the church-path); 'next week it will be another. This week, today, this hour this wine is perfect. You know what they say of pears – from under-ripe to over-ripe in the passing of a night – it is true, far more true of wine. I have the greatest vineyard in the world; it has made the greatest wine – but only for a moment, only from the *Fuder*, only under the Knight's Hall.'

He fetched glasses, a thief, a crowbar. He swung his three hundred pounds up on to the wood blocks supporting the barrels to reach the bung. He knocked out the bung, plunged in the thief, filled the three glasses with care. He was right.

The pears, the flowers, the high intoxicating scent of Riesling sang in the glass, like leaves and buds, utterly spring-like. Instead of ending there, though, with the simplicity which all new wine can usually offer, it started, it suggested, it slowly disclosed harmonies. It was not Riesling alone which gave that scent. Not youth alone which gave that freshness. It was not the oak, not the earth, not the sun alone, not the vintner, not the vintage. It was grapes re-born from ancient, exquisite early-landed cognac-quintessential grape-flesh, full-blooming, leaf-dappled, warm with the spent sun like the stones of a wall. If it was sweet it was as a face is sweet. My throat, my lungs and stomach could taste it. It hung between tongue and teeth and lips like the Pentecostal gift.

We left the cellar then, marching upstairs in solemn procession, bearing our glasses, still perfumed, in front of us like chalices in church. We were led into the Knight's Hall, through its echoing length, armour-hung, up wide and shallow stairs, through archways and on to a terrace. We might have been on a balloon. The world was far below. The river, not even a very impressive worm now, had one touch of silver, like the mercury in a thermometer, right under the sun's eye. Its dark bends might be among factories or forests.

We sat, and a table was brought out in pieces; two trestles – much sawn-on by the look of them – and a big scrubbed board. Bread and butter were brought out – the maid, following the two young men who brought the table, was vast-bosomed for her age, serious and plain under her lace cap. Another trip back into the house and she came out with wine, in a wooden pitcher hooped with iron.

If in the cellar it had been mysterious, that lovely mounting perfume, here in the sunlight it was beautiful.

'We will drink my wine with lunch', said Herr H. 'And maybe this afternoon some bottled wine.'

I don't know what had come up with us in the car in those Schlichter & Schreiber packages. It must have been bath soap and baby powder. Nothing that was ever in a shop came out on to the terrace. There must, I thought, have been a brook up here, even at this altitude – the trout cannot have been out of it more than half an hour. The birds we ate still seemed to have the wind rushing through their feathers, the vegetables to be rooted in the ground. And the wine still seemed to be the blood of growing grapes.

The Kurdirektor hardly spoke, but sweated gently in his heavy suit, and when he took his eyes off his plate looked side-long at the view. There was nothing to say. We were feeding, like animals, on perfection.

Nowhere, least of all in Germany, can animality remain ethereal for long. Lunch was over. The vision faded. We were not to drink bottled wine out there on the terrace; the proper place for bottled wine is in a parlour, and into a parlour we trooped. The windows were shut, and curtained, too, with yellowing swags of lace. Green fronds jetted up from what-nots of that peculiar orange-brown wood. By the time we were in, and the doors shut, the Kurdirektor had lit a long cigar.

The cellar-master was called in, and sat, cap in hand, in his green knicker-bockers and huge shoes, by his master's side. Bottle after bottle, brought up from the cellar in wicker baskets, was opened.

Many of the bottles were blue – the colour of glass in which fine middle-Moselles, Saar and Ruwer wines used to be bottled. The labels of the Bischöfliches Konvikt, the Bischöfliches Priesterseminar, the lush landscape and heraldry of the von Schubert estate, the austere steel-engraving, black on white, of Scharzhofberg, the river-scene, faded to sepia on parchment, of an old Bernkasteler label, were all there. Vintages, bright on the neck-labels of the 1959s, were fading on the '49s and '34s, dim on a '21, almost obliterated on a '96. The words *Beeren Auslese* and *Trockenbeeren Auslese* were repeated like the wandering bass line of a fugue, in wreaths and tendrils of gothic lettering. *Originalabfüllung, echt, Eiswein, Schlosskellerei, Kabinettwein, feinste Auslese, Originalabzug* seemed like a Wagnerian code for some dangerous secret.

Behind the soft popping of corks the Kurdirektor was murmuring to himself, like the baritone running through his part in the wings, the saga of names, growers and vintages. He picked up each bottle, cradling it in his huge hand as he read the label, pausing an instant and then putting it down in its place in the row. With an after-thought he changed the places of the Scharzhofberger feinste Auslese 1934 and the Ayler Kupp Beeren Auslese '37. The bottles clanged together briefly as he put them down in their new order. He picked up a Brauneberger Juffer, its vintage obscured by age, and moved two bottles aside to make room for it on the table.

'A rare experience now awaits you', he said, with the air of a ring-master cracking his whip. He motioned to the bottles with his cigar – that Brazilian tobacco smells like a bonfire of cream cheese – 'These are my orchids', he said.

The air, indeed, was like the air in an orchid-house; still, sickly and thick.

The least wine that was opened that afternoon was a *Beeren Auslese* seven years old. We raced down the Moselle, up the Saar, up the Ruwer. The golden, glutinous, flower-sweet productions of back-breaking effort in Bernkastel and Piesport, Graach and Wehlen and Zeltingen, Kanzem and Wiltingen, Ayl and Ockfen, Eitelsbach and Maximin Grünhaus were laid before us.

I felt like a queen bee; glutted with honey, choked with pollen. The rose and carnation scents of the wines became intolerable, nauseating. The Kurdirektor and his cellar-master drank them all, greedily, smoking cigars, until the table was covered with glasses and corks and ashes.

It was growing dark when we left the parlour – yellow-dark with the foggy fall smell of a summer evening in the Wald. We went out to the Mercedes without speaking. The cellar-master bowed. We sped away down the mountain.

'Herr Kurdirektor', I said 'you have taught me more than I ever knew about Germany.'

'Ah, Herr Johnson', he said, 'you have seen its glories now. You have tasted the greatest wine of the world.'

VERMOUTH

Piero Sardo

*V*ermouth is as old as wine. First evidence of a rudimental aromatic wine dates back to the year 4000 BC, on mount Ararat. Black berries and elder berries were added to wild grape juice kept in holes dug in the ground. Nowadays we would hardly call that drink wine, since the wineskins it was kept in must have imbued it with some fairly unpleasant flavours even before it started to go sour. To make it drinkable it had to be dressed up with strong aromas. This primitive manipulation was followed by more scientific practices: medicinal wines were obtained by adding herbs and plants to wine. Hippocrates is believed to have invented *vinum absinthiatum* (Hippocrates' wine), by letting dittany and *artemisia absinthium* flowers soak in the wine. This is practically the basic recipe for vermouth, which was enriched with the spices brought by Venetian merchants from India, Indonesia and East Africa: cardamom, cinnamon, cloves, nutmeg, rhubarb, myrrh, ginger, and sandal wood; subsequently, vanilla and cinchona-bark from America were added to the infusion. Venice, the capital of the spice trade, soon became one of the most important production centres of aromatic wine: in 1549 Costantino Cesare de Notevoli printed the *Ammaestramenti dell'Agricoltura*, with the first recipe for its preparation.

Yet it was in relatively recent times that the first written document pertaining to the preparation was drafted in Turin, the city that was to become and has remained the capital of vermouth: *vinum absinthites* is mentioned in the *Pharmacopea Taurinensis* in 1763. Actually, Piedmont had already become the leading region in the production of aromatic wine. It was the availability of dry and sweet white wines and wild herbs from the Alps and Pre-Alps (in particular, alpine yarrow and gentian, besides artemisia) that contributed to the development of this particular branch of the liquor industry. At the turn of the 17th century, a book called *Secrètes du seigneur Alexis Piemontois* had been published in Lyon: the herbalist Alessio gave his recipe for a Hippocrates' wine with the addition of alpine herbs. It was so enormously successful that Alessio was summoned to the Bavarian court, where the wine made by 'Herr Alexius' became 'Wermut Wein' from 'Wermut', the German word for *absinthium*. At the court of France it was then turned into 'vermouth' and as such it came back to the French-speaking court of Turin.

Here the infusion was named 'vin d'honneur' and in 1786 Victor Amadeus III of Savoy declared it the 'court aperitif'. In those years, many local liquor makers declared that they were the original authors of the recipe, but the process had been widely applied in Turin for many years; certainly since well before 1786, when Benedetto Carpano proclaimed its invention. Carpano devised his own particular recipe, just like all vermouth producers, including Martini and Cinzano. The shops of the most famous ones were all in Turin city centre, where the well-to-do were wont to take their aperitifs.

As the historian Valerio Castronovo has pointed out, the commercial fortunes of vermouth began in Turin: 'Besides silk and organzine, which had been very popular in Lyon and London, another product, vermouth, became popular in the early 19th century as a typical product of Piedmont[1]'. In the mid-19th century, the wine and liquor industry – together with silk-factories, tanneries, foundries and arms factories – played an integral part in the industrialization of Turin. And since this city had become the capital of Italy and the leader of national unification, it also required a stable productive structure. The domestic market was largely limited to basic foodstuffs, so the firms involved turned to export. They managed to create a strong brand image and their success was huge, spreading throughout Europe and overseas as well. Big names like Cinzano, Martini, Gancia, Riccadonna and Bosca not only made fortunes for themselves, but also indirectly provided thousands of little wineries all over Piedmont with business. The largest companies set up plants all over the world, especially in South America, where some of those names are now playing an active part in the wine renaissance of countries like Chile, Argentina and Uruguay.

From the 1840s to the 1960s, vermouth accounted for a good share of the 150 million litres of Italian wine exports.[2] After the Second World War, however, product image and consumption began to decline. Aperitif drinking took on new forms and meanings, and young people were no longer drawn by the flavour and connotations of the old 'vin d'honneur'.

Since then many producers have closed down, and others have tried to adjust to the new tastes by diversifying their production. And yet, at present – when practically all the historic brands in the industry are controlled by foreign capital – every year more that 100 million litres of Italian vermouth are consumed the world over. The new course began in 1964, when the European Common Market was established: from less than 50 million litres to nearly 200 in 1974; a fall below one hundred million between 1987 and 1992 and then a new increase in 1993 and 1994. Today vermouth represents 25% of Italian wine exports.

Notes

1 *Le origini della Torino industriale e la Martini & Rossi*, in *Martini è*, Turin, 1996.

2 Data taken from A. Niederbacher, *La vite e il vino in Italia in cifre e in immagini*, Cologno Monzese, 1994.

THE ORIGINS OF CHAMPAGNE

François Bonal

*I*n 1718, Canon Godinot of Reims, a philanthropist and owner of vineyards, wrote a book entitled *Manière de cultiver la vigne et de faire le Vin de Champagne*: 'For the past twenty years,' he declared, 'the taste of French people has confirmed the success of sparkling wines from Champagne'. We can therefore assume that Champagne was invented around 1690. This is also supported by the appearance in 1700 of the first literary text to mention the wine. In a poem entitled *Epitre à la duchesse de Bouillon*, Guillaume de Chanlieu invites a lady to come to his home and drown 'tomorrow's troubles in the sparkling froth'.

The appearance of froth in wines from the region of Champagne was the result of new wine-making techniques. In the late seventeenth century, and in all wine regions, people began to realize that wine would keep and travel better in bottles than in wooden vats. Heavier bottles were thus produced, inducing the economist Savary de Brulons to write that some glass-makers had specialized in the production of 'thick bottles, whose use and demand have rapidly increased since everybody knows that wines keep better in them'. Producers also started to bottle at the onset of winter, when the wines had yet to complete their fermentation. It was a process of trial and error which generated residues of yeast and sugar. With the warmth of spring, fermentation started up again, producing carbon dioxide that accumulated in the bottle. In 1801, the famous chemist Chaptal wrote that 'sparkling wines derive their properties from being shut in glass before fermentation has been completed'.

The frothiness of the wine could vary considerably from one vineyard to another. The cold climate of northern areas – it was colder than it is today – enhanced the effervescence of the wine for two main reasons. Firstly, the grapes were never perfectly ripe at the moment of harvest, so they were rich in malic acid, which fostered malolactic fermentation. Secondly, fermentation was slowed down by the cold and thus far from being over at the moment of bottling.

Champagne was not invented by a single person. Indeed, the English journalist who wrote, with typical British humour, that Champagne invented itself was pretty close to the mark. As I have shown in my book about Dom Pérignon[1], the wine revolution responsible for the birth of Champagne appears to belong to a framework of collective changes whose origins are still unknown.

Froth was initially considered an entirely negative phenomenon, and much effort was put into preventing it from forming, as many texts of the time reveal. However, a few producers understood the potential of the new drink. The joyous impertinence of Champagne was likely to attract the young Lords intent on pursuing the pleasures in life during the last, gloomy years of the reign of Louis XIV. The production of this new sparkling wine thus became deliberate, and Champagne eventually became popular at the dissolute court of the Duke of Vendôme. In 1715, Philippe d'Orléans and his lovers assured the lasting success of Champagne at the convivial dinners held at the Palais Royal. As Richelieu himself wrote in his *Mémoires*, '. . . orgies did not start until everybody was in the state of beatitude brought on by Champagne . . .'.

The fashion for Champagne soon conquered England, Germany, Russia and Italy, where in 1727 Paolo Rolli included the following lines in his *Di canzonette e di cantate*:

> *In buona compagnia,*
> *Un fiasco di sciampagna*
> *Che i labbri e il cor vi bagna*
> *Col vivo suo liquor.*
>
> *Smozzata pria la fiamma*
> *D'ogni penoso assetto*
> *vi pon la gioja in petto;*
> *E l'allegria nel Cor.*
>
> *Gorgoglia in bianca spuma*
> *E fino alla pupilla*
> *Vivace vin zampilla*
> *Dal colmo del bicchier,*
>
> *Va poi dal seno in mente*
> *E grato a chi ti beve*
> *Le sue più care idee*
> *Risveglia nel pensier.*
>
> *(Book I, Song XVIII)*

By the early eighteenth century, Champagne had become the perfect wine for high society parties. However, its organoleptic qualities fell far behind its great renown. It was produced by means of a process of continuous fermentation, and unlike today, no sugar was added at the outside. Indeed, to achieve greater sparkle the juice of unripe grapes was used. As late as 1799, Cadet-de-Vaux wrote in his book *L'art de faire le vin* (The art of making wine) that '. . . sparkling Champagne wine is produced with grapes harvested when they are not fully ripe . . .'. So those early Champagnes must have been incredibly acid. In fact it was only later that sugar was used as a sweetener prior to adding the liqueur d'expédition. And it wasn't until the beginning of the twentieth century that wine-makers began to remove the deposits formed by the agglomeration of vegetal organic matters. Champagne was originally acidic and so cloudy that a modern wine expert, Emile Manceau, did not hesitate to define it 'revolting dishwater'.

And yet, incredibly enough, that horrible wine was terribly expensive, since so much in its production depended on chance. Nobody knew how to control it, though it was found that it kept its sparkle best when bottled during a full moon in March, possibly even in April. In 1816, a good century after the appearance of Champagne, André Jullien made the following comment in his *Topographie de tous le vignobles connus*: '. . . the events that bring about the sparkling character of this wine are so astonishing that they cannot be explained . . .'.

In those days it was taken for granted that wines either produced too much froth, or too little. Some producers turned to all sorts of additives to give flat wines the right sparkle. In the treatise mentioned above, Godinot himself refers to some alarming practices: 'It is also true', he relates, 'that there were wine merchants who, in the light of the ever increasing success of these sparkling wines, added alum, wine spirits, pigeon excrement and other drugs to make them extraordinarily frothy'. When wine was too effervescent, the bottles exploded. This was the scourge of the casse (breakage). Out of a thousand bottles placed in the cellar, as many as 800 might burst at the start of the second fermentation.

Because of the irregular production of bubbles, there were various kinds of Champagne on the market that differed in relation to the intensity and quantity of the froth. The *mousseux* was the most common product, with a pressure of about two atmospheres; then there were the *demi-mousseux*, whose light froth vanished rapidly; and the *grand-mousseux*, also known as *saute-bouchon* (cork-poppers), which were highly appreciated by party-goers.

In the nineteenth century, Champagne was still fairly expensive. In 1850 its price was 6 francs per bottle, while a Saint-Estèphe or a Pommard were sold for

2 francs . . . Nowadays, if we consider the price of a non vintage brut Champagne, the ratio has been reversed.

Thanks to an annual production of over 250 million bottles and reasonable prices, everybody now has the chance to taste this king of wines. Since proven techniques have replaced the earlier trial and error methods, the quality of Champagne is now flawless and constant.

Notes
1 François Bonal, *Dom Pérignon Vérité et légende*, Editions Dominique Guéniot, Langres

THE REVIVAL ROUTE
Michel Smith

*I*n France, a new fashion is about to take the world of enology by storm. New labels extolling neglected or forgotten grapevines are sprouting up everywhere. The following is a brief *Tour de France* encompassing some of the unrecorded vines of ancient times.

Are you fed up with your Cabernet? Tired of the Chardonnay? Then why not celebrate the sweet *Arbane Champénoise* and sing the praises of the good old *Carignan* from Languedoc! In every French region, all the most renowned wine-growers have been smitten by the urge to rediscover our underestimated viticultural wealth, saving neglected and often endangered grapevines from oblivion. The movement actually began in a rather tentative fashion back in the Eighties.

I can still recall a number of learned colleagues sniggering at a Burgundian wine-grower complaining about the systematic elimination of indigenous vineyards such as those producing the *Pinot Beurot* (the younger brother of the Alsatian Pinot Gris, also known as Auvernat, or Malvoisie along the banks of the Loire) or the *Pinot Lieubault* (a red grapevine virtually erased from the grapevine description and classification maps). We will be lucky if we still have any of these grapevines left at the end of the century, so there was nothing to laugh about. Yet nowadays a great many wine-growers have decided to revert to earlier species, to exploit their forgotten grapevines as an effective subject of communication. And an equal number of experts and consumers have succumbed to their charms.

Autochthons and emigrants
I started my search in Champagne, in Aube to be precise, a department not held in high esteem by established merchants such as Krug, Bollinger and the like. A rather ungrateful attitude, since the grapes grown in Aube largely contribute to the mixes of the great brands, whatever may be said in exclusive circles about premium grapes coming from Marne! Some time ago, François Moutard, the manager of a small Champagne-producing company, decided to focus on a few *Arbane* grapevines which had been planted in 1952. The Arbane is a vinestock which used to be regarded as twice as precious as the common and highly prized

Pinot Noir and Chardonnay. This year, for the first time, Moutard has decided to make a separate wine from this peculiarity which, he believes, is going to yield 1,500 bottles a year. The result is a golden wine, with an intense and complex nose, lively on the palate, marked by hints of dried fruit and great persistence.

A few steps from Champagne is Burgundy. Around Chablis, in the village of Irancy, the *César*, a black, hard-skinned grape producing a white juice, continues to yield coloured, full-bodied wines rich in tannins on the farms of traditional wine-growers like Patrice Fort. The Yonne is the only department where growers can produce a red or rosé Burgundy from this type of vine, which is said to have reached these hills with the Roman legions. Moving eastward, the rather touristy vineyard route of Alsace leads to Heiligenstein, an immaculate little village which takes pride in being the cradle of the *Klevener*, not to be mistaken – God forbid – for the Klevner, the Alsatian word for the Pinot Blanc, also called Auxerrois. Given that nothing is simple in Alsace, the true name of Heiligenstein's Klevener is Traminer, the local name of the Savagnin rosé, from which the Gewurztraminer is made. This grapevine is so warmly supported by the wine-growers of the village that in the surrounding area the 2-hectare vineyards of the Seventies have gradually expanded to around eighty. 'Apparently, it was transplanted here by some Austrian settlers a long time ago', explains Charles Boch, who cares for nothing but his Klevener. Michel Mastrojanni, a French expert who knows Alsace fairly well, reminds us that the word Traminer derives from Tramin, the name of a Tyrolean village in Italy. Whatever its root, when vinification is performed correctly, the Klevener is an excellent white wine with a strong candied fruit aroma mixed with hints of *pain d'épice*.

A Splendid Gamay

Between Alsace and Blois Castle there is only a small gap . . . on the road map, of course. A few kilometres south of the banks of the river Loire, not far from the woods and ponds of Sologne, the Cour-Cheverny denomination protects less than 100 hectares of the bold *Romorantin*, the vinestock of a white grapevine which is said to have been introduced by the French King Francis I, who brought it from Burgundy to the small town of . . . Romorantin. Whatever its history, this grapevine presently yields rare, precious and highly delicate wines, such as those produced in the old vineyards of Michel Gendrier.

Not far from there, Henry Marionnet, an expert in fruity wines, has become a past master of production using carbonic maceration of the Gamay, which is also found in the Beaujolais. He is also committed to protecting old vineyards through the marketing of three original *cuvées* at reasonable prices. His 'Cépages Oubliés' (Forgotten Grapevines) have revalued the red juice Gamay (the one used for the Beaujolais gives a white juice), with its deep flavour and soft tannins. 'It is the traditional grapevine of the Cher valley whose fruits we used to drink when we were teenagers. We would tap it from the *demi-nuid* of our parents. When the DOC officials turned down its request for recognition, it ran the risk of disappearing forever. When I realized that my neighbour was about to uproot the last plots, I persuaded him to rent them out to me.'

Another *cuvée*, named 'Vinifera' (the equivalent of 'wine-producing'), is the fruit of a non-grafted Gamay from a French vineyard that Henry vinifies through intracellular fermentation, as he does with his classic Gamay. Oddly enough, this wine looks much darker, besides being marked by great persistence and a spiced black cherry aroma. It is a light wine which makes you merry if you are wise enough to drink it cool, with a few friends, on a summer evening, eating grilled meat on skewers and avoiding intellectual exertion. Besotted with his Gamay, Henry has also vinified an extraordinarily fruity 'Première Vendage' (First Grape Harvest) with no added sugar and sulphur. As he himself likes to say, this eleven-degree wine must be drunk without reserve! And, believe me, he is absolutely right.

A few steps from the Charmoise area, where Marionnet lives, Paul Buisse, a shopkeeper, is busy bringing back distinction to the taste of the *Fié*, a grapevine which is grown on less than 50 hectares all over France. Fié is the local name of the Sauvignon gris, the younger cousin of the Sauvignon blanc, a renowned grapevine of Sancerre and Pouilly-Fumé. Paul presents his delicious white wine in a beautifully eccentric bottle. The delicacy, body and fruit of the contents are remarkably well balanced.

While we are on the subject of Pouilly-Fumé, we should also add that since 1937 the village renowned for this white wine has also hosted a much less pretentious controlled denomination featuring the name of the village itself: Pouilly-sur-Loire. This is a light white wine, often pleasantly flowery, only produced from the *Chasselas* grapevine. Nowadays what remains of this species is apparently only sufficient to produce a few thousand bottles a year, which are mostly managed by Guy Saget, a wine-merchant who makes an 'old vineyard' *cuvée*.

Let us continue our trip to the Jura and Savoy, where certain grapevines such as the *Poulsard* and the *Trousseau* are presumably endangered since they grow nowhere but in their places of origin.

As we head down the Rhône valley, we will come across a micro-denomination at the gates of Aix-en-Provence. Its name is Palette and derives from a 23 hectare vineyard in which René Rougler has lovingly preserved a few *Manosquin* vinestocks beside his other grapevines.

At the tip of the Côte d'Azur, the *Niçois de Bellet* (a wine produced in a 45 hectare area) can still boast a few specimens of the *Folle Noire*, which owes its name to its fluctuating yields, and the *Braquet*, named after a local family. We strongly recommend tasting the wine of this vinestock at Ghilslain de Charnacé's cellars in Bellet Castle. The sparkling version is produced in nearby Piedmont (Brachetto), where it is usually savoured together with the first strawberries of the season.

The lavish Carignan

If we make a U-turn along the Mediterranean coast, toward Montpellier, we will come across the first vineyards of Languedoc and Roussillon, two French regions whose Cabernet and Chardonnay have attracted the attention of Mondavi and Gallo. This is the home of Olivier Jullien, a sort of mischievous elf and a poet entirely devoted to his vineyard. He was the first to name one of his *cuvées* 'Les Vignes Oubliées' (The Forgotten Vineyards) in the Eighties, and since then he has been emulated by innumerable vine-growers. A great joker, unable to take himself seriously, insensitive to the siren calls of the media, he dresses its bottles with his 'Etats d'âme' (Moods), as he has called one of his *cuvées*. Jullien obtains his 'Vignes Oubliées' white wine from several ancient species, including the *Terret-Boulet* and the *Carignan blanc*. The result is a wine with a full-bodied finish which almost resembles honey after some years in the cellar.

Originally grown in the Cariñena region of Spain, the Carignan was introduced into southern France in the 12th century. It is not exactly a rare grapevine, since it is widespread in France and until very recently ranked fifth worldwide for its crop. Largely exploited from the beginning of the century till the Sixties to obtain industrial wines from flat land vineyards, where it used to be planted for maximum yield (200 hectolitres per hectare), the Carignan is presently abhorred, and indeed uprooted by most grape-producing farms which tend to favour popular grapevines such as the *Syrah*. These wine-growers have evidently forgotten that the Carignan can yield excellent wines when the vines are relatively old (between 30 and 100 years) and the grapes are harvested fully ripe from vineyards grown on the poor hills of the French *Midi*.

Sylvain Fadat is a welcome exception to the general rule. He produces a deep Carignan as a *vin de pays* that can be pleasant in spite of its strong but harmonious tannins. Such tannins are the emblem of his 1994 red wine, maliciously sold at a few francs more than his extremely elegant, DOC-labelled Côteaux-du-Languedoc-Montpeyroux. The Carignan is also flourishing again in Minervois thanks to the Domergue family, whose 'Carignanissime' *cuvée* bears fine witness to the grapevine. They have also rehabilitated another ancient grapevine, the *Cinsault*, with an excellent *cuvée*.

It is a widely held conviction that the South is unable to produce a good white wine. Nonsense! Simply taste the bright, sweet Malvoisie which Suzy Malet and her son Jerome produce just opposite the prison of Perpignan. This Catalan grapevine known as *Tourbat*, which is harvested rather late in the season and presented under the nice label of 'L'Abandon' (The Desertion), produces a tender, mild, light wine.

Toward the Spanish border, in the Banyuls denomination region, Christine Campadieu and Vincent Cantié are reviving the *Grenache gris*, which was once regarded as destined exclusively for the production of specially fermented or alcoholic wines. A thick, spicy, full-bodied, powerful *vin de pays* (14 degrees) which goes well with many Mediterranean dishes.

Toward the end of uniformity
This *Tour de France* could stop at many other locations. Still in the south, we should not forget the Pyrenees and the famous South-West region, where many denominations include such odd grapevines as the *Fer Servadou* for Marcillac, the *Petit Manseng* for Juranon, the *Négrette* for the Côteaux-du-Frontonnais area and so forth. Robert Plageolles is almost a local landmark, renowned for his extraordinary knowledge of these ancient grapevines and the causticity of his humour. He is also a first-class wine-grower for the Gaillac denomination. After rehabilitating the *Len de Lell* (i.e. *Loin de l'oeil*, Out of sight), a rigorously local grapevine, Robert has now fallen in love with another white, indigenous vinestock, the *Odenc*, which he has planted over 2.5 hectares of land to save it from oblivion. The product is divided into three *cuvées* which produce a golden white wine whose fragrance may range from over-ripe to candied apples. Three grape harvests are made for a threefold sorting. The first offers a rather dry white wine with a ripe, intense fruity flavour; the second, the 'Grain d'Ondenc', is even more explosive, while the third, called 'Vin d'Autan' (the Autan is the hot, dry wind which dries grapes) tends to be fortified with a honey touch. Each *cuvée* produces no more than 3,000 50cc bottles, much sought after by collectors.

Coming to the end of our quick *Tour de France*, we can say that this wealth of unusual grapevines on our labels – and many others should be mentioned –

may indicate a turning point in vine growing as if, at the dawn of the third millennium, wine-growers felt bored and somehow sick of banality and uniformity. The curiosity shown by wine-lovers towards the forgotten French grapevines is perhaps also a sign of the incipient contempt felt for the soulless international wines which are flooding the planet. Wait a minute! Isn't that Bacchus pointing a reproaching finger at the Chardonnay, Cabernet and other Sauvignon wines? . . . You don't believe me? Well, dreaming is not forbidden . . .

Les bonnes Adresses des Cépages Oubliés

Champagne Moutard-Dilligent
10110 Buxeuil
Tel. ++33/3/25385073

Patrice Fort
89530 Saint-Bris-le-Vineux
Tel. ++33/3/86538633

Charles Boch
6, rue Principale
67140 Heiligenstein
Tel. ++33/3/88084126

Michel Gendrier
Domaine des Huarts
41700 Cour-Cheverny
Tel. ++33/2/54799790

Henry Marionnet
Domaine de La Charmoise
41230 Soings
Tel. ++33/2/54987073

Paul Buisse
41402 Montrichard
Tel. ++33/2/54320001

Patricia et Daniel Domergue
Campagne de Centeilles
34210 Siran
Tel. ++33/4/68915218
    Tel. ++33/4/68567238

Vincent Cantié et Christine Campadieu
Domaine de la Tour Vielle
3 avenue du Mirador
66190 Collioure
Tel. ++33/4/68824220

Guy Saget
La Castille
58150 Pouilly-sur-Loire
Tel. ++33/3/86391637

René Rougier
Château Simone
13590 Meyreuil
Tel. ++33/4/42669258

Ghislain de Charnacé
440, route de Saquier
Saint-Romain-de-Bellet
06200 Nica
Tel. ++33/4/93378157

Olivier Jullien
Mas Jullien
34150 Jonquières
Tel. ++33/4/67966004

Sylvain Fadat
Domaine d'Aupilhac
28, rue du Plô
34150 Montpeyroux
Tel. ++33/4/67966119

Suzy et Jérôme Malet
Domaine Sarda-Malet
12, Chemin de Sainte-Barbe
66000 Perpignan

Robert Plageoles et Fils
Domaine de Très Cantous
81140 Cahuzac-sur-Vère
Tel. ++33/5/63339040

SHOPKEEPERS AND PEDDLERS
Nelly Krowolski

*W*hat makes Hanoi's or Saigon's streets different from what they were ten or fifteen years ago are the places where you can buy something to eat, where you can always eat, from early in the morning till late at night. The restoration of a market economy has revived street business and pre-war eating habits.

The Vietnamese do not like eating while they walk unless they are having an ice-cream. I can still recall the crowd which usually gathers in front of the shop of Hanoi's most famous ice-cream vendor: groups of teenagers and whole families standing and enjoying their cornets. Then they normally throw away the cones, thereby fuelling a small-scale 'recycling business'. They usually prefer to squat down in front of the seller's stall just for the necessary time to quickly eat the food of their choice.

Street dishes

With the exception of breakfast, which people increasingly tend to eat out and alone, meals are a serious matter, normally taking place within the family, at home or at a restaurant, rigorously Chinese in the past; conversely, snacks, which all come under the expression 'eating to have fun', find their *raison d'être* in the street or at the market. If, in the past, a popular saying censured women for their supposed greediness, for 'going to the market to eat dainties and then hitting their children at home', today men do not lag far behind when it comes to 'eating to have fun', though they tend to 'eat to drink'.

What kind of food is offered along the streets? It depends on the time you decide to eat. In the morning, you can find anything which is normally eaten for breakfast: noodles or rice soups enriched with different meats, fish or shellfish; all kinds of rice served with sausages, pâtés or crumbled peanuts, ravioli, eggs, etc. During the day, the choice consists of pancakes, sweet or savoury rice cakes, soy cream flavoured with ginger syrup, 'sweet soups', usually containing different types of beans, local refreshing drinks, ice-creams, fruit, hot rolls (a real delicacy) and even yogurt. In the evening, the streets basically offer the same dishes as in the morning plus anything suitable to fill a temporarily empty stomach or to go with a drink with a friend: roasted quails flavoured with five spices, grilled or lacquered meats, dried and characteristically smelly cuttlefish grilled on request, hot pâtés, steamed brioches, etc.

Food is sold by peddlers or inside shops. In the first case, you can sit under the verandah of the vendors who have prepared the dish, under an arcade, on the sidewalk, at the entry of an alley, in the surroundings of or inside a market. The food is eaten on the spot or taken home to satisfy a whim or to have something to offer to an unexpected guest.

Peddling

Peddling is a traditional business animated by a well-known repertoire of cries. I still remember my first stay at Dà Nang, back in the seventies. Time was beaten out by the cries of the peddlers who passed along the street, praising the nature of the goods in the baskets hanging from the yoke they carried on their shoulders with their sing-song; soy cream around ten in the morning, crusty bread late in the afternoon, still warm newly laid eggs around ten or eleven in the evening . . . not to mention the van of the Chinese vendor you could hear in the distance thanks to the wooden castanets knocked together by his son, to allow his prospective customers to get their bowls ready for the *my* (a wheat noodle soup), his speciality. This door-to-door sale still goes on but with difficulty since the noise of urban traffic no longer allows people to hear the call of the vendors. Besides, their vans, equipped with a stove and everything necessary to serve food, find it harder and harder to make their way through the congested traffic. This is why street catering is now provided by food shops.

Shops and restaurants

Sometimes it is hard to tell peddling from the trade of shops and restaurants: the demarcation line is often blurred. Thus, the *com binh dân* ('popular rice'), dives where the clients make up their menu by choosing from a number of already cooked dishes and eat in a small room often overflowing onto the street, are much more similar to the so-called *com bui* ('dust rice'), whose name recalls the dust on the sidewalks due to the heavy traffic.

Sidewalks mostly bustle with people in the morning hours. Soon after daybreak, women peddlers set up their stoves to cook their specialities on request or to warm up the soups they have prepared at home. The customers sit on tiny stools to eat their food. When the peddlers run out of broth or other ingredients, they leave their place to other vendors or will come back later on, to sell different delicacies. Throughout the day, anyone can therefore be sure of finding a dish 'to entertain' their taste buds. Even fruit sellers are ready to prepare grapefruit, water melons and pineapples for people to enjoy squatting in front of their stand, holding a plate of salt and chilli to make unripe fruit tastier.

While this habit of eating on the sidewalk or under an arcade may delight the customer looking for different tastes and fragrances, it can be a nuisance for pedestrians, especially in Hanoi, where the sidewalks are often narrow and the streets are a forbidden land, crammed as they are with bicycles, mopeds, motorcycles, cars and trucks. Periodical civil 'clearing' campaigns are launched by the local authorities in an attempt to streamline the display of goods and throngs of people. But the sidewalks do not normally remain clear for long. After just long enough to avoid annoying the police, the sidewalks become packed, the tiny stools find their former places and the clients can have their favourite dishes on the spot once again, but only with chopsticks!

SUNDAY MORNING IN LIMOGNE

Annie Hubert

$\mathcal{T}$o feel the pulse of a village, district or city, there is no better place than the market. It's a place of exchange for material goods and intangible realities, a space-time in which human dynamics can take shape and become manifest. Markets also often draw out the visual, olfactory and auditory aesthetics of a given population. Moreover, they offer the inquisitive visitor a marvellous opportunity for 'getting inside' a different world. Our planet is full of markets, each different from the next. Though they may initially appear to be chaotic, they actually embody all the logic of specific social intercourse.

I have visited innumerable markets – some exotic, others ordinary, some far afield and others near at hand. I tend to use them as a way of getting to know the wider universe around them that transcends the immediate realms of sight and smell. And every time, even if the hundredth, the experience is all-embracing and intense. These are places of embryonic dishes, of food in its raw state, of vegetable, animal and crafts products. They lead me into a world that I can slowly decode through its tastes, shapes and techniques. And as I get to know it, I may also learn to love it.

In the South-West

The 'markets of my heart' are those of South-West France, which I have elected as my homeland. They are the quintessence of this region, each one a stage for the food most representative of local production. And not only are they venues for the display and exchange of food, but also for the circulation of news, the narration of stories and the celebration of a wide range of events. In such distinctly rural areas, the weekly markets in the main square of the village are also primary meeting places; in fact nowadays they tend to replace the church square for the purposes of socialization.

Limogne is a case in point. A small village on the Causses du Quercy, it consists of around one hundred houses, a butcher's shop, a baker's shop and a bazaar that sells practically everything. There is even a minute supermarket, which has survived over the years without getting bigger. Expansion has probably been thwarted by the vivacity of the Sunday morning market. Whatever the season, the market in Limogne is what quickens the heartbeat of the local community. By seven in the morning, the farmers of the area are already to be seen with their vans setting up their stalls in the square facing the church and along the street leading into it. Not only the small producers meet up for the occasion, but also the pensioners who sell the produce of their vegetable gardens, orchards and courtyards. The itinerant stall-holders usually turn up a bit later, their vans packed with work gear, aprons, clothes and items of that sturdy underwear much favoured by the elderly. There is also a pork-butcher from the nearby Aveyron, a cheese-maker from Cantal whose van turns into a stall, and a trader from the Maghreb whose olives, spices, fruit and dried legumes fill the air with pungent smells. From ten o'clock onwards, the activity is in full swing. All the able-bodied oldies gather in their Sunday best, while men and women rally in small groups in the middle of the street to exchange views and news, their empty baskets still hanging from their arms. You have to elbow your way along the street and through the square to reach the stalls, and this is all part of the socializing. Young women pushing their prams stop in the middle of the crowd to admire their respective offspring. Younger men tend to gather on one side of the square, in front of the café, where coffees and glasses of *pastis* are served apace. And among the crowd, in the tourist season, groups of vacationers stand out, particularly the 'foreign strangers' who are not 'from these parts', as opposed to the 'domesticated' strangers who have houses in the area and have been coming back for many years.

In this restricted area – a few hundred square metres – stalls display pyramids of fruit and vegetables in their natural state. This produce doesn't look selected, washed and polished as it would in supermarkets; instead there's plenty of colour and pleasant smells that fill the air with a heady mixture of garlic, the spicy green magic of tomato leaves and the pungent presence of potatoes still sheathed in a film of nourishing soil. Smallholders proffer a few boxes of fruit: apricots, peaches, apples or pears, cherries and strawberries, including the delicious *mara des bois* – a variety reminiscent of wild strawberries that I first came across in this very region. In front of the stalls, close to bunches of scallion, braids of pink garlic and the piles of zucchini, tomatoes and aubergine, the country women sell large bunches of flowers from metal buckets: iris, dahlias, daisies. The *habitués* queue in front of the cheese van, and conversation flows on and on, eased by the smooth, sonorous accent of the area.

The cheese-maker is an important person because he 'does' a number of markets in the region, and can thus convey information very quickly. Live conversation beats boring old phone calls any time for animation, taking on dramatic tones abetted by gesticulation and some responsive audience participation. The vendor is perfectly acquainted with his customers' tastes, successfully dealing out huge slices of a fresh, cream-coloured Cantal and a tasty golden Salers. Impressive portions of Roquefort also find their way into shopping baskets: in this area, sheep's cheese is only ever eaten in industrial quantities. The small, round locally produced Cabécous cheeses are particularly appreciated by 'tourists', who consider them a cult-product of the Quercy plateaus. Then there are the few stalls reserved to *pastis* makers. This is not the anise drink of the same name, but a delicious cake made from very fine, transparent pastry, rather like Austrian *Strüdel*: toothsome proof of a Saracen legacy that is reminiscent of *baclava*, *pastillas* and *briks*. These *pastis* are filled with apple slices soaked in plum brandy. To make them, pastry-makers knead and roll out the dough on a large cloth-covered table. Further down, on small foldable tables, country women sell a couple of chickens, ducks or rabbits, gutted, cleaned and wrapped in transparent plastic bags. Alas, plastic holds sway everywhere: all stallholders have a stash of plastic bags for their products. Long gone is the age of the newspaper and paper bag, much to the disgust of the older people who complain more about the waste than the pollution.

Salami, confit, cucumbers

On the pork-butcher's stall, the ever-present and emblematic pork sausage is accompanied by salami large and small, fresh and seasoned, along with large chunks of salted ham and salted and smoked duck breasts. Various pieces of *confit* (cooked meat preserved in fat) of duck and pork are heaped up in the enamelled containers: they will enhance soups or be grilled and served with potatoes *sautéed* in lard. A bit further along, a wine seller displays a full range of bottles of a good Cahors and a few glasses for tasting . . . this for the 'foreigners', those who are not from the area. Virtually all those who are have a vineyard on their land and produce wine for family consumption; it is certainly not Cahors DOC, but in good years these homemade wines can be delightful. In the appropriate season there are also mushroom gatherers who bring their baskets of scented *porcini* or orange chanterelles to market. In spring they also sell bunches of *respountchous*, young hop shoots that taste rather like small, wild asparagus, slightly bitter and aromatic. Connoisseurs boil them and serve them with a *vinaigrette* and boiled eggs. Then there is the herb and 'organic' produce vendor. This is an elderly farmer who discovered one day and to his considerable satisfaction that foreigners regarded the produce he grew without chemical fertilizers in his vegetable garden as being organic. He lost no time in making a nice cardboard poster claiming his role as a grower of natural products. And the tourists could not have been happier.

There is also a cucumber lady: on a foldable table she sells one or two jars of home-made pickled cucumbers, some small trays of raspberries, red currants or blackberries toward the end of summer, and a few jars of jam in winter. All this is a far cry from industry, from regulations and mass-consumption. The word 'trade' is reductive for this kind of exchange. For these are products which mirror both the vendor and the customer, who are acquainted with all aspects of production and find the time to chat and joke together. The word used in food and farm talk is 'traceability', and there's plenty of it here. The provenance of these products is a known quantity, and this makes them effective, simple and reassuring. The outcome in the kitchen will be dishes that hearten us as they nourish us.

The crowd is so thick that you can only move a few steps at a time, and very slowly. All around you hear the singsong local accent, and occasionally the notes played by a small band playing in a corner of the square. A white truck parked in front of the small supermarket draws many a customer. Pizza only made its appearance in the region fifteen years ago, but since then has never looked back. Not only among the tourists is it successful, but also among the country folk. Driven by curiosity, they must first have thought they were about to sample a sort of *quiche*. They now include it in their Sunday lunches as an element that lends a little extra colour. Patrick the pizza-maker has even invented a local version using Roquefort, Cabécou and the ubiquitous salami.

People's shopping baskets fill up and the roads gradually empty. By about 1:30 the little village has returned to its usual quiet and sleepy ways. Everyone has gone home for Sunday lunch, and since this is a farming region where good food is still an essential part of the joy of living, the post-market repast continues to be an important family custom.

FALAFEL

Philip Sinsheimer

$\mathcal{T}$he origins of the falafel are obscure, controversial even. In open polemic with an article on the popularity of falafel in Israel, published in the Tel Aviv daily *Ha'aretz*, an angry reader wrote in that 'Falafel only has one real homeland: the Lebanon.' Unabashed, the magazine answered back that 'falafel is to be found throughout the Middle East. It is Lebanese as much as it is Egyptian or Palestinian, and the Israelis have adopted it as their national dish.'

The purpose of this article is not so much to establish once and for all the true origin of falafel as to recount what I managed to find out about the identity of the speciality in Israel during a stay there. It is worth pointing out, first of all, that the controversy is partly the result of a linguistic muddle derived from metonymy. The word falafel is used to refer to two distinct entities: a round fritter of mashed chickpeas or other pulses (in Egypt they use butter beans) and the Arab bread sandwich (the round, flat kind that opens like a pocket) filled with the fritters and miscellaneous garnishes. In Israel, the second usage prevails, whereas in the Lebanon the word is used to refer almost exclusively to the fritter, which combines with other dishes to form the traditional *mezzé*.

In Israel, you find falafels all over the place; they are a fact of life. As soon as I arrived in Tel Aviv, I saw falafel adverts everywhere. The chickpea fritter is on sale from one border of the country to another, in big cities and small villages, and even at gas stations in the middle of the desert. Israeli as opposed to Jewish, it is loved by all the different communities that live together in the country, irrespective of religion. The Palestinians of Jerusalem and those of the Arab quarter of Jaffa, south of Tel Aviv, serve and eat falafel just as Israelis of Jewish origin do. The kosher precepts governing the eating and preparation of all meat and dairy foods consider the all-vegetable falafel neutral. Whether you are Jewish or not, you can eat falafel at any time of day. Nutritious and cheap, it is ideal for eating in the street and it also happens to fit in very nicely with a certain image of Israeli civil society as hard-working, united, always on the move and ready to fight.

The spirit of the place

At which point, one may wonder whether this vegetable fritter is made the same way throughout Israel. In other words, is one falafel worth another? In Jerusalem, I heard talk of an exceptional falafel – the Shlomo – 'the best in town, possibly the best in the country'. After walking round the new town for ages, I eventually came across the district they had told me about, Mea Shearim. It's a place inhabited by orthodox Jews; the men dress in black and women cover their heads. I kept getting lost, and the people I asked for directions all replied with a hasty wave of the hand that I found hard to interpret. I moved out of narrow streets into wide avenues, and got lost again. It was more by good luck than good management that I found myself in Shlomo Mosayof Street, the one I'd been looking for. About a hundred metres away I could see a tiny shop with a queue of six people standing in front of the counter, patiently waiting their turn. I joined the queue. I had come to the right place. In front of me was a Jerusalem Israeli with two American friends whom he had brought to initiate into what he considered the 'best' falafel in Israel.

As I waited, I observed. There were two men working behind the counter. One, a plump little guy of 30 or so, was preparing the chickpea fritters and tossing them into a vat of boiling oil. When they were golden brown, he would dry them off on an old iron draining board. Beside him, a man with a white beard (I later discovered he was the uncle) would pick up fritters and stuff them into Arab bread rolls, garnishing them with a mixture of cubed cucumber, tomato and onion and a tablespoonful of Tahini (sesame paste) – plus a hint of red pepper paste, for those who asked for it. This was a rigorous version of falafel, without any frills.

As I waited for them to prepare my order, I told the two men behind the counter about my falafel survey. Without looking up from their work, they simply pointed up at the prize they had received for the best falafel in Israel. I paid my 9 shekels (about €1.30, the standard price) and popped a few discs of cucumber in brine and a long pickled yellow pepper into my falafel.

The moment of truth had arrived. I opened my mouth and bit off a lump of the giant sandwich. The fritters combined crunchiness and softness and blended to perfection with the garnish and the sauces. Neither too dry nor too damp, the sandwich is a model of equilibrium. No flavour prevails over the others, and the taste buds are not overworked or overpowered. I asked one of the other guys in the queue what he found outstanding about this particular falafel. 'It's clean,' he replied. By that, he was referring not so much to hygiene as to a sort of purity.

This is a simple straightforward falafel – the genuine article.

It is the benchmark for a dish that is now made in the most wild and wonderful variants. Apart from the cucumbers in brine and the pepper, which you can add at will, the Shlomo falafel is unalterable and unique, always produced the same way. It is light years away from the stuff served in restaurants, where punters are fobbed off with a pocket of Arab bread filled with falafel and can add all the ingredients and sauces they want. The widest choice of ingredients and garnishes I found was at the Elat Mixed Grill at Elat. There the falafel sandwich can be filled with red cabbage, white cabbage, sauerkraut, cabbage in mayonnaise, beetroot, carrots in brine, cucumbers, olives, fried aubergine, pickled peppers, fried peppers and *shug* (Yemenite pepper purée) and can be dressed with Tahini or curry and mango sauce! In this case, the chickpea fritter becomes a sort of symbol of the plurality of the Israeli people. In the confined space of a pocket of Arab bread open to the Mediterranean, the garnish evokes all the various communities. The variety of the ingredients and the total freedom in combining them faithfully reflects the spirit of the place. Elat, a pretty seaside resort, is famous for its liberalism. Here sauerkraut and fried peppers are free to party and dance together at any time of the day or night in the dancehall of your choice!

At Mea Shearim, the *genius loci* is altogether different. The search for origin and respect for tradition are key values in this quarter of Jerusalem. Here the political and religious environment is reflected in the local falafel, connoting it with a claim to purity and immutability. Prepared 'in the family', the same unchanging recipe excludes all excess and incongruous mixing, so that the Shlomo falafel is designed to reassure. Books of ritual prayer are set out on the counter for customers to read. The 'elect' falafel participates in the sphere of the sacred, though you don't have to be an orthodox or practising Jew to appreciate it!

With culinary preparations that come in a thousand different variations, it is only natural to seek out and promulgate the 'authentic original'. Take pizza, for example: since it is now available on any continent and garnished with any sort of sauce and ingredient (in California even with Thai chicken), it becomes a sort of gastronomic ritual to taste a *pizza margherita* or a *pizza marinara* in a back street in Naples. Likewise, the simple, straightforward Shlomo falafel has adapted to all sorts of mutations. Objects of cult such as these can whet the appetite of even the most secular gastronome.

Recipe for falafel
(found on a postcard)

Ingredients
600 g dried chickpeas soaked overnight
1 tsp powdered cumin
1 tsp powdered coriander
1-2 tbsp cayenne pepper
50 g white plain flour
1 clove of garlic, crushed
salt
oil for frying

Method

Drain the chickpeas and combine with the spices in an electric mixer. Add the flour and mix well. Shape into balls with a diameter of about 3 cm, and fry all over in hot oil (190°C) for two to three minutes until they are golden brown. Stuff into a pitta bread and garnish, using lots of imagination.

KHAO SOY AND OTHER NOODLES
Annie Hubert

Southeast Asia is a heaven for street food. In every town and village food stalls appear at street corners. They are in fact portable kitchens of two kinds: a two wheeled cart containing a charcoal stove, utensils, pots, ingredients and crockery, or in its simplest version, two baskets carried on each end of a bamboo pole, one containing the stove and cooking pot or wok and the other ingredients and bowls. Men, women and sometimes children operate these small trades characteristic of urban life, and the majority are of Chinese ancestry. One can wonder in fact if the street food culture did not come from China to Southeast Asia over a century ago, in the wake of the first great migrations of coolies from the south encouraged by the various colonial governments in search of cheap labour.

In Southeast Asian towns one can eat at any time of day or night, a light snack or a heavier dish, in the middle of a busy street, sitting on the curb, standing or squatting on a low stool. Most urbanites, including children, eat in this manner at least once a day, the very low prices making it affordable even for the poor; indeed, for the destitute it might be the only form of meal.

But the triumph of street food occurs in the 'evening markets'. Each city has its street or area reserved to tradesmen of all kinds operating at night, the majority of which provide local food specialities. At sunset, stalls are set up, rough tables and benches scattered around them, and kerosene or electric lanterns provide the necessary light. In the refreshing coolness, families or groups of friends stroll around and can share food which is the traditional way of expressing conviviality. Smoke fills the air, delicious smells entice one from one stall to the other, sounds of sizzling, frying, sautéing are barely heard above the din of loudspeakers diffusing syrupy love songs sung by the local stars of the moment. Wide eyed children conscientiously eat their syrup flavoured shaved ice, fried bananas and other such treats, while their fathers or mothers inspect the various stalls. Each one has a speciality, and a night market can be a good sample of all the types of 'eating out' cuisine typical of the country or province. Street food should not be confused with home food. Only what is cooked in a home kitchen and consumed with a rice base corresponds to the concept of 'meal'. Street food consists mainly of snacks, or of foods which one does not prepare at home. Thus, at a night market, a family can enjoy a series of dishes which will take the place of the evening meal, but with a totally different content, since rice will not be the staple base. Sitting at one of the tables, shared with other customers, each one can create his original menu.

Chiengrai

One interesting area for street food is Northern Thailand, and particularly the town of Chiengrai: a crossways of Shan, Chinese, and Thai cultures, including some ethnic minorities. The food stalls offer a large choice of dishes: grilled chicken or pork served with fresh herbs and chilli peppers, rice gruel, glutinous rice in coconut cream with fresh ripe mangoes or durian, glutinous rice cooked in a bamboo with black mung beans, grilled beef in a savoury sauce of the Muslim Han (the Hui) from Yunnan . . .

But the main, all-important fare is the noodles. These were probably introduced by the Chinese centuries ago. They are of two types: made of rice flour, white, slightly transparent, of every width, or of wheat flour, yellow, and thinner than the rice kind. There are endless ways of preparing them, the most common being soup. In a chicken, pork or beef broth, they can be mixed with fish or meat balls, beef slices, chopped vegetables, pieces of chicken, *tofu*, and are accompanied by fresh aromatic herbs like Asian basil, coriander, dill, mint, green onions, hot sauces or fresh chillies, and always a slice of lime. The taste is hot, salty-sweet-sour and aromatic, a delight for nose and eyes as well as for the palate.

The characteristic and most popular noodle soup of Chiengrai is *Khao Soy*, thought to be of Shan origin. It consists of a thick spicy brown curried sauce with minced beef or chicken and a touch of peanut paste for additional taste. Thick wheat noodles of a bright yellow colour sprinkled with fried onions and fresh herbs complete the dish. This soup somewhat resembles the Laotian *Khao Pun* (Laos is not far away, across the Mekong), which consists of rice noodles served with a spicy peanut sauce. *Khao Soy* is a favourite with children and often acts as a snack lunch.

But noodles can also be sautéed, and the possibilities are as varied as for soups. Rice noodles may be sautéed with vegetables, onions, chillies, and the fragments of roasted peanuts that are a Thai classic. They can also be fried crisp with a sweet-sour sauce and bits of pork. Wheat noodles can also be fried or sautéed, with or without sauce, with chicken, fish or pork, with any variety of fresh herbs and the juice of a lime. Each cook at his stall develops his particular blend of flavours, which becomes his trademark. Reminiscent of their Chinese origin is the fact that these soups and most noodle dishes are eaten with chop sticks and a spoon, which is not otherwise common in Southeast Asia, except for in Vietnam. Such consumption is a noisy business involving sucking in the noodles while pushing them in with the chop sticks.

Until the advent of mass tourism in the area and the recognition of local cuisines, street food was the only cheap food outside the home. Restaurants were Chinese, or European. But street food remains, resisting the fast food invasion, too expensive and tasteless for cultures who take a major interest in cooking and flavour and manage to achieve the best with the bare minimum.

Recipe for *Khao Soy*
Ingredients (for 4 people)
1 clove garlic
1 tsp coriander ground seed,
1 tsp ground cumin seed,
$1/2$ tsp chilli powder
$1/2$ tsp ground cloves
1 tsp turmeric
450 ml chicken stock
1 large onion, chopped
300 g of chopped cooked chicken meat
1 tsp sugar
2 tbsp soy sauce
450 ml coconut milk
4 tbsp chopped onion, deep fried so as to be crisp
4 'nests' of Chinese egg noodles

Method

In large pan sauté the chopped onion in some oil, when transparent add all the spices and sauté for a minute. Add the pieces of meat (bite size), add the stock, sugar and soy sauce, bring to a boil, and add coconut milk at the last minute, it should not boil.

Cook the noodles one minute in boiling water, and put in soup bowls. Add the liquid over and sprinkle with crisp fried onion. Serve on the side some chopped green onion and wedges of lime. If not salty enough, add a few drops of fish sauce (*naam plaa*).

5000 VARIETIES

Manfred Kreiner

*G*ermany currently produces 5,000 types of beer, but the big names are becoming increasingly similar.

Suckling pig with vinaigrette sauce and mustard grains – it goes without saying, you should drink a tasty Kölsch with it. Rollmops of red mullets on a bed of hop shoots go very well with a light, low-alcohol ale. Smoked cod with large beans and chanterelles? Nothing better than a stout Bock. A duck stew cooked in the oven with three different types of cabbage is just fine with a bitter, sour Pils, whereas goat's cheese from Baden wrapped in bacon requires a full-bodied Altbier. As a dessert, a beer timbale with plums sprinkled with a Weizen, rich in yeast. Six dishes, six different types of beer – and six audacious gastronomic feats. This menu has been created by the chef of the Taube of Grevenbroich, Dieter Kaufmann, and his sommelier Oliver Rasper, with a view to demonstrating that in Germany – the land of beer *par excellence* – beer can be something more than the drink that usually accompanies a shank of pork, or roast chicken. They wanted to demonstrate that, to a certain extent, beer can even hold its own beside sophisticated cuisine.

Oliver Rasper has summed up the basis for a successful marriage: 'The food must have strong aromas.' Sweet, soft and subtle flavours clash with the tannic acid contained in beer. 'I cannot drink beer with a *poché* fish, but I certainly can with smoked fish.'

Nevertheless, menus including beer still tend to be an exception, even in Germany. True, many sophisticated restaurants utilize beer froth in their preparations, making beer soups or zabaglione with Altbier; nevertheless, they invariably suggest wine to go with their dishes. For instance, renowned Berlin chef Siegfried Rockendorf has drawn up a drinks list comprising over 100 wines, but no more than one beer, 'mainly consumed by the kitchen staff'. Sommeliers in the most famous restaurants tend to relegate beer culture to beer festivals. A dish that goes with beer is practically beyond their ken.

200 litres per year

Learned disquisitions are largely lost on the average German drinker. Last year alone, his thirst was quenched by 132 litres of beer. And since this estimate of per-capita consumption also includes teetotallers, new-born babies and grannies, we could easily bring the figure up to 200 litres. Germans traditionally compete with Czechs and Belgians to bear the palm as the biggest beer-drinkers. Certainly they are world champions as far as the number of breweries (1254) and the different beer types they produce (over 5000) are concerned. As Mark Twain was to say, 'German beers are as different as hens in a yard: pale, dark, even black. . . .' In recent times, however, there has been a constant fall in the number of breweries, year after year. Big fish swallow small ones.

Yet those who actually enjoy the endless range of products are relatively few. The delight of experimenting, the quest for the new, the parallel tasting of different beer types – all this is a real exception among beer-drinkers. How sad it is to stick to the usual sour and bitter Pils (the most widely consumed beer in Germany) when there are so many things to discover. And talking of Pils, in a parallel tasting session organized by the TV network ZDF, Pils brewery owners sampled fifteen different types of Pils and were largely unable to recognize their own products. Famous beers all evidently taste pretty much the same. At the end of this alcoholic marathon, by which time many participants were visibly drunk, Henninger owner Peter Lämmerhirdt drew the following conclusion: 'Just like cars, beers are doctored to such an extent that it is impossible to tell one from another.'

But beer connoisseur Dietrich Höllhuber maintains that 'only the most narrow-minded people consider beer as a drink for narrow-minded people.' In his opinion, beer is much richer in shades, colours and facets than its image as a popular drink would suggest. Moreover, beer embodies the same regional differences as wine. Hence the plain charm of a light Kölsch, the creamy froth of a stout Bock, the crimson-bronze reflection of Alt, the toasting aroma of black ale, reminiscent of coffee, the clove aroma of Weizen . . . the beer flavour may be fruity, sweet, bitter, yeasty, hop-like, fresh, sparkling, smoky, bitterish, and each with any possible alcoholic content. Yet, unfortunately, when beer is old or badly made, it may also taste of bread, paper, oxide, milk, or have a rotten or stale flavour.

Cold, in small tankards

Experts have traced over a thousand aromatic substances in beer, the most important of which are esters, aldehydes and ketones. During the tests which are regularly carried out by DLG (the German society for agriculture), the examiners review the range of aromas through smelling and tasting. They analyze the porosity and stability of froth, the fineness of bubbles produced by carbon dioxide, the quality of bitterness, the effervescence, the fullness of taste, smell and flavour. A Pils should have a bitter taste, but this bitterness should not be too tangy. It should be clearly felt as an aftertaste, yet without lingering too long in the mouth, and without leaving the throat dry.

More aromatic beers – that is, those with a higher extract and alcoholic content – should have a fuller, stronger taste. A Weizen should be fizzier, thus containing a higher level of carbon dioxide. Nevertheless, carbon dioxide forms very fine bubbles in a good Weizen, and is thus not excessively aggressive or predominant.

But what are the distinctive features of a good beer? 'A beer is truly good,' maintains Dietrich Höllhuber, 'if its aspect, the first sip and aftertaste are distinct and complex. A monotonous beer suggesting no significant mix of aromatic elements is acceptable, but not good.'

A good beer must be – first of all – fresh. Beer cannot grow old. A few months after bottling it already loses vigour, and is not as fizzy. This is why beer produced by small breweries and drunk locally has a fresher, more lively taste than some of the classic prestigious German ales exported overseas and stored for a few more months.

Beer often loses its freshness due to faulty tapping. It must be served chilled, at 8°C, and poured carefully. A good Pils does not last seven minutes – as many will insist – it lasts no more than two. Those long taps that plunge into the tankard shoot shafts of air into the beer with disastrous consequences: the carbon dioxide comes out, and the beer loses its strength. Another common deadly sin among bartenders is to pour beer into various glasses to keep the froth down, and then mix two half-filled tankards to get a full one. If this is the case, customers should head for the exit, or content themselves with a glass of mineral water.

Another suggestion: even when extremely thirsty, you should drink beer in small tankards. The typical huge one-litre tankards of Bavaria, famous worldwide as the symbol of the Oktoberfest, are a complete denial of beer culture. Freshly tapped – and even at the third sip – a good beer maintains all its flavour. And at the fourth, the glass should be empty.

ALE MOVEMENT
Lesley Chamberlain

'What two ideas are more inseparable than Beer and Britannia?' observed the wit and epicurean Sidney Smith. But since the eighteenth century the beer market in this country has become infinitely more complicated. The biggest modern upheaval in terms of social habits came about a quarter of a century ago, when the British turned *en masse* into wine-drinkers, who preferred wine bars to pubs. Beer risked losing its clientele. But now pubs themselves have changed the drinks they sell, public taste is catholic and adventurous, and beer is enjoying a new comeback. Top of the small, independent brewers' range, aimed at the 35-55 age group, are authentic ales. Next down are trend-conscious bottled beers with unusual names, aimed at the 18-24s. Finally for non-connoisseurs, come the cans.

Authentic ales are made by traditional methods. They list all their ingredients, though there is no legal requirement to do so, and they have a relatively high alcoholic content at around 5%. Their marketing in Britain as choice beverages matched to and drunk with good food takes its cue from a US entrepreneur Charles Finkel. Finkel, who had always sold wine, launched his campaign to give beer a higher epicurean profile in the late 1970s. Beer lists alongside winelists are now common in US restaurants, with over 100 different bottled beers available.

Last year I tasted Pure Brewed Lager from Samuel Smith's Old Brewery in Tadcaster, northern England, the ingredients of which are listed as malted barley, hops, yeast and water. It was a personal revelation. A single mouthful was packed with the flavours of a whole meadow. Samuel Smith's recommend drinking their lager – or continental beer – at 7°C 'with trout amandine, fresh or smoked salmon, all white fish, chicken and *quiche lorraine*'. Discerning drinkers though swear by the same brewery's even more traditional Taddy Porter. This is the famous type of dark ale that was the origin of commercial brewing in Britain and much featured in the novels of Dickens. A dry, full-bodied beer which derives its character from black roasted malt, porter goes wonderfully well, drunk at 13°C, with mussels, oysters or clams. Nut brown ale, also served at 13°C, is the ideal aromatic complement to Stilton cheese.

Claret and Labour Party

The authentic ale movement helps tickle the tastebuds of its clientele by actively rediscovering beer history. Tacitus writing about Britain in the first century mentioned a beverage brewed from barley, and the Whitbread brewers have just put their first Roman beer on the market. Ale Caesar has a joke name (a pun on 'Hail, Caesar') but otherwise its intentions are serious. The ingredients include cardamom, rosemary and honey and the price is a modest £1.50 compared with the £50 asked by another brewery for a resurrected ancient Egyptian beer made with a rare grain called emmer. This Tutankhamun Ale was sold by the bottle in Harrods last year.

To switch from taste to technique, part of the interest in authentic beers is how they are made, avoiding all additives and opting against modern industrialized practices and in favour of the open fermentation of all ales. A Manchester restaurant which has its own unique in-house brewery actually puts the beer-making process on show as part of its service to customers. The brewery rises up through the centre of the building according to the food writer Clarissa Hyman 'like a tangerine-coloured urban spaceship'. The restaurant takes its name Mash and Air from technical brewing terms.

Incidentally when Sidney Smith made his pronouncement above about the inseparability of beer and Britannia he didn't reckon with a snobbishness which for most of this century meant beer was the working-class drink, shunned by the wine-drinking middle-class which had more money to spend and knowledge of the wine-growing countries of Europe (or at least wanted to pretend that it did). The writer George Bernard Shaw was typical of his upper class when he spoke of being 'only a beer tee-totaller, not a Champagne tee-totaller'. An earlier poet, anxious about the self-destructive habits of the lower orders, spoke of beer's 'muddy ecstasies'.

But just as things have been changing in the 1980s and 1990s in the world of beer, so they have in British class politics. It has been a kind of side aim of the marketing of new styles of beer, commented Samuel Smith's manager Christian Horton to me, 'to bring the class distinction down'. Personally I would say that the demise of the old snobbery finally owes less to marketing than to the Labour victory in the 1997 General Election. Before that there was always an old symbolism to hang on to, and when the New Labour Party was trying discreetly to throw off its socialist past without offending the workers, antagonistic newspapers loved nothing so much as to catch a Labour politician drinking wine. Traditionally Labour was the party of 'beer and sandwiches' and for a long time that gesture of solidarity mattered. An historian writing recently in *The Times* pointed out how much in the 1960s the prominent socialist Antony Crosland was resented for his love of claret. Last year a *Times* leader even marked New Labour's ending of its traditional deference to the Trades Unions with the headline: 'Beer and sandwiches are not the food of a good relationship.' One might say *The Times* has not yet heard of the revolution in beer, or just that authentic ales in Britain are simply good in themselves. For better or worse, they have not yet acquired a social image.

HOLLAND, PILSNER
AND THE OTHERS
Grazia Solazzi

*O*rdering a beer in a café in Amsterdam almost certainly entails being served a Pilsner. There are no other draught beers – at the most a couple of bottled ones, and they are always the same. Like saying that Holland is synonymous with Heineken. Yet, strolling along the canals in a quiet, characteristic district not far from the Central Station, you come across the Brouwersgracht, the beer-makers' canal, which derives its name from the numerous breweries once located there. The Netherlands were renowned for their breweries back in the Middle Ages, when their number increased throughout the country, and even small villages were able to produce their own strong, dark beers.

Present-day Holland doesn't initially appear to have retained much of that early independence of spirit. The Dutch market underwent a large-scale concentration process in the sixties. A decade later there were only 14 breweries left and they produced less than 40 different types of beer, 25 of which were normal Pilsner. The handful of brewers who did endeavour to produce something special had quite a hard time, while the beer-lovers themselves had to turn to beers from Belgium to appease their thirst for typical, high quality products. Luckily, in the last few years, things have changed considerably. Though finding a really well-stocked bar is still difficult, Holland currently counts approximately 50 active breweries, supplying no less than 500 types of beer. They all produce – except the giant ones – less than 100,000 hectolitres per year, and many of them hardly reach 1,000 hectolitres.

Output varies according to personal taste, and the master-brewer's penchant. Generally speaking these beers are neither pasteurized, sterilized, stabilized nor filtered, thus their characteristics remain unchanged. In the Netherlands (and in the rest of the world) the most widely distributed beer type is Pilsner, and a large number of micro-breweries produce various versions of it, with a higher or lower hop content. Then there are many other varieties, from white beers – prepared with wheat, thick, milky in colour and pleasantly bitter – to darker ones (Bock is typical), full-bodied, low in fermentation, strong in malt, and over 6.5 proof alcohol. Some products are restricted to specific periods of the year, and artisan breweries have lately started to take their customers by surprise with 'autumn' or 'winter' types, usually dark, fuller in body and more aromatic than the typically summery ales that are light and refreshing. The Maximiliaan brewery in Amsterdam offers a new beer every season which is only produced for the following three-to-four months.

Holland also boasts a Trappist monastery. 'Trappist' beers are typical products, high in fermentation and thus also fairly alcoholic. This is perhaps why they are known as 'meditation beers'. Such beers are produced by adding yeast before bottling to obtain a second phase of fermentation. There are only five beers in the world that are recognized as true Trappist beers, and the other four all come from Belgium. The monks of the Onze Lieve Vrouw van Koningshoeven Abbey started their production in 1884 and nowadays their beers – which are still prepared following ancient recipes – are distributed under the name La Trappe. Another brewery which managed to withstand the sixties' take-overs is Alfa, founded in 1870 by Joseph Meens and still in the hands of his descendants.

BAR·RESTAURANT·BAZAAR

Lesley Chamberlain

*W*hatever happened to the English pub? Situated in King's Road, the heart of fashionable London for the 20-35s, Jim Thompson's, an imposing three-storey villa faced in black marble, looks like a once typical Victorian local. Inside there's the familiar sight of staff pulling pints of draught beer behind a crowded bar. But there the illusion ends. Look again outside and you'll see no painted wooden sign with a traditional name, swinging in the wind, and, back inside, the old division of public and saloon bars has gone. The rest of the building, full of earsplitting music, is given over to a large Oriental-style restaurant where each piece of decor carries a price tag, as a potential souvenir. Meanwhile the whole front wall of JTs, transformed with glass doors, is flung open to the pavement. The warm nights now often last in London from April to October and there is a passion for sitting outside.

To my mind it's global warming, along with international travel and youthful prosperity, which have utterly changed what the British expect of bars and restaurants these days, and especially in the metropolis. New British restaurant food should be 'interesting', almost infinitely culturally varied, and good value, and it should also be informal, so one person can have a snack while another enjoys a full meal. Above all Britons want to feel they have been entertained. This is the message the marketing departments have got. Successful popular establishments now have a highly crafted image, or theme, which, borrowing a term from classical music, I would call a through-composed package of food, decor and ambiance. The aim is to send customers away with 'a total experience'.

The Jim Thompson theme grew out of the life story of an American prisoner of war in Japan, who revived the Thai silk-exporting industry in the 1960s and filled his Bangkok home with native art, before disappearing mysteriously in the Malaysian jungle in 1967. Hardly a single customer knows the story, or takes home a wooden mask or a glazed vase, but the bustling dining room, with informal, polished modern service is not easy to forget. The vast array of available dishes from Indonesia, Vietnam, Burma and elsewhere could not be further from the traditional meals served in pubs even twenty years ago. Gone are the plates of steak and kidney pudding with carrots and peas, to be replaced by dishes of Tiger prawns, sesame chicken, wok-fried vegetables with coconut, and everywhere fresh ginger, lemon grass, onions, and chilli. The Southeast Asian cuisines have moved strongly into the market occupied in the 1960s and 70s by good-value Chinese and Indian cooking. With the craze for healthy, predominantly vegetarian or fish diets ever-growing, they look set to expand their custom indefinitely. True, the tastes of individual dishes are smoothed out to suit what a connoisseur might depressingly call 'the general palate' and the wines are the bland, easy-drinking end of the New World range. But the cooking itself is genuine and wholesome, and the new-style British clientele, never in the country's history so passionate about cafe life as it is today, laps it up.

Panorama postimperiale

Any one of hundreds of new bars and restaurants and pub conversions would probably be just as symbolic as JT's of the country's latest mood and aspirations, though the social historian might specifically link this place with the booming 'Tiger' economies of Southeast Asia which Europe both admires and fears. These cultures have a strong presence in London, thanks to the Imperial past and the financial present. The semiologist would surely agree on the condensed meaning of the sign. But he might additionally conclude we have simply become more and more self-conscious about living in a cultural world consisting only of signs. Indeed, we have happily turned them into our entertainment 'reality'.

This intellectual culture shift, now filtered down to popular commercial levels, has hit all eating and drinking establishments, requiring them to wake up to the times. But, because of other additional factors, including the Conservative government's relaxation of the regulations governing pub ownership back in 1989, it has hit the traditional pub most directly. New market freedoms combined with fashion have meant that all across the country pubs have been shedding those old names, like the Duke of Cumberland or the Fox and Hounds, which related either to royalty or to rural life. In their place have come formulaic names like the chain of establishments called Pitcher and Piano; names without cultural roots for establishments which are always noisy and packed with revellers. A contemporary pub has a theme when its decor echoes its name, and the music and the events follow suit. It's the big leisure industry conglomerates like Grand Metropolitan that have taken over ownership of many pubs from the old breweries and no doubt they are in their element.

Complaints at the changes have come in the press, not only from old-fashioned punters who just want a pint and a cheese sandwich and a game of darts, but also from those who point out that rural English pubs used to double as landmarks. Renaming them makes it impossible now to give lost motorists directions. But the old guard is unlikely to win back what has been lost, if only because time has moved on. The postmodern theme-as-substance world is our consciousness. One old-fashioned brewer eager to capture the retro market told me proudly his firm had returned to 'sawdust on the floor' in one of London's oldest pubs, The Cheshire Cheese. He didn't realize that sawdust too is just a theme which you can buy or reject, as you choose.

It isn't a bad scene, this post-imperial revelling. There seems to be a heightened appetite everywhere for life-as-instant-participatory entertainment. It's as if bars and pubs and restaurants had suddenly moved much closer to show business, while welcoming contributions from the floor.

BELGIAN PARADISE
Davide Faggioli

$\mathcal{I}$t is practically impossible to say how many types of beer are produced by Belgium's 111 breweries. Probably over 400; certainly over the last 10 years the Belgians have marketed the princely total of 3600 different labels. Such figures, accompanied by a per-capita consumption of 104 litres, ranking Belgian drinkers fifth in Europe, after Germany, Denmark, Austria and Ireland (Italy comes last, with 25.4 litres per head), make Belgium the 'paradise of beers'.

The world of Belgian breweries is highly varied. It goes from international giants like Interbrew, Leuven (the fourth largest brewery in the world with a production of 36 million hectolitres per year), to tiny breweries, like Les Artisans Brasseurs in Namur, whose plants only produce 250 hectolitres of beer per year, and whose beers will never be advertised or marketed outside the region. Some beers have only one commercial outlet. This is the case of the Trappist beers of Sint Sixtus, which are exclusively sold at the abbey of the same name (Sint Sixtus Abdij, 8983 Vleteren, tel. ++32/57/400376).

All breweries, big or small, help keep the time-honoured national tradition of beer-making alive. Until the beginning of the century, each village had its own brewery. In 1900 there were 3223, and they produced 14,617 hectolitres per year, nearly the same amount as the 14,833 hectolitres produced in 1995 by 'just' 111 breweries. Per-capita consumption in the first few years of the last century was higher than it is now: 121.6 litres as opposed to the 104 of 1995. Both figures are modest when compared with the 260 litres per year consumed by the inhabitants of Antwerp in the late seventeenth century, and a mere nothing in relation to the 400-litre all-time record reached in 1620. Antwerp was no exception: in Mechelen in 1660, per-capita consumption amounted to 404 litres, and went down to 'just' 250 litres at the end of the seventeenth century. In the second half of the sixteenth century, Lierre hospital allocated 16% of its budget to the purchase of beer.

Faced with such a marked drop in per-capita consumption compared to the beginning of the century, how can overall production have remained stable at nearly 1.5 million hectolitres? The answer is simple. Exports of Belgian beers have increased constantly over this period, from 5000 hectolitres in 1900 to 4,880,000 in 1995. Italy imports over 206,000 hectolitres per year, Japan absorbed 248,483 hectolitres in 1994, when exports to Russia accounted for a further 120,631 hectolitres.

New beers

Over the last decade, many traditional beers have disappeared from the market and have been replaced by copies. Some breweries have marketed non-filtered beers, and new production techniques have been experimented with, as well as new ingredients, like smoked malt. Up until ten years ago, essences and aromas were rarely added to the traditional ingredients of malt, hops, yeast and water, whereas now the production of fruit-flavoured beers (the banana-flavoured Chapeau Tropical, for instance, or cherry-flavoured Belle-Vue Kriek) is fashionable, as are honey-flavoured beers (Cuvée d'Ariste and 't Smisje, produced at a rate of only 100 litres per week by De Regenboog, tel. ++32/50/373833) and beers flavoured with various herbs (the mint-flavoured Minty). Traditional beer-lovers are not impressed.

Another interesting development of the last few years has been the acquisition of medium-sized breweries by large ones, with the aim of expanding their distribution network and consolidating a difficult domestic market. This has led to a decrease in medium-sized producers and, as a consequence, to the disappearance of certain beers, while the number of small companies has noticeably increased. To make up for the disappearance of beers that were once produced by no longer extant breweries, large companies have discovered the so-called 'speciality beers', like Abbey and Trappist beers, Gueuze, sour beers and white beers, which are all in growing demand.

It is now also common to release specific beers for each season (the special Christmas or Easter beers, for instance) as well as for special events.

Beer has always accompanied the best Belgian cheeses, but it has now returned to the kitchen, and is used in the preparation of mouth-watering dishes such as *les carbonnades Flamandes, les fricadelles à la bière, les oiseaux sans tête au Lambic, le lapin à la Bruxelloise,* and *les pruneaux à la bière.*

Styles

To explore the rich universe of Belgian beers, you need to be familiar with the way beers are classified. Peter Crombecq has written *Bier Jaarboek,* an excellent

456-page guide to Belgian beers, unfortunately available only in Flemish (though in November the English version of its CD-ROM *Belgische Bieren* will be sold in Belgium for 995 francs, with information on 1100 beers and 1400 pictures. For further information: tel. ++32/3/7755473). He classifies his country's beers according to 44 different styles. Without mentioning them all, we can group them into three different categories: basic style, substyle and label.

1. The *basic style* denotes the inner properties of a beer. It depends on its main ingredients and brassage process. It can be organized as follows: national styles, those considered a national peculiarity, different from regional ones; styles inspired by foreign products; international styles.

2. *Substyles* are a subdivision of one style into categories based on different intrinsic features due to the addition of extra ingredients. Fruit and herb aromas fall into this category. A substyle can even mean a fine-tuning of a specific main style.

3. The *labels* often feature words like 'cuvée', 'grand cru', 'spéciale', 'single', 'double', 'abbey' or 'Trappist', which may or may not mean something. Often they provide no additional information ('cuvée', 'grand cru'); sometimes they offer an indication of the basic style ('double', 'triple').

Trappist beers

The so-called 'Trappist' beers deserve a chapter of their own. They should not be confused with the various 'abbey' beers (for example Leffe produced by Interbrew or St. Feuillien by Friart), which originated at an abbey and are now produced by ordinary breweries. Only five Belgian beers can legally claim to be 'Trappist': Chimay, Orval, Rochefort, Westmalle and Westvleteren. To guarantee their authentic character, each has created its own brand. They are still produced in monasteries by Trappist monks and nuns, who normally belong to the Cistercian order. Trappist beers are all high-fermentation beers (the wort ferments for four-six days at a temperature of 15-25 degrees) that ferment a second time in the bottle. Their alcohol content is usually fairly high, from 5.2% proof for Orval to 12% proof for Rochefort blue cap.

THE POST-INDUSTRIAL PINT
Michael Jackson

*C*rush fruit (usually grapes), run off the juice, ferment it and you have wine. Steep grains (usually barley) in water until they begin to sprout; arrest this at the optimum point by drying them in a kiln. The grain has now become malt. Make an infusion or decoction of this malt in water; ferment that. Now you have beer.

Wine is in some respects a simpler drink than beer. Both are products of equal antiquity, dating at least from the first civilizations of the fertile crescent. Wine may have spread west through the temperate but warm, grape-growing climes of Turkey, the Balkans, Italy, France and Iberia. Beer may have followed a cooler, grainier, path, through Armenia, Georgia, and southern Russia to brewing regions like Bohemia, Germany, Belgium and the British Isles.

Why is the simpler drink the more readily revered?

Perhaps southern Europe's soft, fleshy, voluptuous, grape, and colourful meal-time companions like tomatoes, aubergine and peppers make for a more sensuous tableau. The north's tougher grain, and underground foods like potatoes and turnips, are less obviously exciting.

Some people argue that wine was the drink of the Imperial ruling classes: the Romans, Burgundians, Normans and Napoleonic French. Although Tacitus was rude about beer, my feeling is that the snobbistic distinction between the two drinks came later, when Northern Europe was first to industrialize, especially in the mid 1800s. Breweries took up steam power and produced beer on an industrial scale; railroads distributed beer far and wide; coal-miners and steel-workers, dehydrated from their labours, drank it in vast quantities.

The wine grape, nearly wiped out by the aphid phylloxera, was vulnerable and valued. With its dusting of local wild yeast, it was reluctant to travel. Grain was hardier, a staple, and commonplace.

Imported wine was the luxury of the bosses; beer the ever-present, less expensive, drink of the working man.

Beer, sweet and sustaining when accented toward barley, is rendered tart and quenching by the use of wheat; silky-smooth by oatmeal; spicy by rye; nutty, toasty, roasty or smoky by the style of kilning . . . but these variations began to diminish as artisans gave way to industrial brewers.

Like ancient wine-makers, brewers had once used a wide variety of tree-barks, leaves, herbs, spices, berries and fruits to flavour their product. Now, most restricted themselves to the cone-like flower of the hop vine.

Beers fermented with wild yeasts survived only in very traditionalist regions after the work of Pasteur. (Belgium's Lambic family is the obvious example). Fermentation at warm temperatures became less common after the invention of refrigeration. (The technique did, though, survive in ales, stouts, wheat beers and styles like the Alt of Düsseldorf and Kölsch of Cologne).

Cloudy and blond

All beer had been either cloudy or dark before the technology was developed to use indirect heat in kilning the malt, and to precipitate yeast. In the days of stoneware, metal or wooden drinking vessels, colour and clarity were not an issue, but mass-produced glass was becoming available when the world's first golden beer was launched in Pilsen, Bohemia, in 1842. This beer, Pilsner Urquell, is still produced. It is noted for its flowery, herbal, dry, hop aromas and flavours, balancing a deliciously sweet maltiness. Pilsner Urquell has lost some character in recent years, but is still a fine beer.

Elsewhere, today, the great majority of the world's beers are very distant, blander, imitations of that Pilsner style. These international brews are designed for easy consumption, rather than character or complexity. In that respect (though not necessarily in production methods), they are the 'fast foods' of the beer world.

Golden beers first spread through Europe, and were then exported by breweries like Beck's (in Bremen, on Germany's short coastline), Carlsberg and Heineken (both in countries with small local markets, lots of sea, and a consequent trading tradition). In the 1870s, the American brewers Anheuser-Busch introduced Budweiser, named after a great Bohemian brewing city, as the first nationally-marketed beer in the US. At the time, every immigrant community in the US brewed its own native styles of beer, but these would largely be wiped out, especially by Prohibition.

On both sides of the Atlantic, the two World Wars closed small breweries and left a conflict-weary public seeking unity and sameness. In the English-speaking world, it was the era of white, sliced bread, television dinners, processed cheese and instant coffee. But the bland 1950s, with their peak of mass-marketing, were followed by the 'alternative' 1960s and the rise of the first post-war teenagers. When the Woodstock generation got their hands on the levers of power, in the 1970s, a century of mass-market growth faced its first challenge.

Urban modernization gave way to conservation, the unquestioned power of the car was challenged by concern over the ecology . . . and people began to care about what they ate and drank. A consumer society became also a consumerist society.

In Britain, a spontaneous consumerist movement called the Campaign for Real Ale, formed in 1971, fought against the filtered and pasteurized beer made by ever-larger national brewers, and favoured the cask-conditioned products of smaller producers. In 1973, the German-born economist E. F. Schumacher, who spent most of his life in Britain, published his book *Small is Beautiful*. It was a major influence in his adoptive country.

Revivalist brewers like Peter Maxwell Stuart, at Traquair House, a castle in Scotland, and Fritz Maytag, at Anchor Steam, in California, proved that Schumacher had a point. At a nuclear submarine base in Scotland, a young American, Jack McAuliffe, decided to go home to the United States and start a small brewery, in California. He called this first new-generation brewery New Albion, in recognition of its British roots. It was founded in 1976/7, and began what came to be known as the micro-brewery movement.

Other young Americans who travelled in the military, as students, or on vacation, tried in the US to create British, Belgian, German and Czech styles of beer. In doing their utmost to be authentic, they often made beers more traditional in character than their European models, and still do. They also evolved new American styles, counterpointing the blandness of the mass-market brews by featuring the intense aromas and flavours of hops from the Pacific Northwest.

Many of the new beer-makers began as amateurs, often inspired by Charlie Papazian, a schoolteacher who founded the American Homebrewers' Association. He later added an organization for micro-brewers. These amateurs turned professional were like lovers of good food who open their own restaurants. When I began writing about beer, there were fewer than 50 breweries in the United States, and only a handful of (hard to find) speciality beers. There are now about 1,300, each producing anything from three or four styles to a dozen or more.

An early source of information on traditional styles was my book *The World Guide to Beer*, first published in 1977, with an extensive update ten years later. As the influence of revivalist American brewers has spread worldwide, this has been reflected in a newer work, *Michael Jackson's Beer Companion*, first published in 1994, with an update in 1997.

In researching my early books, I felt like a musicologist travelling the Mississippi Delta to record elderly blues singers before they died. I wanted to describe traditional beers before they vanished. I discussed not only their flavours (often using wine comparisons) but also the ways in which they were served, and the moments at which they were (or might be) best enjoyed.

The new drinker

The appreciation of beer requires a diversity of styles (not just taste-alike golden Pilsener derivatives) and an understanding that each has its uses. In almost every economically-developed nation, there is a growing diversity, though only Japan approaches the United States in this respect.

In the opposite direction, the polarization toward blander brews reached its extreme with 'clear beer' in the US four or five years ago. This colourless, virtually tasteless, product was a failure.

When I began writing about beer, the world's largest single brewery, Coors of Colorado, had only one product. The biggest producer, Anheuser-Busch, with a dozen breweries, had four beers, notably including Budweiser. Each now has 30 or more, and their introductions in recent years have ranged from hoppy Pilseners and malty Bocks to Belgian-style spiced or fruited beers, English-accented Porters, sweetish 'Irish' brews and far drier, aromatic new American styles. The mighty Miller company now controls three smaller breweries, making good examples of lagers, ales and wheat beers respectively.

These giants have no shortage of brewing skills, though it is difficult for them to make small specialities economically worthwhile. They are trying to do so because they are sophisticated marketeers. They know that, while they can sell huge quantities of their mainstream beers, the days of a largely uniform American culture are gone. So is the era when millions of thirsty steelworkers emerged from shifts in cities like Pittsburgh. This is the post-industrial period. Once, Budweiser could send every prospective (male) consumer to the refrigerator at an appointed moment by advertising on three national TV networks during the breaks in (for example) football games. Today, viewers tape programmes and watch them when they feel inclined, often fast-forwarding through the commercials. The networks are losing audience to cable and satellite stations, rented videotapes and the internet (which is full of talk about speciality beers).

Today's workers labour at computer screens. They are not dehydrated at the end of their working day, but they still fancy the reward of a drink, perhaps one that is less quenching but more satisfying in flavours. For reasons also of health, or simply the need to drive, people are drinking less – but tasting more.

Older drinkers may not change their habits, but a new generation is doing so. A majority of the beer-lovers who attend my seminars in the big American cities are young professionals, a good number of them women.

The new American beer-lover may choose (for example) a wheat-beer, in a vase-shaped glass, as a quencher; a Belgian ale, in a Burgundy sampler, as an aperitif; a whole range of beers with meals or in cooking; a snifter of barley wine after dinner, or with a book at bedtime. These are choosy, critical consumers. They want real information on the beer they are drinking.

They are more knowledgeable than their counterparts in Britain or Belgium, and far more questioning than those in Germany or the Czech Republic. German beers are becoming blander, and those in the Czech Republic even more so.

The United States has long been a global influence, but never more than now, in the post-Communist era. We Europeans may find ourselves being reintroduced to our tastiest traditions by the Americans. Or we could succumb to the blandest products of Coors, Anheuser-Busch and Miller.

In a world as free as we have ever known, do we want real diversity or an endless 'choice' of samey, bland beers? That will be determined not by the marketeer but by the consumer. It is for us to decide.

THE DEVIL'S AVOCADO
Daniel Chavarria

'$\mathcal{H}$e hasn't a clue about eating'. Those were the words my father once used to dispatch a French friend of mine who refused to taste his *chinchulines* (the word used in Argentina and Uruguay for grilled cow's innards). We had invited my mate to a barbecue on the patio of our house. He wanted to understand what all the different meats, fresh and cured, my father was turning on the grill actually were: chops, steaks, cutlets, liver, kidney, heart, chicken's innards, sweetbreads, brain, sausage, *morcilla*, or black pudding, bacon . . . When I told him that the best *chinchulines* were the ones that hadn't been washed too well, that when a moderate amount of a herbivore's fecal substances roasts with the fat of the intestines, the result is a bitter taste of Olympic fragrance, my friend smiled, went all pale and changed the subject.

My father, it is only fair to say, would never have dreamt of eating a piece of Camembert or sucking snails. Contrast of this kind, combined with the Socratic concept that virtue is something to be learnt, induced me to a series of reflections on hedonism.

My personal experience has taught me that the unknown – whether it's food or liquor or women or ideas you're talking about – dispenses no pleasure until it stops being unknown. There's nothing superfluous in pointing out that, in some cases, the enjoyment of pleasure demands perseverance and even educational discipline.

There are of course exceptions to the rule. Alexander von Humboldt succumbed at his first taste of a *guanabana*. The pleasure of tasting it, he wrote, was worth all the privations he had suffered on his journey to the Orinoco. It was a passion without a preamble. Instantaneous bliss. Another exceptional example of immediate, outright pleasure was that of a Hungarian Jewish friend of mine. At the age of just eight, while his family was fleeing from the Nazis (it was 1940), during a stopover in Rio, he tasted his first ever banana. After the first bite, he fell into ecstasy and thought of paradise (it's no coincidence that *Musa paradisiaca* is the botanic name for the fruit).

On account of their excessive sweetness or sourness, or of their unusual taste or scent, other tropical fruits are disagreeable at first for the inhabitants of other regions.

Gastronomically speaking, apart from all the grilled meat we eat and our habit of drinking *maté*, we inhabitants of Montevideo and Buenos Aires, the Temperate Zone, are a mixture of Italian and Spanish. The bases of our diet are corn, meat, vegetable, sometimes olive oil and wine.

Almost all the rest of Latin America right up into central Mexico alternates white rice, beans, sweet corn, manioc and plantain and, apart from the odd privileged pocket, produces virtually no wine at all. Instead, they drink beer and fermented cereals.

Moving on to tropical fruits, the southern cone of America regularly eats bananas from Brazil. But other fruits such as pineapple, mango, *guyaba*, *zapote*, *mamey* and all the great variety of custard-apples are very expensive and exotic. They are hard to conserve and are very rarely eaten in Uruguay and Argentina.

This is also the case of the avocado which, in Montevideo and Buenos Aires, is only to be found in characteristic restaurants. Oddly enough, in Chile, where a gastronomy of European origin prevails, a small brownish red avocado known as *palta* is highly popular. Wherever it grows in Latin America, the *palta* is an object of veneration. The poorer people are, the more they appreciate it. A couple of avocados, with or without salt, with or without pepper, will sate the hunger of any local. Yet during my first stay in Santiago, the taste was new to me and I found it repulsive. It was like nothing I'd ever eaten before. To my palate, it tasted of medicine or antibiotic mould.

I was very young then, a heroic hitchhiker with very, very few resources to my name. In Santiago, I stayed in a very cheap boarding house where you had to eat what you were given, without any choice at all. The food was meagre, but there wasn't a salad or a stew or a soup in which they didn't add that damned little avocado. I was unlucky enough to get there in the heart of the *palta* season. The salads I ate consisted of eight to ten pieces of avocado garnished with little bits of tomato, lettuce, raw onion and boiled white beans. Yes, I often suffered the pangs of hunger in that boarding house.

My conflict with the fruit reached its climax a year later in Peru. There was a group of us, Uruguayans and Argentineans, who had the habit of meeting up in a private club in Lima to listen to music, drink *maté* and cultivate our nostalgia. One evening at dinner, the cook prepared us some small shop-bought *ravioli* with a very piquant meat sauce. All very Peruvian but eminently edible. He swore in advance that he wouldn't be using any coriander, a herb Peruvians add arbitrarily and ruthlessly to all Italian sauces.

When we started eating, I waxed all nostalgic about my grandmother's homemade *ravioli*, which were very big, irregular in shape and size and stuffed with meat or brain or Swiss chard and boiled eggs.

One of the people listening to me – Maestro Ruffo – was almost driven to tears.

He was an Argentine accordionist of Italian origin whom we had invited with a guitarist to accompany him. With his tangos, he had been stirring up our nostalgia since the middle of the afternoon.

'Listening to this music can fatten you', commented one irremediably skinny type.

I can assure you that any left-wing Rio Plataman, as most of us were that day, is proud to be Latin American. No way does he feel European. During our long exile in the Seventies and part of the Eighties, we learnt to settle down in pretty well any Latin American environment. But when we were together as a group we used to hurt each other with our tangos, and we ended up regretting and sublimating often banal things and habits. Sometimes we went over the top.

When it came to food, we used to try to cook our way, but something was always missing. The cut of the meat was never the same, we couldn't find cheese as hard as what we were used to, the basil was always too aromatic, and there was no one who could make pasta like our mothers and grandmothers used to. In the beautiful, hospitable cities of Latin America, from Rio de Janeiro to Havana to Mexico City, faced with panfuls of the omnipresent, usually sticky white rice, beans and sweet corn transformed into *arepas*, *tortillas* or *tamales*, or overawed by spicy, sweet and sour Indo-American food, we wept at the memory of our barbecues and pastas. Yes, OUR pastas. Because every Rio Plataman who has grown up in Montevideo or Buenos Aires or Rosario – even those of Spanish, Jewish or central European origin – considers Italian pasta a national dish.

As I reminisced, Ruffo assured us that his wife Emma could make real *ravioli*. Lima-born Emma was a singer, a lovely women Ruffo had met 20 years earlier, when he first arrived in Peru. Listening to him, it sounded as if Emma's *ravioli* were exactly the way I wanted them: uneven, biggish, some plumper, others less so, sometimes with holes and other imperfections from which the succulent fillings oozed out.

Emma also made *cappelletti*, *agnolotti* and I don't know what else. All things she had learnt from Ruffo's mother, an Emilian peasant woman who had emigrated to Buenos Aires before the war. Mamma kneaded her pasta proudly, overloaded with cultural responsibilities, careful to conserve the traditions of her forebears. She was so passionate about it, sometimes her eyes would well up with tears. That's when she would remember her family back home. And Ruffo's voice used to quiver just talking about it. It's a good job he stopped because otherwise we would all have been crying.

A few days later, Emma offered to make us her *ravioli*. The same group as before met up at Ruffo's place. Some of us helped to make the pasta. Aided and abetted by two young mestizo girls, Emma began cutting and filling the *ravioli*. The rest of the party, all men, bantered and drank *grappa* and *maté* and played cards.

Later, when the smell of the sauce was beginning to torture us, I asked Emma's permission to taste it. It was a Bolognese meat sauce. Authentic, slightly on the piquant side, but well-balanced with the aromas of Mediterranean herbs.

When the serving bowls at last reached the table, Emma's *ravioli* had all the adorable asymmetry of my grandmother's. As soon as we hurled ourselves over our plates, there were expressions of surprise, alarm, wild glances, furrowed brows, strange chewing movements, turned heads and, ultimately, general consternation.

Emma had added a personal touch, an Incan addition of green avocado, to the filling of Swiss chard and boiled eggs Ruffo's mamma had taught her. She assured us that after ten minutes' cooking, the little chunks of avocado would ripen and give a very intense flavour to the filling.

To avoid offending her, two or three of us managed to eat a full plateful. Others mopped up the sauce with their bread. Indeed, so as not to waste the sauce, others asked if they could cook some plain pasta. But the *ravioli* were a disaster.

Emma started crying and Ruffo took the blame to buck her up. After years and years in Peru, he had grown accustomed to avocado. He liked the filling, but he knew that no fellow countryman of his would be able to stomach it, and he ought to have warned his wife about that. Poor Emma was humiliated. She apologized and said she'd never met anyone who wouldn't eat avocado. It just hadn't crossed her mind. She wanted to give us a surprise.

On that occasion, I was very annoyed, not with the avocado but with myself.

Ever since I was a kid, I'd been conditioned by a precise cosmopolitan vocation not to trust regionalist hyperbole. Every time I came across someone convinced his country, his music, his women, his wine, his food, his language and his way of living were the best and prepared to argue about the fact, for me that person was either stupid or ignorant. A nobody.

I believe that tolerance is the supreme sociocultural virtue. Without it, there can be no communication, and other human virtues can't develop.

As a traveller with few resources, I was already experienced in having to adapt to things which repelled me at first. Baseball, for example. I would have nothing to do with it at first. I thought it was static and boring. But today it's one of my favourite pastimes. Football also excites me. But it's a different thing. I enjoy it in a different way. To enjoy a baseball match is to learn a new form of enjoyment. So why couldn't the same thing happen to me with the flavour of avocado? After all, I'd learnt to eat snails, frogs' legs, roast monkey, mouldy cheese and fat-assed ants!

After the disastrous ravioli experience in Lima I was adamant that avocado would never ruin a meal of mine again. I was going to make peace with the fruitiest. I was going to discover its secrets and I was going to become one of the millions of inhabitants of the American continent who adore it.

A few days later an acquaintance suggested I go to a deli in Callao where they do a dish of avocado with assorted peppers. It sounded great. Who knows, maybe a good dash of piquant would cover that awful medicinal taste.

It was true. I had at last learnt to appreciate how that mass of oily tissue caresses the taste buds. OK, it was more a tactile pleasure than a question of taste. But I was making progress. Working stubbornly with my palate, I gradually discovered a symphony of subtle flavours. In the space of a few months, I learnt like every inhabitant of the tropics to become a passionate consumer of avocado.

Since then, avocado has become a regular ingredient in my salads. I subsequently learnt to prepare it as a refined hors d'oeuvre, stuffed with lobster, with crabs' nippers, with different sauces and with a variety of types of piquant dressing. I became almost addicted to it, and at home I ate it simply, dressed only with oil and lemon. To this day, I have the habit of celebrating a rite which fills me with great pleasure. I cut the avocado lengthwise, then I take the half containing the stone, which I hit with a knife. It's a foolproof system for making sure the stone sticks to the blade and comes away from the pulp. Then I use a spoon to scoop out the lumps which I add to sweet corn soups and bean stews the way the common people used to do in Peru.

In Lima, I never managed to convert my fellow Rio Platamen to the wonders of the avocado. To eat an avocado you have to be either a mestizo or an Indio, they used to say. How ignorant can you get? Years later, in Cuba, I was to repeat the same things about Rio Platamen who hated baseball. Among the many compatriots who lived in Havana in exile during the fifteen years of our mass exodus, I never met anyone who was capable of appreciating baseball. I'm proud to be the exception.

In 1964, following the political winds of the decade, I went to live in Brazil. In San Salvador de Bahia, I used to lunch in a university canteen. It was the season of avocados, huge, shining and green, and I got into the habit of buying them on the street and taking them to the canteen with me. I used to drop in the *feijoada*, With this very cheap, highly nutritional fruit, I was thus able to strengthen the anaemic student soups, white rice and manioc flour, ever present on the tables of the Brazilian *Nordeste*.

When they saw me arriving with my avocado under my arm, the others used to grin and elbow each other. Some would saunter up to my table with an insolent air. Others were scandalized. Would I really dare to . . .? I had a great time leading them along.

Brazilians eat avocado with sugar. In Portuguese, it's called *abacate*. *Abacatada*, a drink of avocado, lime, milk and sugar, is the most popular *batido*, or shake, in the country. For Brazilians, the idea of using avocado in a soup is like, for Italians, the idea of putting honey in their minestrone. Or, for someone from Madrid, the idea of putting slices of ripe mango in their chickpea stew together with the usual sausage, *morcilla* and raw ham. They all thought I was an eccentric or a troublemaker. I used to tell them it was a common habit for at least two million people in the countries of America, but in vain. They wouldn't listen. For them, it was an absurdity, a piece of bad taste and nothing else.

In Bahia, I continued to put avocado in soups and stews and mix it with fish and shrimps. I also learned to love *abacatada*. It's a delicious drink. I grew so fond of it, I've never stopped making it since. I like drinking it in one go. As I feel it go down, I have the impression my insides are being massaged with a cool, purifying cream. What I like best of all is the very delicate taste that comes back up to the lips. It's better than that of the original *batido*, like a benign echo from by gastric caverns.

Alas, I've lived in Havana for 30 years, but I've never managed to persuade a Cuban – not even members of my family – to accept it. The few who have dared to taste my avocado batido take one sip, then hand me back the glass with the same horrified expression the Brazilian students used to have when they saw me putting avocado in my soup. It's a real pity: Cubans miss out on sweet avocado and Brazilians miss out on the savoury variety.

I console myself by thinking that one day a juster, prejudice-free society will take possession of the world. I dream that children will learn from the cot not to cling stubbornly to regular habits. That they learn to love and defend what's theirs – their country, their traditions – but also appreciate that many other good things exist in the world. And you can't expect to arrive at good things without a bit of hard work. Educationalists will teach children to appreciate diversity and cultivate tolerance. That way children will be more intelligent with more respect for their neighbours.

In conclusion, I'd like to recall that in pre-Revolutionary Cuba, the poor were used to eating a dish called 'the blonde girl with green eyes'. It consisted of boiled corn flour and enriched with pieces of avocado.

When I have guests who like very piquant food, I cook a personal creation of mine inspired by that 'blonde girl'. First, I prepare an avocado cream and add a very strong chilli pepper (there's a small, conical green or red variety in Cuba called '*ají de puta madre*'). I then mix it well with *polenta*. The result is more green than yellow. At the end, if I don't want to reveal the presence of the avocado, and to intrigue my guests – always astonished at the silky texture of my *polenta* – I add some saffron, just enough to restore the corn to its natural colour.

FROZEN FAST FOOD

Pier Lorenzo Tasselli

*T*he Hercules C130 was flying over the Antarctic. We were wedged into our seats along the walls, all wrapped up from head to foot in our Polar outfits, in accordance with the regulations. In the case of an emergency landing, we'd be leaping out fast to stay alive, with no time for rummaging through our equipment in search of the right gear.

The Hercules landed without me even realizing. As a side door opened we were struck by a blinding light and the biting cold. We disentangled ourselves from our harnesses and swarmed towards the exit, picking out our own luggage from the heap. I shot out of the craft, all bundled up and laden down, and I found myself right in the middle of a very hostile environment. A snowstorm was raging – or at least, so it seemed: the wind was blowing in strong gusts, the snow whirled in the air slapping my face without respite, and it was unbelievably cold. I put on my snow goggles, which immediately misted over. In the middle of the snowstorm I could see a hut, indistinctly, a dark spot in the midst of an endless white landscape.

I stepped into a large rectangular tunnel – as black as the outside world was white – which led to a large dome, still quite cold. Under the dome there was a series of prefabricated structures that looked like containers.

A door opened and the travellers went through. I did the same. It was the canteen and kitchen room, a place I would soon come to know so well. We sat down here and there, and I poured myself some coffee – from your usual transparent pot into your usual paper cup.

A pale, skinny lad arrived. He said he was the head of the logistics section (it went without saying that he was military personnel) and gave us a series of explanations that he regarded as essential. I made very little sense of it, but I did understand one thing, which was weird: if visitors arrived from the outer Antarctic area on an unofficial basis – be they travellers, explorers or whatever – we were to give them a kick in the butt instead of a welcome, to leave them helpless outside, possibly without even so much as a civil greeting. Such was the Regulation which loomed on the board. This being said, the man went back to sleep because according to the official time it was 3 'a.m.'.

So no one was going to see us to our dwellings; not that we really understood where they were. Outside, apparently. So I plucked up all my courage, poured down another coffee, put on my goggles, zipped up my parka, covered my head with its fur-lined Eskimo-style hood, and eventually went out.

There was no snowstorm out there at all – just a blinding white plain and a deep blue sky. Not a single breath of wind, and the cold was not really biting. Getting off the craft, I had simply found myself in the middle of a fake storm: all that snow-whirling and wind-gusting was caused by the rotors, which are never stopped lest they freeze.

The Hercules had gone, and the snow was scattered with luggage and bags, including my boxes full of tools, so carefully nurtured during the trip from Los Angeles. All around us the ice stretched out as far as the eye could see, perfectly flat.

So where were our dwellings? Far away on the horizon I could see a series of dark green containers. Surely it couldn't be those. The was space everywhere, too much of it, and the installations were scattered all over the place. Here I am, I thought, stranded in the middle of the Antarctic, 34°C below zero and 700 kilometres from the nearest human settlement, with my luggage at my feet and 3,000 metres of ice beneath them.

Minute against the horizon, somebody was walking towards the huts. Cursing in my disbelief, I set out in the same direction, moving one large foot after the other in the snow.

From closer to, the dwellings resembled a row of small hangars, much like those seen in war movies like *Mash*. It was weird to find them even at the South Pole. Despite the similarity to their tropical counterparts, they were equipped with a robust insulation system: a heating plant was attached to each one, noisily channelling hot air inside. Entrance was via a double door.

Inside, the darkness seemed even darker, after all that blinding sunlight and snow. I found myself in a narrow corridor, among drop-curtains of the usual green material, behind which people could be heard snoring. It looked very much like the dormitory in the hold of a galleon, or submarine. I eventually managed to find an unoccupied place.

The hangar-dormitory was split by partition walls into single rooms, which opened on the front towards the corridor. When occupied this opening could be closed with a wide oilcloth curtain. Finding such a cloth for my cubicle required considerable effort in the days that followed.

Diarchy

After a sleep I went back to the canteen room, where I met the scientific head of the base. A really nice person – quite the opposite of the military head of the base. He was an astrophysicist with broad interests that transcended the domain of physics. Somewhat melancholic of character, he was often brought to despair by his military alter ego. And when explorers eventually arrived from the outer Antarctic area, he dashed to greet them, he personally saw them around the base, he made sure they would be cared for, nourished and hosted. He physically placed himself between them and the military head. The base was thus ruled by a diarchy distinctly reminiscent of the relationship between the military and political commissars in the Red Army, where a similar dualism also prevailed.

I spoke to the scientific head about the feeling of neglect I felt on arriving at the base, and he sighed: he had experienced exactly the same sensation. He told me it was the first sign of an unexpected reality – at the South Pole, daily life was entirely self-managed.

The first activity I took part in was the excavation of a trench in the snow for laying cables, which took a couple of days. Then, my conscience decided it was high time I had some fun, so I started my photographic report.

In the hangar where the 'Amanda' experiment was taking place (neutrinos through the ground) there was also a wonderful camera tripod, perfect for using with the self-timer. I took some nice shots of myself next to the South Pole sign. It was a sequence, really: in the first shot I was tucked up in my head-to-foot Eskimo gear, in the second I was zipping down my parka and – just like Nembo Kid coming out of Clark Kent's clothes – I eventually appeared wearing tights and my Arcigola Slow Food T-shirt. In the last shot, I was clutching the bottles of Barolo del Castello di Verduno that Arcigola had given me so that I could bring them down to the South Pole. Mission accomplished.

My couple of dozen readers may wonder why Arcigola had entrusted me with this task. Well, perhaps you didn't know that the Barolo di Verduno was brought to the North Pole by Umberto Nobile on the Norge airship. Now, thanks to my endeavour, the other Pole was also a *fait accompli*.

Alas, History mistreated this feat. There is no proper documentary evidence of it left at all: as soon as I set foot in my home country – Termini railway station, in Rome – the bag containing my photographic material was swiftly stolen from me. To tell you the truth, a few pictures do exist which other members of the expedition sent me afterwards; they were taken on New Year's Eve, when the bottles were opened. They show a handful of deranged men in pitiful conditions crammed around a table scattered with left-over food – including several cans of Budweiser. In the background, an anonymous partition with a picture on it. And there I am pouring wine from a bottle, with the Castello di Verduno label turned towards the lens. Except that a picture like that could have been taken anywhere, in any dull room in any part of the world. Still, I swear it was taken in the canteen of the Scott-Amundsen base, South Pole, on New Year's Eve 1992-93. But no evidence of this is left.

A Communist Society

The T-shirts I used to wear bore the Slow Food logo, thus my mission was soon discovered. And this raised a wide range of expectations: being Italian, I was supposed to be a great singer and an excellent cook.

The kitchen at the Scott-Amundsen base was endowed with a small team of professional cooks and aids; still, it needed further staffing, no experience required. It was a fatigue duty that all the people at the base made on a shift basis. It was not compulsory, really – just *noblesse oblige*. Regardless of rank, everyone enrolled for a shift; the head of the scientific section also made his appearance behind the counter, wearing an apron and clutching a ladle to serve us the soup (I had no doubts about him, and to tell you the truth, even that shit of a military head did his shift).

On my arrival, a gorgeous Mexican woman – indolent and charismatic – was walking around the kitchen. I immediately decided to volunteer.

Once a week cooks were off duty and the kitchen management was handed over to volunteers, who cooked whatever took their fancy, and were convinced they were able to cook. That day was usually awful, and you had to make do with a series of pseudo-pizzas, tasteless mush, would-be-lasagne. And when our turn came, I made it clear right from the start that my relationship with cooking basically came down to sitting at the table and eating. Thus, I accepted to make salads and cut the pies in six perfect slices. The fruit pies were absolutely delicious. Cinnamon-flavoured apple pie is typically American, and the cherry and blueberry pies were just as good. More unusual versions were also sometimes available: pumpkin pies and treacle pies. The pumpkin pie was really superb. Extolling the virtues of the food, I asked in a pompous tone: 'Who made these delicious pies?' With a slight aura of embarrassment, the woman helping the cook had to admit it was her. So I asked her what the secret was. Well, easy peasy: you simply had to take the package pre-cooked in California from the refrigerator and put it into the micro-wave.

The quality of the cooking depended, clearly enough, on the virtues of the head cook. Sometimes there were excellent cooks seeking adventure on the other side of the globe, other times you were stuck with whoever applied for the job. In any case, the raw materials were excellent and deserved proper treatment, and this was not always the case.

At the South Pole supplies are always first-class: craft land bringing all sorts of things at least a couple of times a day, including fresh vegetables and meat (but not milk, God knows why – you only get long-life milk, of the hardly drinkable sort). Apart from the larder, food was stored on the ice floor under the dome (–20°C) or outside, in the snow, in the sun (–34°C): pyramids of turkeys that looked like rugby balls, whole sides of beef, piles of half-kids, boxes and containers with all sorts of foodstuffs. The refrigerator was used for warming things up: when you had to cook some food, you put it in the refrigerator to bring it from an outside temperature of minus 30-20°C to a suitable temperature of minus 5°C.

The members of the Antarctic community ate their meals in the canteen, during various time brackets. Even so, the canteen and larder were open 24 hours a day, and accessible on an everyone-caters-to-his-own-needs basis. You could find all sorts of rations for snacks, breakfast, and drinking: the ever-present transparent coffee pot, tea bags, the Ovaltine tin . . . In the self-service refrigerator, there were a few special neatly-labelled dishes wrapped up in transparent film bearing the name of the owner. But if anyone wanted to take a whole turkey from the pile and cook it in the oven (or eat it raw!) there would be no problem . . . but it never happened.

A market as such still survived, in the form of the shop at the base. Its features were singular. It opened for an hour a day selling toiletry articles, stamps, Antarctic gadgets and alcoholic drinks. The role of the 'salesman' was played in turn by the various members of the community, as happened in the kitchen. Prices were not real, they were a sort of token. When I bought a packet of disposable razor-blades, the voluntary person on shift checked on a special book, which said that the price was 20 cents for the whole packet. We both laughed, I paid the 20 cents while he took note of the sale. Soaps, toothpaste, wine and tequila were also available, at ridiculous prices.

All this is to say that at the South Pole, where 'freight' costs are among the highest in the world, there is a shop with the lowest prices in the world, and most foodstuffs can be obtained for free, and are available in huge quantities.

The token you pay at the shop has the same function as entering an item sold in the ledger – that is, rationalizing the distribution of some specific commodities, which are not 'merchandise' as such in that they have no real exchange value. The items requiring this particular technique were really just a few. Among these, alcohol had a special place: it was the only foodstuff that came under a controlled regime, and indeed for a short while it was restricted. In the Scott-Amundsen base, once the working shift was over almost everyone went around carrying bundles of beer – I am not saying single cans or six-can packs, but whole suitcases of cans! The standard packaging held 24 cans and had a side handle for carrying. For us Italians, who also enjoy our tipple (albeit of a different sort), such behaviour was almost incomprehensible, and sometimes also obnoxious, particularly in view of the fact that it focused on watery US beer.

Happily for us, our *winter-over* was Andy Calohun, a Scottish lad, though very Mediterranean in looks and style. His job was to spend six months of Polar night at the base to nurture our experiments. Perfectly suited to surviving the Antarctic winter, he had brought with him all the equipment necessary for home brewing. We waited for the outcome of the first wort, which was fermenting in a liquid gas cylinder, and extensively celebrated on the occasion of the first tapping – a Stout ale, robust and aromatic.

In the meantime, I kept looking for an oilcloth curtain for my cubicle. Nobody was able to give me real help; it seemed they had all found theirs by chance. I also ended up finding one by chance, and not only this. One day, needing some writing paper, I was told where I could find it. I went there and opened a small door. There before my eyes was a dream-like vision: an endless stretch of shelves piled with potentially useful items, all the spare parts of all the machines. An eternal light shone on them. No human beings were around. 'I like the South Pole because the doors here have no keys', one of my colleagues once told me. 'If you need something all you have to do is take it off the shelf.' Who would possibly 'steal' anything? And what for? To sell it to whom? To take it where? We were 700 kilometres of ice away from the nearest human settlement, 3,000 from South America. And why should anybody take more than what was truly needed?

Why pile things up, if what you need is always at hand? There were useful items at everyone's disposal, even beyond their actual needs. Such objects were thus devoid of any exchange value! That was Communism Accomplished!

As a matter of fact, Bucharin and Preobrazenskij, in the *ABC of Communism*, maintained the following: 'The Communist production system is not based on production geared to the market, but to production geared to satisfying everyone's needs . . . there are no longer "goods", only "products". These products are manufactured, but they are not exchanged, purchased or sold. They are simply kept in common stores and distributed to people needing them. Therefore, money will no longer be necessary'. And a few lines later: 'All the products will be available in abundance, all the sores will be healed, and everyone will be able to take as much as he or she needs. But will people try to take more than is really needed? Certainly not. Nobody nowadays, on getting on a train, would pay for three places and leave two free – there will be no need for it. And the same will go for all the products: everyone would get from the common store what is really needed, and nothing more. Nobody will be interested in selling goods in excess, because everything it takes to satisfy people's needs will always be available. And money will have no value either.'

This is exactly the way the Scott-Amudsen base worked. I experienced a long moment of ecstatic emotion – I had come a long way, was foot-sore, grief-ridden and weary. I had reached the South Pole, and found the Communist Society there! Unwittingly set up by the Americans.

If there is a mysterious reason underlying the unconscious labouring of men, I was almost led to believe that the whole thing had been created FOR ME.

There I was – and at last everything took on a real meaning.

MAPPING WHAT WE EAT
Marco Riva

$\mathcal{B}$efore the revolution induced by food technology (modern preservation, cracking and reconstituting processes of ingredients) and by the opportunities offered by advanced transport, the drive towards globalization in the food economy was limited to products with high added value (spices, tonics, alcohol, exotic fruit, cheeses, meat and preserved fish), as well as cereals (which were already crossing the Mediterranean at the time of the Roman Empire). These days, in the most industrialized regions, 1000 kilometre journeys are quite normal even for fresh meat and fish, vegetables, milk, eggs, oranges, strawberries and apples, in line with a trend that is continually increasing the distance between production and consumption. The evolution of food preservation, the consolidation of manufacturing processes such as cracking and reconstitution and the reduction in transport costs have radically changed the provenance of the food in our refrigerators: Irish meat and Norwegian salmon, German milk, Slav cherries, Tunisian olives, Chilean wine; and then there is Canadian or Australian flour in our bread, pasta and biscuits, Dutch or German potatoes in the purée mix, Russian malt is used as the basis for Scotch whisky, Japanese tuna inside the cans.

Most consumers have only a rudimentary knowledge about these 'food routes': some are obvious and well-known, while others are quite surprising. Not all current labelling regulations comprise a compulsory declaration of provenance. In an Italian fruit and vegetable market they will always say that the lettuce is locally grown and never admit that the oranges come from Spain or the mushrooms from ex-Yugoslavia. Again, in Italy, 80% of the meat is imported, but I challenge anyone to find a butcher who admits to Slovenian rabbit or Polish escalopes!

Packaged products show where production took place: but the ingredients, where do they come from? This is no trifling question: many proposals have been put forward to find an international coding method which would make it possible to discover the origin of the raw materials – even in products that are transformed twice – particularly for reasons of safety (the vicissitudes of mad cow disease should have taught us something).

We were saying that some of the routes are surprising. My job has brought me into contact with an interesting case in point: that of yogurt destined for distribution in Sicily and produced bearing the name of an important Italian company with its headquarters near Milan. The raw material – milk – comes from Bavaria; it is produced in an associate company near Rome (a company that has its own brand and was recently taken over by the sector's leader) in central Italy; trucked north by road to the Milan headquarters, and then air freighted to its destination in the extreme south. But is Sicily nearer to Milan or to Rome? In this case, the added value easy covers the costs of this meandering route. Yet it is reasonable to point out that yogurt is not a highly sophisticated technological product, and that to produce it near the consumer area (which would also ensure greater 'freshness' when retailed) would not be such a far-fetched idea. Here is another miracle arising from the global village: in Italy (where there some 300 registered, active and exploited natural water springs, evenly distributed throughout the territory), half the mineral water travels from the southern and central regions towards the north and half does the reverse journey. In this case there is no doubt that over half the price of the water is due to transport costs.

Then there is the case of *bresaola* (dry-salted beef), which is representative of another problem entirely.

This delicatessen product is the pride of the food economy in the Valtellina area. It is a locally characteristic product, protected by the IGP rules (Protected Geographical Marks). However, 90% of the *bresaola* marketed is made from rounds of beef which, although top quality, come from Brazil or Argentina. The local character is assured by the curing methods which are indubitably those of the Valtellina. The same thing happens to Parma or San Daniele ham, where the pork itself is anything but local.

These examples are not pleas for protectionism, but just the right to know and the chance to check. It may be an illusion, but some of the more distorted models ought to regain lost balance, with greater focus on the development of the kind of integrated systems (profitable, on a small scale) that make the best of local resources and production opportunities: from small-holdings to baking products, to the miniaturization of some dairy processes. By way of consolation, at least the British and American 'microbreweries' are making a substantial stand with their 'fresh' and 'diversified' beers brewed at home or in small local works.

Food game

Just a little upset by what appears to be going on, I decided to take a closer look at things myself, ascertaining the origins of the food that makes up my normal daily fare. To carry out this 'food game', I was helped by many colleagues and friends involved in food technology. As we have already pointed out, the legally required indications (that is, the declarations on the label) are, on the whole, insufficient.

I should start off by saying that my daily fare is what you might call modern but traditional, nothing very exotic, and fairly free of food fads, dietary or ideological. Just contemporary 'Mediterranean' fare, deliberately inclusive of fish, carbohydrates, vegetables and salad, and open to preserved products. A further note: the recorded consumption took place on one June day (the provenance of many foods depends on the season) and the geographical reference is Como, Lombardy, Italy, Europe.

What did I eat? For breakfast: a cup of fresh milk, 2 biscuits (Italy's best-known brand) coated in chocolate and hazelnut spread, with sweetened coffee. For lunch: a dish of pasta with tomato and basil sauce, followed by a grilled beef escalope with a side-serving of *soncino* (the cultivated version of 'lamb's lettuce' or corn salad of the genus *Valerianella*), and lastly a kiwi-fruit. Other ingredients also featured in the lunch: parmesan cheese, bread, olive oil, salt, pepper, and mineral water. Mid-afternoon I had a vanilla ice-cream (the commercially-produced sort, covered with chocolate). Lastly, for dinner: a frozen pizza topped with tomato and mozzarella, a boiled sole with a spoonful of mayonnaise and a side-serving of french fries, followed by a peach. The accessory ingredients were: bread, wine (Sardinian Vermentino), vegetable oil (for cooking the chips), salt. After dinner I succumbed to the desire for a little chocolate and a small glass of whisky.

Separating the data on the provenance of the food (collated with patience and a couple of dozen phone calls) I prepared 3 summary charts (see figures 1, 2 and 3) which respectively indicate food or ingredients from national, European and intercontinental sources.

The product that took the shortest route to get to my stomach was the fresh milk. Actually I am lucky to live in an area where milking and packing take place within a radius of 20-30 km. Next (over 50 km) comes the *soncino* salad (picked and dispatched from around Cremona). One of the ingredients in the pizza (the yeast) had about the same distance to cover on its way from Pavia. Broadening the range, but still within the Italian borders, we find the eggs (Vicenza in the province of Venetia), the basil (Imperia, in Liguria), and then some of the flour, mixed in the ingredients for the pizza and the bread (the Po Valley Plain). Again, it was about the same distance for the parmesan. The sugar came from over 300 kilometres away (Ferrara, in Emilia) as did the peaches (Cesena in Romagna). Around a hundred years ago this would have been the geographical limit for collecting together the ingredients for the meal. Add the sunflower oil (an ingredient in the mayonnaise and used for the french fries, Umbria), salt and some of the semolina (Apulia), the wine (Sardinia), the mineral water (the naturally fizzy sort, Campania), the tomato purée (again, Campania), and the lemon (Sicily), and that's it for the national larder: a goodly store of flavourings and secondary ingredients, but weak on basic ingredients, at least from a dietary point of view.

We need to go over to the European chart to discover something more substantial: milk, the ingredient for the ice-cream and the pseudo-mozzarella for the pizza, come from Bavaria; the flour for the biscuits is British, as are the malt and the distillate (whisky); French bran for the pasta, Turkish hazelnuts (chocolate and hazelnut spread), Dutch potatoes, Irish beef, and sole from the Atlantic. My luck must have been out: the olive oil, even though the label was Italian, had absorbed the hot sun of Spain!

Even further flung were, obviously, the tonics: cacao (chocolate) from Equatorial Africa and the Antilles, coffee from Columbia and Brazil. Then there was the pepper, from the Far East, the kiwi (in June it came from New Zealand) and the Canadian, American or Australian flour and brans. So, my meals spoke many languages, albeit with an Italian accent.

Imported proteins

This survey is well documented, but not very objective. Nonetheless, it closely approaches the truth. Macroeconomic indicators suggest that over 60% of the proteins and carbohydrates consumed in Italy (such as meat, milk, fish and flour) come from imported sources. We know that in heavily industrialized areas agriculture is now a marginal activity. No wonder the Agricultural department at the University where I work, in the centre of Milan, has to arrange daily student visits to the sheds to see the cows.

Basically, the intercontinental transport and marketing of food is an unavoidable aspect of the economy – but this is not the same as saying it is a 'good arrangement'. A 'softer' and more 'responsible' development could considerably reduce the distortions which force food to travel too much.

After looking, with a certain dismay, at the charts enclosed with these notes, like many inhabitants of metropolitan areas I sowed basil and sage seeds in two pots (my wife is having a go at growing a tangerine tree, but I frankly think this is a no-hoper). In a few months, these will be the products that take the shortest road to get to my table.

Table 1

Italy

Foodstuff	Provenance	Foodstuff	Provenance
Fresh milk	Lombardy	Basil	Liguria
Salad	Lombardy	Sunflower oil	Umbria
Yeast (frozen pizza)	Lombardy	Tomato (purée)	Campania
Egg (mayonnaise)	Venetia	Mineral water	Campania
Flour (biscuits, bread)	Po Valley	Bran	Apulia
Parmesan	Emilia	Salt	Apulia
Sugar	Emilia	Lemons	Sicily
Peaches	Romagna	Wine	Sardinia

Table 2

Europe

Foodstuff	Provenance	Foodstuff	Provenance
Beef	Ireland	Hazelnuts	
Malt (whisky)	Great Britain	(chocolate spead)	Turkey
Flour (biscuits)	Great Britain	Olive oil	Spain
Sole (frozen)	Atlantic	Bran	France
Milk (mozzarella		Potatoes (frozen)	Holland
for pizza)	Germany		

Table 3

World

Foodstuff	Provenance	Foodstuff	Provenance
Flour (pizza base)	Canada	Cacao	
Bran	United States	(chocolate spread)	Antilles
Cacao (chocolate)	Equatorial Africa	Pepper	Far East
Coffee	Colombia	Flour (bread)	Australia
Coffee	Brazil	Kiwi	New Zealand

MORE FROM LESS

Vic Cherikoff

*T*wo centuries ago, the only food eaten in Australia was 'bush tucker' – food that grew in, on and around the land then populated entirely by Aborigines. These native inhabitants herded no animals (some may have used dogs for hunting and certainly used them at night for warmth) but intimately knew the life cycles and managed the populations of animals they hunted. Neither did they plant crops but encouraged natural regeneration of their food plants by digging water channels aiding flood irrigation or through the use of fire. In hard times, in some of the most inhospitable inhabited deserts in the world, survival through drought depended on no more than three species of plants and finding water was an all-consuming activity. More typically, Aborigines forming nearly 600 different nations chose their foods from between 150 and 600 different animals, river and seafoods, insects, fruits, seeds, nuts, tubers, gums, nectar, honey, herbs and spices. Life was long (by comparison to Europeans at the time), relaxed and rich in art, music, songs and stories which maintained the connection of Aborigines to one another in their family groups within their clans but more importantly, with their land.

When the white man came, everything changed. Driven from their lands and into conflict with their invaders as well as their neighbours, Aboriginal culture altered radically. Disease and dislocation disrupted Aboriginal ways and their diets constricted to more closely resemble that of the colonialists – a simple reliance on white flour, white sugar and meat from introduced animals which were often eating traditional bushfoods as they grazed. Next to no attention was paid to the native foods and even less to Aboriginal preparative methods, until now.

Recent research into the nutritional composition of bushfoods conducted at the University of Sydney, has revealed quite a few surprises. The Kakadu plum (a new marketing name for the unflattering but more common colloquial, billy goat plum) is now the world record holder for the fruit with the highest content of vitamin C, blitzing the previous contender, the Acerola cherry, by several percent. It has been nearly 14 years since this discovery and yet the market for the Kakadu plum is still undeveloped and currently supplied entirely from wild harvested stocks. As a vitamin source, the Kakadu plum is also endowed with high levels of folic acid and iron, both of which assist the absorption of ascorbic acid. How much do you need? The vitamin C in a single olive-sized fruit will provide three times our daily requirement and a spreadable fruit manufactured here in Australia under the Australia's Own brand still consistently has 1% vitamin C in it despite all the cooking and blending.

Another discovery was the protein content of wattle seeds which were used as a flour-substitute and made into a seed cake. Although heavy and most like a full-grain bread, wattle seedcakes had an interesting oily flavour particular to the species being used. Australia has nearly 1000 wattle species but Aborigines used only around 50 of these for food. The protein content, along with the oils and complex carbohydrates make for an interesting nutritional and flavour mix. Today, wattleseed or just 'Wattle' is used as a flavouring in a roasted and ground form not unlike coffee but with many more uses. Wattle can 'bush-up' whipped cream, ice cream, pancakes, breads or even a red wine based meat sauce. Some cafés now serve Wattleccino™ flavoured cappuccino as a caffeine-free drink with a coffee, chocolate, hazelnut taste.

Many of the new generation of bushfoods now becoming popular around the world include the herbs and spices Aborigines used either as meat flavourings, accompaniments or tonic foods and medicines (inhalants commonly). Nutritionally, these are not significant but as functional foods they can influence the net nutritional effect. By flavouring a nutritious but low fat, low sugar or high carbohydrate food with herbs the palatability can be improved and enjoyment enhanced. Without the flavourings otherwise nutritious foods may rarely be consumed.

More exciting is the nature of the complex carbohydrates in wattle and many other bushfoods. Aborigines, like other similar groups around the world, have never needed physiological adaptations to a diet high in simple sugars since even ready sources of sugars say, in wild honey, came along with waxes and proteins which slowed absorption of sugars. Modern Caucasians, who rely most on sugars (and saturated fats) are even beginning to show some intolerance to these basic nutrients as the incidence of diabetes and its complications begin to escalate. Yet traditional foods of most races seem to offer the key to good health. The complexity of the carbohydrates appears to play a protective role by being slowly absorbed as they are digested and the simple sugars released from starches and other polysaccharides (sugar matrices). In the body this slow-release sugar is more easily handled than the deluge of simple sugars released after ingesting refined, processed foods of the modern world. Perhaps we should all be eating more wild carbohydrates, zero fat bunya nuts and tubers, low fat (high iron) game meats and seafoods (with their beneficial cardiovascular effects), nutritionally dense seeds, nuts and fruits and all benefit from minimally processed simple foods with natural flavour.

As for us modern foragers, more used to food halls than food trees, we are now able to add back wild ingredients in culturally appropriate ways. Bunya nuts can be boiled, puréed and blended with soy milk (organic of course) and then refried to bring out the characteristic chestnut flavour of the bunya while turning the natural waxy-potato texture into a more versatile choux pastry-like consistency. This refried bunya nut can be used as a pie crust, made into dumplings, toppings or garnishing for savoury or sweet dishes. Fat-free cooking with paperbark, Aboriginal style, could be used for a game steak (low fat and high iron as for most game meats). Having seared the meat, topped it with a layer of refried bunya nut and wrapped it in a piece of paperbark (a layered papery bark from a swamp tree), cook on the hotplate of a BBQ or dry fry in a pan until the meat feels spongy but bounces back when pressed. Some steamed vegetables of any type 'bushed-up' with a combined sprinkle of mountain pepper and native peppermint would complete the main course.

For dessert, a rainforest parfait, made with a Kakadu plum jelly over-layered with a low fat fromage blanc flavoured with lemon myrtle (a rainforest herb with a delicious lemon/lime and lemon grass taste). A dollop of wattle cream (high fat this time but just use a little) which is simply whipped cream through which an extract of wattle is folded to turn the cream into a coffee/chocolate/hazelnut delight. For texture, a crumble of wattleseed Anzac biscuits finishes the treat.

THE BANQUET
Raymond Buren

$\mathcal{G}$eorgia is an unusual country. It boasts an alphabet and a language of its own, a centuries-old history rich in legend and epic deeds, and, on top of that, the most seductive convivial traditions. It is said to be the country of the Golden Fleece, meaning that the modern-day province is none other than ancient Colchis, where Jason led the Argonauts. It is also rumoured that here gold prospectors used to immerse sheep's fleeces into the river water to make specks of the precious metal stick to them. It is no accident that jewellery is still a flourishing business in these parts.

But to get back to the myths, Zeus had Prometheus chained to a lonely rock in the Caucasus, where an eagle came to peck at his liver. The Prometheus myth is at once cruel and ambiguous. Prometheus, whose name in Greek means 'forethought', stole fire from heaven for men, and later refused to open Pandora's box. Infuriated by his repeated insolence, Zeus banned him from Olympus and sentenced him to the torture from which Heracles later released him. Perhaps Prometheus is the symbol of revolt against all despots? Perhaps he is the hero of progress who freed man from his miserable condition? Or perhaps he is simply the Artisan capable of creating harmony and reconciling heaven and earth with sociality and conviviality? In other words, wasn't Prometheus, to all intents and purposes, a Georgian?

The qualities that he exhibited are still undeniably safe and sound among the people of Georgia. Neither Slav nor Latin, they are warm, loquacious and joyful, as well as being endowed with brilliant intelligence. The new Barbarians, armed with their astounding technologies and mass produced goods (Coke and Fanta, to name but two), have still failed to destroy the deep roots and traditions of a country which has often been devastated by marauding foreigners from both north and south. To tell the truth, Georgia isn't the most accessible of places, and tourism (the tourism of tour operators, that is) is still in its infancy. The fact is that pilgrimages in pursuit of the treasures of humanity have long been hard to manage.

No tourist guides are available for this splendid country, with the exception of publications from the period of Soviet occupation, and the *Guide des Routards* still considers the area too risky for a journey or a stay. The best approach is thus to take stock of information picked up on the spot. If you are lucky enough to know the Georgian language or Russian or, in the towns and cities, English or German, you should get by. In any case, group tours are organized by agencies such as Caucasus Travel Ltd (fax ++995/32/987399-931175), capable of fielding whole battalions of Georgian guides with charming smiles. A number of different airlines serve Tbilisi, the capital, with the lion's share going to Turkish Airlines. By land, the route from Turkey is still the best, though it's pretty impervious.

Wine and conviviality

So why go to Georgia? The answer's easy: to discover a simple, still unadulterated country, full of good wine and fresh, wholesome food. Georgia is a place where they are oblivious to the artificial manipulation of foodstuffs, a place of refined customs, where the women's long dark seductive brows shade eyes of velvet. In short, you come here in search of the treasures of humanity.

To say that Georgia is the country of wine is to state the obvious. Since time immemorial, they have cultivated grape varieties here – mtsvane, rkatsiteli, tsitsaka, tsolikauri, krakuna and saperavi – that are totally unknown in the West. Situated on the rocky outcrops of the Caucasus, Katelia is the wine-growing area par excellence, but vineyards are to be found everywhere. In Tbilisi, I even saw a vine growing out of the pavement with its leaves creeping up to the second floor of a house. Saint Nino, who brought Christianity here in the third century, bears a cross with two vine-shoots entangled in her hair. Even the graphic volutes of the Georgian alphabet, very complicated for the uninitiated, evoke vine tendrils. Georgia also happens to be the only country I know where an official holiday is celebrated during the grape harvest. Wine (*ghvino*) is, without doubt, the lifeblood of Georgian patriotic love.

Wine is made using archaic methods. After pressing with the feet, the must, or *kvevri*, is left to ferment with the skins and stalks in large terracotta pitchers buried in the ground. The Georgian naïf painter, Niko Pirosmani, has produced lively pictures of his method of wine making – organic ante litteram. To this day, the wine is still drunk from the horns of animals. Everyone knows that the horn is the ancestor of the glass that was modelled on the breasts of Helen of Troy. Desiring both glasses and breasts, it was Paris who ended up starting the Trojan War.

The Georgian table is fantastic, always over-abundant, but never heavy on the stomach. Olive oil is entirely lacking and meat is rare, but dairy produce, vegetables and fruit abound. The national snack, eaten at all hours of the day, is *katchapury*, a delicious wheatflour galette flavoured with cheese from Imericia, which is now to be found everywhere. Shelled walnuts are often used in Georgian cooking and, during the grape harvest, long 'sausages' of them dipped in grape juice and flour are hung over the doors – a pick-me-up known locally as *tchutchkela*. Other noteworthy delicacies include stuffed aubergine, horseshoe-shaped sausages stuffed with meat, barberries and pomegranate. So there's no risk of dying of hunger in Georgia!

The Georgian banquet of today derives, of course, from the Roman *cena* and the Greek *deipson*. There can be no faithful without a banquet, and there can be no true banquet without a ritual. This is how man has decided to honour the gods and the fruits of the soil. All this of course was before we were overwhelmed by the horrible plethoric practice of standing, tray in hand, in endless queues in front of the counters of canteens or fast food joints.

In his *Symposiaca*, Plutarch tells us that the women of Sybaris used to receive invitations to banquets a year in advance to give them time to think about the clothes and jewellery they would wear. He then warns that, '. . . those possessed of common sense do not take part in a banquet like a jar to be filled up; for if a dish is bad it can be left, and if the wine is not good one can drink water; but a fellow guest who gives one a headache, who is unbearable and uncouth, destroys and ruins the pleasure of any wine, of any dish and of any music.'

We know that the Greeks loved banquets, when they unleashed their appetites to the full and wholly indulged their Dionysian spirit and their intelligence, though they remained sober throughout. A master of ceremonies, the symposiarch, established the number of kraters it was correct to drink and how the wine had to be diluted (often three parts water to one part wine). The Greeks never drank pure wine, which they considered poisonous, leaving the practice to barbarians like the Shiites or the centaur Eurytion, who died as a result.

The role of the *tamada*

The Georgian banquet, the great feast, is known as the *supra* and is presided over by a master of ceremonies, the *tamada*, who directs the sequence of events without fear of contradiction. In Telavi, the capital of the wine-growing region of Katelia, I had the honour of taking part in a *supra* presided over by the governor of the region.

Supra in Georgian means tablecloth and many are the occasions to bedeck tables for feastmaking. Such occasions may be happy (*exinis*) – engagements (*nisnoba*), weddings (*korc'ili*), christenings (*natloba*), the first birthdays of children (*jeoba*) and birthday parties in general (*dabadebis*) – or sad (*c'iris*) – funerals (*kelexi*), the fortieth day after the death (*ormoci*) or the first anniversary of the death (*clistavi*). Of the many other occasions I might list, I shall cite one in particular: the presence of a guest of honour.

The ritual of the toast (*sadgegrjelo*, or 'long life') is the most important moment in the *supra*. You never drink without being explicitly asked to do so, often with a lyrical, evocative speech by the *tamada*. Nor can you drink before sitting down at the table: no exchanging small talk standing up with glass in hand here.

The qualities which the *tamada* has to possess are eloquence and an ability to hold his drink. He has to praise the guest (or the reason for the reunion) in honour of whom he empties his glass, though he must not get drunk. His role is to keep the atmosphere convivial, without drowning it. The participants at the banquet never propose toasts. The *tamada* stands up with his glass in his right hand, then the person to whom the toast is addressed stands up too. No one drinks before the *tamada* (who usually empties his glass: *bolomde*). The other diners remain seated, each drinking only when it is his turn, never all at the same time. Then when everyone has drunk, the person in honour of whom the toast has been made in turn dedicates a toast of gratitude (*samadlobeli*) to all those present. Sometimes up to twelve or fifteen toasts may be made during the *supra*; the last are usually dedicated to Georgia and the Holy Virgin, the mother of God. The rules of the celebration change according to the solemnity of the event.

The *supra* is a typical expression of the Georgian lust for life. This dignified and joyful ritual is in no way formal and, from one toast to the next, envisages lots of lively conversation and laughter.

EN SEVILLA
Enrique Bellver

*T*he queen of the *tapeo* is Seville, where living and eating follow rules of their own. Here time takes on a new dimension, becoming a luxury unknown elsewhere. Living the Seville way means experiencing and interpreting life in a manner that is both grandiose and intimate, magical and detached.

In Seville, 'tomar copas' is a true ceremony. The ubiquitous bars and *tabernas* are the stage on which social life is enacted, and the local population weaves in and out from the streets to play its part in the performance. Seville is a mystery until you join in with its ritual activities.

People do not eat here, they savour, conversing rather than chatting. A local may spend hours in front of a glass of wine and hardly taste it. And that is why the *tapa* was created: traditionally a small portion of food brought with the drink, not the massive servings that the bars tend to offer today, Madrid-style. There's an anecdote that explains the origin of this word. The people of Seville have always enjoyed drinking and chatting in the open, where hosts of insects and butterflies tend to commit suicide in the nearest glass, thereby spoiling its original contents. That is, until one day somebody asked the landlord for a slice of ham or salami, or a piece of cheese, to cover (*tapar*) the glass and protect it from the buzzing hordes. This sort of edible lid subsequently took the name of tapa and became a common practice that gave rise to a rich Andalusian culinary tradition.

According to the writer Juan Carlos Alonso, '*tapear* is cheating the ceremony of eating; having fun with food; acting freely without constraints; enjoying the light-hearted pleasures of the spirit.' 'Going for *tapas*' means savouring rich and varied tastes in an alcoholic and gastronomic crawl through bars and *tabernas*; socializing during a pilgrimage from squares to taverns; and talking for hours of matters human and divine. *Tapeo* is a baroque, sybaritic game which delights the five senses with the flavours, conversations, smells, handshakes and beauty of the streets of Seville.

RULES

Like any serious ceremony, tapeo has its own rules. First of all, there should not be too many people taking part if you want to find a place at the counter or a small table to sit. Moreover, small groups are more conducive to good conversation than larger numbers, and can move more easily from one bar to the next. Secondly, tapeo lovers must appreciate that the virtue of tapa consists in its being a mouthwatering appetizer, not a loaded plate. Lastly, tapeo must be well organized: no repeating tapas at the different 'stations'; and plenty of discernment in selecting cold or hot, stewed or fried, fish or meat tapas, eating everything in the correct sequence so that you will have had a full meal by the end.

Varieties

The range of tapas is extremely wide. It includes simple cold snacks with olives, cold meats or cheese as well as many vegetable, meat and fish dishes cooked in different ways (stewed, fried, marintated).

What follows is a map of the most common tapas that you can find in the tabernas of Seville.

Vegetarian

Olives can be stuffed aliñadas (marinated with herbs) or stuffed peppers (these are called rellenas). Both the fruit (alcaparrón) and the bud (alcaparra) of the caper are eaten.

Vegetables

Spinach esparragadas (cooked with asparagus) and chick peas. Asparagus trigueros (a variety cultivated together with wheat) and bitter grilled amargasos. Broad beans with ham. Russian salad. Tomatoes marinated with green peppers and onion. Anchovies in vinaigrette sauce. Aubergine.

Pulses

Chick pea soup. Cocido (boiled meat and vegetables) with lard.

Preserves

Tuna in oil and en escabeche (marinated with vinegar and herbs), salted anchovies, mussels escabechados.

Cheese and chacinas (dried meat)

Mature cheese. Spanish ham. Cold meats. Pork loin en adobo (that is, preserved with herbs or spices) and pork loin caña. Ham serranitos (mouthfuls) with fried green peppers.

Fish

Fried: cod or salt cod pavia (breaded and fried fish pieces). Hake. Plaice. Mullet. Sardines. Squid. Anchovies. Salt cod omelettes.
Grilled: cuttlefish. Swordfish.
Stewed: dogfish (shark-like fish also called ëseadogí) with potatoes. Cuttlefish with broad beans. Tuna with onions. Salt cod in tomato sauce.
Aliñados: Aliñada is a marinade used to flavour fish (anchovies, octopus) and eggs.
Seafood: stewed, grilled and breaded shrimps. Bigaros (whelks from the Cantabrian sea). Boiled scampi and squills.

Squill omelette. Clams with garlic sauce. Mussels steamed and with a spicy sauce.

Meat

Stewed meat or meat with tomato, potatoes or wrapped in lard. Stewed pork loin. Breaded chicken breasts.

Tripe and offal

Bull's tail. Black pudding with onions. Mixed offal with onions. Stew. Fried chicken livers. Kidneys with sherry and grilled kidneys. Marinated spare ribs.

ITINERARIES

At tapeo time, the most crowded areas are La Macarena, Santa Cruz and Triana. If you have to choose, we definitely recommend the latter, a thoroughly devout working-class district: Seville's own barrio, with myriad bars whose tapas express the town's particular style of cooking. Here are four itineraries in Triana to discover the secrets of traditional cuisine:
● calles de Rodrigo de Triana, Betis, Santa Ana, Pagés del Corro and Pelay y Correa;
● calles Altozano, San Jacinto, Castilla, Pagés del Corro, Patrocinio, Santa Cecilia, Arellano and San Vicente de Paul;
● calles Barrio León, El Tardón Sanchez Arjona, Lopez de Gomara, Evangelista and Trabajo;
● calles Salado, Paraiso and plaza de Cuba.

The following are just a few of the many places where you can tapear to your heart's content.

Calle Altozano
Puesto Las Flores: fried hake, squid and puntillitas.
Los Parientes: shrimps, squills and whelks.
Calle Betis
La Albariza: cana de lomo, ham and cheese.
Los Chorritos: charcoal grilled sardines.
Bar Diego: spinach, soups and offal.
La Boteguita: cod en adobo, snails.
La Primera del Puente: pavías, chipi plancha, mushroom omelette.
Rio Grande: tacos merluza en adobo, sausage.
Calle Pagés del Corro
Bar Begu: tuna alino.
La Flor de Triana: pickles, chacina.
La Canera: peas, ham caballito.
Bar Santa Ana: shrimp omelette, egg flamenca and fried green peppers.
Calle Pureza
María del Puerto: rabbit, chick peas and salt cod, gurnards, shell-fish omelette.
La Trianera: potato omelette, snails and pringá.
El Maravilla: black pudding with onions, chicken manudillo, salt cod in tomato sauce and potato aliño.
Calle Alfareria
Bar Zapato: fried salt cod, grilled shrimps, fried eggs.
La Giralda: fillet montado, serranito.
Calle Manuel Arellano
Bar Felix: croquettes, cod in garlic sauce, salpicon salad.
Bar Fermo: beef briskets, pavías.

Kar Kío: meat in tomato sauce, eggs bechan, breaded mero.
Bar Rio Quema: snails and hake.
Calle San Jacinto
Los Dos Hermanos: shell-fish, whelks, galeras, crab and mojama.
Bar San Jacinto: tripe with Sherry wine, chicken ham, swordfish.
Bar Duero: seafood (berberechos, navajas) and bonito with onions.
Bodega Mananilla: snails, potatoes alliolo, cod pavía.
Calle Evangelista
Bar Tetuan: pinchitos, grilled fillet and aliño de bonito.
Bar Paletas: shrimps in garlic sauce, stew and black pudding with onions.
Plaza de Peñaflor
Bar La Amistad: beef olives, carrilada de merluza.
Bodegón Los Curros: asparagus omelette, home-made sausage, bull's tail.

PLACES

Ultramarinos Casa Moreno
calle Gamazo, 7
It still retains the structure of the typical wine shops, true to both environment and style. High-quality pickles are lined up on the counter, together with hams and cold meats. Very few places are so cosy and attractive. Tapas: liver morcilla, Spanish ham and pâté. Closed on Sundays.
Casa Morales calle Garcia de Vinuesa, 3
One of the few remaining typical tabernas in town, with an enormous cask to serve Valdepenas wine. Tapas: squid, pijotas and cold meats.
Casa Robles Calle Alvarex Quintero, 58
The best tapeo bar in Seville, the watering hole of 'guapa people'. Marinated olives and hams are the real counter speciality. Tapas: swordfish, caldereta, Sevillana rice, lamb stew.
El Mero plaza Altozano
A very cosy bar overlooking the Guadalquivir, where the best Malaga-style small fish are served. Tapas: clams, anchovies and salmonetitos.
Sol y sombre calle Castilla, 151
It is a little distant from the centre of Triana, but its tapas are worth a slightly longer walk. The place is decorated with bull motifs, its stews delight the finest palates and the raciones are abundant. Tapas: mussel marinara style (with a sauce of garlic, oil and parsley), gurnards, cazuela Tio Pepe.
Bodega Santa Maria
calle Montecarmelo
An unpretentious but popular tavern that represents an island of humility in the heart of the fashionable part of town. It serves traditional Sevillan tapas: black pudding with onions, pig's trotters.
El Noli Calle Pagés del Corro, 39
El Noli is the best tapas 'narrator' in Seville: no one can do better in listing over a hundred varieties without any errors or omissions. The food is as good as the rhapsody. This place is very crowded at lunch time. Tapas: ensaladilla, plaice, breaded swordfish.

REMEMBER SPAIN
Carlos Delgado

*I*n countries such as Spain, where backwardness and hunger were rife until quite recently, popular imagination has made a gastronomic virtue of necessity. This is how the 'cuisine of left-overs' was born. This cuisine, together with the need for preserving food for the cold and barren months, has in time produced several examples of culinary masterpieces.

However, this gastronomic heritage has inevitably been undermined by economic evolution, the process of industrialization, migration towards cities and the wish to resemble other advanced societies despite a huge cultural gap. A few excellent Spanish specialities have already disappeared and others run the risk of becoming extinct.

This is the case of *horchata*, which used to be a very popular drink in Spain until US-style industrial beverages pushed it to one side. *Horchata* was the milk of the poor, and was not only high in nutritional content, but also tasted good and cost very little. Production began seven centuries ago in the Comunidad Valenciana and used to be sold by hawkers. It had one defect, however: it was low on hygiene. This was due to the fact that the *chufa* (*Cyperus esculentus*), the small rough-surfaced tuber it is obtained from, hosted a range of bacterial flora that came from the soil and were hard to eliminate using traditional methods. Moreover, often there was further contamination deriving from back-yard processing methods. And so it was that the traditional almost home-made drink was progressively replaced by industrial, sterilized *horchatas*, to the detriment of the high organoleptic value of the drink. In recent times small-scale producers have improved their techniques, so it is still possible to meet a few hawkers offering excellent, thirst-quenching and nourishing summer drinks to passers-by in big cities.

At the other end of the country there's a special Spanish oyster called a *morucha*. This indigenous species from Galicia's *rias* (sort of fjords) has an unmistakable taste, slightly oily meat and penetrating sea aroma. Oysters have been considered excellent fare since very early times, indeed probably since the dawn of civilization. Empty shells dating back to the Paleolithic Age reveal that the earliest groups of human beings were already big eaters of these lamellibranchs. The Greeks also appreciated them, but it was the Romans who first gave oysters their due. Pliny defined them as *'palma mensura'* (the measure of excellence) and insisted on including them among the main dishes at banquets. With his characteristic insight, the poet Horace called oysters 'sea truffles', and the Emperor Vitellius set an all-time record by opening his libations with a superb hors-d'oeuvre of 5000 oysters.

For delicate taste and fine iodized aroma, there are no oysters to beat those of the Atlantic Coast and especially of the western coasts of Finisterre and Galicia. They are at their best when caught after a few dry days, preferably in winter. The oysters of Arcade, Arosa, Marin, Aldan and La Coruña are in a class of their own and should not be confused with the so-called 'Portuguese oyster', which is neither an oyster nor Portuguese (it's actually another kind of shellfish belonging to the *gryphea* family).

In recent years the sublime *moruchas*, as these oysters are called locally, have looked as though their days were numbered. They were subjected to an attack on two fronts: the voracity of human predators and an insidious virus. Happily all is not lost, however. By decontaminating the water and helping similar species to acclimatize, the *moruchas* have been saved, though at considerable cost. In fact their 70% average death rate makes breeding them far from profitable. This explains why nowadays they are almost entirely replaced by oysters of uncertain origin, preferably from Greece, Turkey or Italy and, until recently, Yugoslavia.

Something similar has happened to eel fries (*angulas*, which resemble whitebait). These tender, slithery worm-like creatures are much beloved of the Spanish, who have never had scruples about gastronomic infanticide: think about the *lechazo* (lambkin) and the *toston* (roast suckling-pig), not to mention the Andalusian dish of microscopic fish which has become widespread all over the world. If this dish is delicious when made with adult eels, it is far better when the fish are still fries.

The small Basque village of Aguinaga has always been famous for its fries. The fish reach these shores after the effort of crossing the Sargasso Sea. They develop a rough backbone which makes the back darker and acquire a crunchy texture which is a sign of quality. Though these fries have not swum in the polluted waters of Aguinaga for years, dealers sell them as if they were a local product for prohibitive prices: as much as 40,000 pesetas/Kg (about £165) in the Christmas period.

Another gastronomic species which has been the victim of the absurdities of modernity are the delicious anchovies of La Scala, from the Rosas Gulf. Such gourmet produce is now only available from a limited number of family concerns, most of them on the verge of bankruptcy despite the very high sale price. The same is true for the *antxoas* of Cantabrico, which are smaller and, some say, more tasty.

Galicia's unique and peerless clams and cockles (*berberechos*) have largely been replaced by tasteless Dutch species. Moreover, the *bonito* (long-finned tuna) in olive oil produced in Pasajes and other places by the fishermen themselves has practically become a relic. The rare and wonderful Levantine artisan preserves that can still be found are a nostalgic marine souvenir: *atun de ijada* (salted tuna, not dried in the open), and *budel* (salted and dried entrails of long-finned tuna).

Spain's gastronomic heritage is seriously under siege. The extinct or endangered products include a variety of items: Castilian bread, 'de trigo blanco sin argana/que de verlo es bendicion', (made of white flour, without bran/a real feast for the eye), as Lope de Vega put it: from the round-shaped *pa de payés* with a brown crust and a soft interior to the *llonguet*, an oval-shaped loaf with a deep cut on the top which unleashed the erotic imagination of those fortunate enough to eat it, or the *pataqueta*, a bread in the shape of a '3' with closed eyelets shaped as if it were looking at its belly-button.

Outstanding charcuterie is disappearing as the sun gradually sets on the traditional delicatessen shops that were once found in all towns. Along with *bisbe*, the queen of *butifarras* (a sort of sausage largely found in Catalonia) and the much admired (and imitated) *txistorra*, the future is also uncertain for the *botillo* of Léon, a delicious sausage made with offal and eaten with savoy cabbage: a dish worthy of a king. Things don't look much better for the *morcon de Extremadura*, either. This is a wonderful Spanish pork meat ball wrapped in fine pork gut. As for the *frutas de sarten* (fruits of the frying-pan), they reconcile the simple with the sublime and in so doing represent equality. Both rich and poor enjoy a taste of paradise when they sink their teeth into traditional home-made desserts such as the *churro* (a sort of pancake) or the *borrachuelo* liquor cake.

We could go on compiling our list for ever. But these few examples – taken from both *haute* and poor cuisine – should suffice to draw attention to the fact that if no serious action is taken these unique products will simply disappear from our tables and our culinary heritage. Though devised by creative cooks to make up for poverty with dignity, they represent an important aspect of our country's gastronomic wealth.

LOS OLVIDADOS

Edited by Carlos Delgado

Santona
Cantabria
Anchoas El Capricho
Darsena, s/n
Tel. ++34/942/671699
Cottage industry anchovies produced in very small quantities. Preserved in salt for six months and prepared only with locally caught fish. Perfectly cleaned and without fish-bones, their taste in intense and well-balanced.
Price: 600 pesetas, 85 g.

San Pedro de Pinatar
Murcia
Huevas de atun (tuna roe)
Salazones Juan Lopez
México, 1
Tel. ++34/968/182454
Remarkable appetizer to be eaten in very thin layers, like carpaccio, and seasoned with a few drops of extra-virgin olive oil. Serve it with roasted marcona almonds. Tuna roe is hard to find, but its admirers claim it is as good as caviar.
Price: 12,000 pesetas/Kg.

Arlanzón
Burgos
Morcilla de burgos cuevas
C.tra De Burgos s/n
Tel. ++34/947/421178
This delicious charcuterie, made of rice (30%), onion, pork blood and lard, paprika, black pepper, oregano and salt, won two gold medals in the Mortagne-au-Perche Competition (Orne). Soft, intense and aromatic, it is produced in very small quanities according to traditional artisan methods. A real rarity.
Price: 600 pesetas each.

Moron de la Frontera
Sevilla
Mermelada de naranja
La vieja fabrica
Avda Del Pilar, 6
Tel. ++34/95/4851200
Time-honoured family firm specialized in the production of superior quality jams (strawberry, peach, blackberry, apricot, etc.). They are prepared in lid-less pots without cooking. The quality and clarity of the texture is outstanding. Excellent balance between the natural acidity of fruit and the sweetness of taste. Excellent value for money.
Price: 350 pesetas.

WITHOUT A TABLECLOTH
Carlos Delgado

*W*hen the gastronomically-oriented customer enters a Spanish bar or *taberna*, he may initially be a little bewildered by the noise, high spirits and tolerable degree of impudence. However, what will astound him far more is the immense repertoire of *tapas* displayed there to tempt the regulars, or described in white chalk on a blackboard. This amazing parade of culinary gems owes its being to a wide variety of ingredients and origins: here come the ineffable Spanish *tortilla*, the grilled *chorizos*, the *salpicón de mariscos*, the *cazuelita de callos*, the amazing Spanish cured ham, the voluminous *empanadillas*, the silvery sardina *en escabeche*, the symbolic whelks, the pinky polpo *alla gallega* and so forth. The fundamentals: good bread, olive oil, pork, anchovies, sardines and mackerel, pulses and vegetables.

Those who are unacquainted with the Spanish *tapeo* ceremony (if the habit has not yet caught on universally, it should be encouraged to do so) are missing one of the world's great gastronomic adventures. Far from being a mere quick lunch to be downed in a hurry, a sort of typically noisy Spanish fast food, *tapas* is an almost ritual meal that can last for hours as participants wend their way from taverns to bars and *tabernas*, enjoying all the house specialities and washing them down with wine. It was probably this particular combination of wining and dining that gave the big restaurants the idea for their rather pretentious 'tasting menus'. Except that they misunderstood the whole essence of *tapas*: inexpensive, unrestricted, unsung.

Tapas offer a winning mixture of tradition and modernity. Though they can provide a quick snack, they are really a way of eating slowly. Customers forsake the pomp and ceremony of tablecloth, dining room and waiters for the bar, the hot pan, a stool (when lucky) and really quick service. The food itself is ready to be served. That's the nature of it. Interestingly enough, some of the tastiest and most significant products of the Spanish culinary tradition have survived in the form of *tapas*: the rich *callos a la madrileña*, for example; strong, plebeian and irresistibly spicy. Other *tapas* such as the *berza jerezana* (a chickpea *cocido*) are like wonderful 'miniature dishes'. Moreover, in towns like Seville and San

Sebastián, where *tapas* pierced with toothpicks are also called *banderillas*, this form of food has practically become an art in its own right.

Slow food without a tablecloth: this is the *tapa*; a never-ending parade of Spanish gastronomic ingenuity; a playful concept unconstrained by time; the quintessence of social eating; a perfect balance of regional cooking and wines. More than a mere quick lunch for people under no stress, *tapas* can become a unique experience, to be enjoyed with a glass of *cosechero* (a young red wine obtained with the carbonic maceration system) in the Basque Provinces, *Fino* in Andalusia, or a young red wine in the other regions. Relax and enjoy a form of eating that transcends time and reaches the very heart of friendship.

A LIFESTYLE
Manuel Vázquez Montalbán

Tapa is a Spanish word destined to enter the universal multilingual dictionary. The other Spanish words that are used internationally have very serious meanings: *guerrillero*, *desperado*, *pasionaria*, etc., while *tapa* is a source of joys in the plural, brief but constant on the palate. In the *Gastronomic Dictionary* by Carlos Delgado, *tapa* is defined as a 'gastronomic delicacy consisting in various nibbles and small portions that come with a drink'. *Tapa* is generally an hors-d'oeuvre served with drinks before eating, or a mixed meal with various little dishes that can be eaten in different bars. The best idea is to crawl bars, taverns, sandwich-bars and inns to taste the best *tapas* in each of them. This provides an itinerant meal, rich in flavours, creative preparations and freedom.

The origins of this unique gastronomic tradition have been variously explained. Historians date it back to the times of a King of Castile, Alfonso X *el Sabio* ('the Wise'): obliged by doctors to eat and drink little and often, he was served dishes with small portions of different foods. According to another interpretation, the word *tapa* derives from the function of the little dish that was used in Andalucía as a lid to close (*tapar*) the wine glass. Apart from keeping insects out of the glass, the lid also contained something to eat: olives, ham, or portions of the dishes served by that particular bar for lunch or dinner.

Each Spanish gastronomic region has its own *tapas* and a ritual linked to wine, generally speaking young wines, though nowadays young people in particular tend to have beer. In Andalucía, the most popular ritual is to drink *finos* from Jerez, that is, young wine from Jerez, accompanied by various kinds of olives, ham, chicken or fish croquettes, *salpicón* (a fish and vegetable sauce), fried fish (a real miracle of oil-based cooking that Andalusians have turned into their gastronomic hallmark, together with *gazpacho*), fish *en adobo*, broad beans and ham, tripe or *mondongo*, an array of *tortillas* (omelettes), but especially potato *tortilla* with or without onions. In Castilla and Extremadura, *tapa* becomes more solid because of the continental climate: *mollica* (bread dough fried with various types of pork or vegetables, sometimes with grapes), small heaps of loin *adobada* (pieces of bread with *lonza en adobo*), *empanadillas*, sweetbreads, fried bacon (pork bacon fried until the fat is eliminated), and *manchego* cheese.

In Murcia and Alicante, vegetable and sea recipes are added: garlic prawns, vegetable *tortillas*, breaded aubergines, baked and *aliñados* peppers, toast dressed with oil and garlic. In the region that was once called Castile, now united with León, that is, the two fundamental kingdoms in the building of the Spanish nation, cold weather has created strong *tapas*, rich in calories: fried ham, spiced salami, Burgos meatballs, spiced salami in batter, river crabs. Catalonians accompany *tapas* with wine, but also *cava*, the Spanish sparkling wine, and give their contribution to the *tapeo* with snails cooked in many different ways, salt cod with *sanfaina* (peppers, tomatoes, aubergines and onions) or simply baked with peppers, garlic and oil, breaded mussels, bread and tomato, mushrooms, salt and mild sausage, and several kinds of cold meats.

In Aragón and La Rioja, there are *ajoarriero* salt cod (cooked with vegetables and, sometimes, served with shrimps), baked bread and ham, mixed vegetable dishes (egg beaten with the produce of the extremely fertile gardens of this area), stuffed peppers (with salt cod or meat).

In the Basque Country and Navarra, we come to the real sanctuary of *tapa* because of the Basque custom of *chiquitear*, that is, drinking a small glass of wine (*chiquito*) with the widest range of gastronomic nibbles: sausage with cider, baked sardines, mixed mushrooms, salt cod *tortilla*, stewed crab, small eels in the *pilpil* way (cooked in hot oil, with red pepper and garlic).

In Northern Spain, *tapa* offers an extraordinarily entertaining itinerary that takes us to Santander, area of sardines and sea food, or Asturias, where *tapa* acquires a lot of vigour in the *chigres*, cider shops where cider is poured into large glasses to oxygenate it, and people drink it together with a wide range of snacks, like Cabrales cheese sandwiches (definitely the best Spanish blue cheese), a vast variety of fish cooked in cider, or even *tapas* of *fabada*, a dish made of large beans, pork meat and almonds, which is the gastronomic symbol of Asturias. Along the Cantabrian belt, we reach Galicia, Europe's 'Land's End', rainy and cold, where *tapas* are extraordinary: loin, lamprey eel, and sea food pies (made of corn wheat), cooked octopus (*pulpo a feira*), peppers the Padron way, Betanzos *tortilla* or *cocido* pork *codillo*.

Madrid should certainly not be left out of our *tapas* tour of Spain, since it represents a showcase of the endless variety offered by this way of eating and the lifestyle it reflects. *Tapeo* is not a Spanish variety of fast food; on the contrary, *tapeo* is a slow and social way of eating whose followers prop up the bar and offer each other tastes of this and that in a reciprocal ritual known as 'paying the round'.

Spain's capital city offers the entire range of the country's *tapas* culture: in taverns, bars, and inns there are Basque, Galicians, Andalusian and Castillan *tapas*, traditionally accompanied by Valdepeñas, a light wine that seems to have been created especially for going with *tapas*.

This city is more than just a showcase for Spain's *tapeo*. It has also made some creative contributions of its own: spicy potatoes (with chilli pepper), ham croquettes, tripe Madrid style, sweetbreads, veal or pork tripe (*gallineja*), anchovies, tuna *en escabeche*, bread dough with fried eggs, potato *tortilla*, coated (breaded) shrimps, and so on without end, because *tapas* are never the same and you can try garlic shrimp *tapas* in all Madrid's bars and be sure that none of them will be the same.

When Mediterranean Conferences are organized and a suitable umbrella theme is required, I cannot understand why nobody ever thought about proclaiming *tapa* the food expression of a lifestyle that involves giving things a try, chatting all the while, drinking with discernment and reaching the unusual conclusion that, in small portions, the world is beautiful.

THE CONVICT'S DIET
Annie Hubert

$\mathcal{W}$e are living in a historical period in which food has become a major issue for the Western world, at times almost an obsession. Where most people are blessed by abundance, we are more preoccupied with food, its quality and its effects than we were in the past, in times of poverty and famine. All Westerners are now aware of the close link between food and health. Incidentally, this truth had already been established a few millennia ago by the peoples of the Middle and Far East, not to mention our direct ancestor Hippocrates and his medical theories. And here we are, two thousand years later, ready to reassert the same principles, especially the postulates referring to climate, lifestyle, food and its preparation, which notoriously have a great impact on our health. At the same time, we have become increasingly convinced that food produced and cooked according to the traditional methods of our forebears is much better from a gastronomic point of view, since it is not 'contaminated' by synthetic chemical substances. This explains the current rage for 'typical' products, prepared according to so-called ancestral methods.

This article will illustrate how a purely biomedical concept with considerable traditional appeal has become a nutritional model that all Western peoples consider ideal, as regards both gastronomy and health.

Epidemiologists and nutritionists have carried out numerous studies of eating habits in different parts of the globe, especially since the Second World War. Such surveys have revealed the close link between eating habits and a certain number of diseases, in particular cardiovascular disorders and tumours. At the same time, epidemiological studies have shown that the populations of certain regions of the world appear to be less prone than others to develop such diseases. Nutritionists have thus concluded that the eating habits of these peoples were 'better'. Now it just happens that the geographical area comprising the southern regions of the Western world, along the Mediterranean coast, was inhabited by peoples whose eating habits landed them with a low ratio of heart disorders and tumours, peoples who lived longer than their northern counterparts. Before going further, let us point out the fact that poor rural populations obviously could not possibly develop the so-called 'plethoric' diseases associated with an excessively abundant diet. Furthermore, such populations upheld local ways of producing and cooking their food. So Greece, Italy, Spain, Portugal and Southern France stood out as privileged regions due to the good health and longevity of their inhabitants.

A gastronomic ideal

Thanks to these studies and the recent focus on them by the media in Western countries, we now have a new and remarkably widespread nutritional concept: the so-called 'Mediterranean diet'. The fact that this concept is somewhat hazy in no way detracts from its almost magic powers. The Mediterranean diet has become a gastronomic ideal, an endless source of goodness and health. Likewise, the underlying ancestral traditions, which are perceived as being closer to nature, and thus traditional and better.

When scientific data is adopted and adapted by non-scientists, what you usually get is a credo that can become a valid model both for the original scientific community and for the man in the street.

So let's take a look at the origins and development of what is now perceived as ideal traditional gastronomy.

The Origins

As far as I know, the concept of 'Mediterranean diet' first surfaced in 1824.[1] A young British Navy surgeon named Peter Cunningham had been entrusted with the task of escorting a group of convicts deported from England to Australia in 1821. Like his Hippocratic predecessors of ancient times, he was convinced that the human diet should be strictly associated with the climate and seasons. Considering the fact that convicts were heading south, where the climate would be hot and dry, Cunningham came to the conclusion that the men in his custody should eat less meat than they were wont to in England. Conversely, their diet should largely consist of cereals, fruit and vegetables. The assumption underlying this conviction was a pillar of early medical theory according to which certain types of food – especially vegetables – were considered 'cold', and therefore refreshing, whereas meat and other products were 'hot' and thus warming.

Doctor Cunningham was in charge of three deportation voyages and managed to complete them without any loss of life among the male or female convicts. Later on, he published two works in which he recommended a 'Mediterranean diet' to all those who intended to colonize Australia: this would enable them to be healthy even in a hot climate, comparable to that of the Mediterranean. By

'Mediterranean diet' Cunningham simply intended more fruit and vegetables and less meat. He never mentioned the fats that only much later, as we will see, were to become a fundamental component of the so-called Mediterranean cuisine. Being the sort of physician that he was, it is strange that he never wondered what the native peoples of Australia actually ate: the diet of healthy Aborigines who had a very balanced relationship with their habitat. You should never underestimate ethnocentrism!

After Cunningham, the subject was dropped and did not turn up again until the 1970s, when the expression 'Mediterranean diet' was resumed by a couple of American physiologists, the Keys, who in 1975 published a study entitled: *How to Eat Well and Stay Well: the Mediterranean Way*[2]. In their work, the Keys suggested that there is a close link between the eating habits of Northern and Southern Europeans and their health, especially as far as cardiovascular diseases are concerned.

Tasty well-being

So what did those eminent scholars mean by 'Mediterranean diet'? They were essentially referring to a diet that was poor in saturated fats but much tastier than the classic low fat menus inflicted on patients suffering from heart disease.

A few years earlier, exhaustive information about the quality and quantity of food consumption had became available thanks to a number of studies carried out in Europe – in particular, the 1960 survey promoted by Euratom. The Euratom study had highlighted the differences between the countries under investigation, especially with reference to the consumption of fresh fruit and vegetables, cereals and meat. Less meat and more cereals in Italy, where the quantity of absorbed fats was the same as in the other countries, but the quality was different: Italians used more olive oil. Other studies followed, one conducted by the Italian, Ferro Luzzi[3] and another by the American Gene Spiller[4], but even these failed to provide a more precise definition of what a traditional Mediterranean diet was. They proved that Italians did not eat more vegetables than northern peoples, yet their rate of cardiovascular diseases was lower: so, there had to be something else apart from vegetables . . . Further studies provided evidence that there was a close link between the long and healthy life of the Cretans and local eating habits. It was only then that researchers started to investigate the role of fats and take olive oil into consideration . . . They began to speak about a 'Cretan model' in a general theory that the scientific community and subsequently the media identified with the attribute 'Mediterranean'.

An epidemiological study revealed that improved socio-economic conditions in Italy had progressively encouraged southern populations to abandon their 'traditional' poor diet and adopt a model known as 'Northern European' which was rich in animal fats, meat and dairy products. They were thus losing their 'natural' protection against heart disease and cancer.

An artificial image

At this point I cannot help but make the following considerations: first of all, the concept of 'Mediterranean diet' was developed in the Anglo-Saxon world; secondly, the Americans and the British were the first to coin the phrase. The concept is thus a haphazard collection of conclusions reached by various physicians and researchers on 'Mediterranean-style' food consumption. However, the conclusions themselves were approximate and general, since they did not take into account the wide range of cuisines and eating habits in the different regions. This 'representation' of a healthy diet was subsequently adopted by the 'Mediterraneans' themselves, especially the Italians, who did not hesitate to exclude from the so-called 'Mediterranean model' all that did not perfectly fit into its scientific definition. I have read an article by well-known nutritionists who have concluded that Northern Italy – though geographically part of the Mediterranean area – cannot possibly be considered a region based on the 'Mediterranean model' (see note 3). Clearly this is a case of deliberate image construction.

It was up to the mass media to seize these concepts and transfer them from the realms of science (not that they were very scientific in the first place) to those of everyday life. Hence the glorification of the 'traditional Mediterranean' model, and thus the myth of a healthy traditional cuisine.

The most illuminating recent work on the advantages of the 'Mediterranean' diet derives from long and exhaustive studies carried out in Crete under the auspices of INSERM[5]. A comparative study of French patients who had had a heart attack was set up in the region of Lyon and involved two control groups. The first group was prescribed the so-called 'Cretan' diet, while the second one stuck to a classic low fat diet. A triumph! The results proved that the patients belonging to the 'traditionally Cretan' control group (as the researchers called it) had no relapses whereas the others had relapses and a few of them finally died. I was curious to find out which characteristics of the diet had been defined as 'traditionally Cretan' by the nutritionists. The answer I obtained was surprising, to say the least:

● olive oil was not used, because its taste was not appreciated by all the patients included in the research protocol. It had been replaced by an olive oil-like type of margarine specially produced by a large food company;

● typically Cretan fruit and vegetables (walnuts and purslane[6], considered by nutritionists to be decisive elements) had been replaced by French fruit and vegetables, or rather typical produce from the region around Lyon, since the study was carried out in Lyon;

● the so-called 'Cretan' model was thus just a diet in which the consumption of bread, noodles and vegetables was encouraged whereas proteins and animal fats were drastically reduced. So here we are, back to the theories of our good Doctor Cunningham!

For an anthropologist specialized in dietary problems and an ethnographer of food such as myself, this generalization was disconcerting. . . .So I wondered:

● do the Cretans have a monopoly of all that is Mediterranean? Remember that the media usually define this model 'the Cretan miracle'. . .

● why are the big countries of the southern Mediterranean area not included in this model? Nobody has ever recommended eating *couscous*, *kefta*[7], typical oriental sweetmeats or other delicious traditional dishes from that area;

● why are there no epidemiological studies analyzing the big differences between diets and cuisines? The fact is that the cuisines that failed to fit in with the model considered as a panacea, a remedy against all evils, a sort of magic potion, had been completely eliminated in the first place.

Magic

I'm not suggesting that this model should be condemned. In fact it is a diet which provides all sorts of benefits to our body. Nevertheless, as a model it has been artificially constructed by researchers referring to the data they collected in specific, circumscribed places, according to well-defined nutritional criteria. So, where is the truth? Wouldn't it be more scientifically correct to point out that the health of a population depends on the interaction of several different factors: lifestyle, bio-rhythms, profession, physical exercise, general conditions, afternoon nap (why not?), a certain attitude towards life? And that we are dealing with a series of cultural and biological factors which make some populations of the Mediterranean area healthier than others?

There is no harm in exporting this 'model', but we should not consider it as traditional, since it is not really deep-rooted at an ethnographic level. Have we ever wondered if a Mediterranean diet would have as positive results in northern countries?

Can the experience proving that the Mediterranean diet is beneficial to patients with cardiovascular disorders be applied to a whole population? And may I also point out that for those who are used to a dull traditional low fat diet, the 'Mediterranean diet' must necessarily produce a positive effect on their general conditions, by simple contrast!

Thanks to the power of physicians and the impact of mass media, certain segments of society in north-western Europe are now coming into line with the so-called 'Mediterranean' model.

In England the 'Mediterranean diet' is beginning to affect daily eating habits. The magic concept is doing wonders and plenty of cookbooks and TV programmes sing the praises of the South. However, brief perusal of the recipes proposed will reveal a sort of transformation and adaptation to British culinary culture. Quite an interesting mutation! Just add a bitter-sweet flavour here, some sugar there, less garlic in general . . . There is no doubt that the well-educated people of the British Isles are eating differently from the past, that the so-called 'Mediterranean' products are having their heyday: tomatoes, olive oil, aromatic herbs, peppers, noodles. According to my British colleagues, a real culinary revolution is taking place, but has still not trickled down to the lower rungs of the social ladder.

Are we not constantly looking for a magic potion to solve all our problems of body and mind? Might we not find solace for our suffering in an ideal diet – gastronomic, ancestral and immutable – and its underlying magic?

Notes

1 B. Santich, *What the Doctors Ordered*, Hyland, Melbourne 1995, p.12-20; P. Cunningham, *Two Years in Southwales Colburn*, London 1827.

2 A. and M. Keys, *How to Eat Well and Stay Well: the Mediterranean Way*, Doubleday, New York 1975.

3 A. Ferro Luzzi, *The Mediterranean Diet: an attempt to define its past and present composition*, Eur. J. Clin. Nutr. 43, 1989, (Suppl. 2) 13-29.

4 G. Spiller, *The Mediterranean Diet in Health and Disease*, Van Nostrand Reinhold, New York 1991.

5 M. Renaud, *Le Régime Santé*, Odile Jacob, Paris 1995.

6 *Portulaca Oleracea*, wild herb very similar to the flower portulaca for its shape and consistency. It can be eaten as a salad. (Translator's Note).

7 Typical meat balls of the Arab cuisine. (Translator's Note).

EITHER MILK OR FISH
Hocine Benkheira

*I*n Arab and Muslim countries accompanying a fish-based dish with milk, buttermilk or curdled milk is forbidden, on pain of contracting leprosy or some other serious illness. Though rarely stated explicitly, this prohibition has not to my knowledge been deemed worthy of attention by Middle Eastern observers, to the extent that it is not even mentioned by travel writers or ethnographers. It is a rule that has nothing to do with the Jewish law stating that meat and dairy products should never be combined. Yet as an interdiction it appears to be scrupulously observed, albeit beneath the euphemistic form of decorum. The rule is clearly stated in early treatises such as the eclectic compilation, *Medicina profetica*, drawn up by the fourteenth-century writer, Ibn Qayyim al-Jawziyya.

Still to this day a widespread popular compendium, *Medicina profetica* owes much to the Greco-Arab tradition in medicine (Galen, Avicenna), pharmacopoeia and ethics. The prohibition is mentioned at the end of the volume along with other dietary rules, yet it is not to be found in the large collections of prophetic traditions or the great juridical *summae*. The fact of being mentioned in devotional works has imbued the prohibition with religious overtones, although it is not a religious taboo comparable to those concerning pork or wine.

In itself it raises numerous questions which we shall try to analyze in anthropological terms here, with a little ethnographic and literary support.

Dairy Products

Although milk is not a fundamental food for the whole Arab world but only for its nomadic peoples, it certainly plays a significant role. Let us start by considering various elements borrowed from the learned religious tradition. There is a famous passage in which Ali, cousin, son-in-law and fourth successor of the Prophet, tells the latter of his previous night's dream: 'I dreamt that you gve me milk to drink'; to which the response is: 'Milk is the symbol of science.' In another traditional text, a dish combining milk and meat is viewed as the food of God's messengers. God says of this fare: 'I have infused them with strength and prosperity.' Cow's milk is considered to be a remedy. There are two more quotations from traditional texts that are of interest: 'There is no believer who has dairy goats near him whose family is not made holy and full of blessings. And if that family has two goats then it will be blessed twice each day. Each morning an angel will rise to tell them, "You are sanctified and blessed, may you have a long and joyful life". And sanctified here means pure.' One day the Prophet said to one of his paternal aunts, 'What is it that impedes you from having a source of blessing in your house? What is this source? An aínimal to milk. A goat, a dairy cow, these are the blessings.'

Nomadic tribes such as the Nigerian Tuareg never sell milk from their herds, but offer it to visitors. In this way, even the poor have something to give to their guests. The herds they rear are mainly dairy animals. Milk is often the favourite food of children, old people and invalids. It is renowned as being an energizing foodstuff. Cow's milk is considered to be nourishing and to produce the rounded forms that are signs of beauty in women of the Sahara regions. The Tuareg believe that camel's milk increases virility, whereas it can cause dysmenorrhoea in women. Although not from the Arab-Berber region, the Peul tribe of Islamicized shepherds also provides an eloquent case. In their culture milk is so important that sharing it symbolizes a whole range of social ties with group members, visitors and even animals. It is a duty to offer milk to passing visitors. Sharing milk establishes a relationship. To refuse to drink the milk which is offered signifies excluding the giver from the group, refusing to establish a social link with him/her. The shared drinking of milk is thus fundamental to communal living. Milk may also be given to domestic animals: horses, dogs or cows that have recently given birth. In the Maghreb, milk contains *baraka*[1]. According to an old saying, 'If you do not have milk in your house, your house is empty.' *Cuscus*, the quintessential ritual dish, can only be dressed with meat sauce, milk, or better still, with a broth containing both. The ideal drink to accompany *cuscus* is buttermilk or curdled milk.

Ambivalent Fish

According to a thirteenth-century medical treatise, fish and seafood cause cataracts. Fish has a 'watery' nature. When salted it loses its wetness and becomes dry. Religious tradition warns against eating fish, since the body labours to digest it. According to another tradition, eating fish causes tuberculosis. Only in a few specific regions of the Maghreb is fish eaten with *cuscus*. Despised since time immemorial, fish is considered inferior not only because it is the meat of the destitute, but also in view of its symbolic value. In fact the Berber-speaking tribes of the Maghreb abstained from eating fish until very recently. All North African and Saharan ethnographers (E. Bernus, Ch. de Foucauld, M. Gast, H. Lhote, P. Marty) mention the nomads' profound antipathy for fish. The Tuareg, whose diet is essentially based on millet and milk, are repulsed by fish, which is widely available and cheap. Nomads have been seen selling the tins of sardines distributed to them during times of famine. A slightly milder form of the same attitude is to be found in all North African tribes. Indeed, Maghreb recipes reveal that fish-based dishes are limited to the absolute minimum. In a study of Casablanca conducted at the beginning of the sixties, the French geographer A. Adam found that Moroccans did not greatly appreciate fish, even though the country has Atlantic and Mediterranean coast lines and fish is therefore widely available.

A Hypothesis

The following postulate may help us understand the reason for this prohibition: since the milk is obtained from animal husbandry, it can be considered to be on a par with meat. Thus milk, like meat, is a ritual food and its consumption involves more than merely practical considerations. In this sense the nutritional value of milk is inseparable from its symbolic value. Just as meat is the food that makes it possible to found social links in the food sphere, so milk can play the same role. Blood and milk are linked by a form of continuity, and it is this that explains the equivalence between milk and meat. Milk can be said to be another form of blood. The learned Muslim tradition of the Middle Ages confirms this theory. The consumption of milk can thus determine a relationship between human beings (the sharing of maternal milk with foster brothers, for instance) just as food at the same table can; moreover this link can also be forged between humans and animals.

The milk-meat equivalence also has other implications. The ritual importance of meat primarily depends on the fact that it comes from animals that are very familiar to man, are considered almost to be similar to humans, and in many cases are full members of the community.

Fish on the other hand is radically different from man, so much so that in the Islamic world fish are not considered animals in the full sense of the term. This is why they do not have to be ritually killed before they are eaten. Moreover, fish cannot be reared in herds, or indeed trained. As a result, fish can never be considered equivalent to meat. Furthermore, fish is something that is bought from strangers. In the Islamic world, animals – and thus milk and the meat they provide

– is at the same time symbolic of fortune, dignity and prosperity. Fish on the other hand, symbolizes poverty, ill health and humiliation.

To conclude, milk symbolizes the higher economic and social status attributed to raising livestock, whereas fish stands for the humbler activities of hunting and harvesting. As a result, milk and fish are not combined in meals since it is simply not possible to mix high and low; furthermore, the barrier between animals of land and water, between wild and domestic, must be preserved. A significant sociological implication of this is the marginal status of those who make a living from fishing, who can never be viewed as suitable marriage partners.

Note
1 For the Arabs, blessing, fortune.

HERRING COUNTRIES

Jørgen Mønster Pedersen

$\mathcal{M}$arriages are often made for love, but every now and again one comes across unions based on reason, calculation or simply need, rather than on passion. The meeting between food and drink is originally founded on geographical, climatic and cultural conditions. As in many marriages, however, the two partners tend to adapt to one another in order to harmonize cohabitation and create a happy life together.

This tendency towards adaptation is not necessarily noticed by the external observer, yet it can prove to be very fertile. New habits lead to new recipes: it is thus that incomparable dishes are born. This process has already taken place in Mediterranean cuisine and is now under way in the cuisine of Northern countries. For foreigners many of the tastes and combinations probably seem like mysterious alchemies . . . but then love is blind, after all.

I shall take several typical Nordic dishes as examples: *Myscost*, Norwegian caramelized cheese, *Skjerpekøtt*, dried mutton from the Fær Øer islands (Føroyar), *Surstrømming*, Swedish fermented herring, or Danish marinated herring. In general you cannot 'learn' to like these tastes: they have been familiar since infancy and they form part of one's genetic patrimony.

Marinated herring, for example, has been eaten in Denmark since time immemorial. The seas and straits surrounding the country were extremely rich in this fish, a distant cousin of the sardine, which was salted and exported to southern Europe in large quantities from the Middle Ages.

Herring is an oily fish well-suited to many recipes whereas smoked herring is a speciality that deserves its international gastronomic recognition. Today, however, marinated herring is more popular. The classic cold *smorrebrod*[1] that is so popular in restaurants and at home, for parties and for everyday, is prepared by desalting and marinating herring, which is then served, accompanied by raw onions, on slices of wholemeal rye bread spread with lard. It can be bought ready-made or traditionally prepared at home.

The marinade – or rather marinades, as there are numerous versions – always includes vinegar and sugar and is spiced according to taste. The sweet and sour taste – a legacy of Medieval cuisine which still thrives in Nordic cooking – is present in many traditional dishes such as marinated cucumbers and marinated beetroot. The latter are often so sweet that foreigners are disconcerted and have been known to eat them like jam with their dessert. They should, however, accompany a *terrine* or a dish of sliced *charcuterie*.

A Small Glass of Snaps

To return to the herring: it is a fish with a strong, persistent taste that can only be married with *snaps*: a good small glass of *snaps*, followed by a glass of beer. You cannot, horror of horrors, combine it with wine! There are approximately twenty types of *snaps* on the market (mainly produced by Danisco Distillers), with varying tastes. Almost all are characterized by a spiciness conferred by cumin, dill or by both. According to European legislation, *eaux de vie* are alcoholic drinks of at least 37° proof, aromatized with cumin or dill.

There is no exact law establishing which *eau de vie* should be combined with which type of marinated herring or indeed any other culinary creation. Consumer preference for specific types of *snaps* (Aalborg Taffel Akvavit) does not take into account the way it combines with food. I believe it is important to recognize the importance of *snaps* since, besides being a national drink, it accompanies Nordic cuisine in general to perfection.

In Mediterranean countries, olive oil is used to dress salads, brown onions and to fry meat and vegetables; in Northern countries animal fat is generally used. Lard, butter and milk (which is often drunk at meal times) are used in the place of vegetable oils and as a result the dishes are so heavy that they require strong alcohol to facilitate digestion.

Unfortunately, the very high alcohol content of *eaux de vie* has meant that it is increasingly rare to see it on Danish tables. Furthermore, the decline in the consumption of high proof alcohol has led producers to update their products, and to cater for the younger generation whose palates are not used to tastes such as cumin and dill. The new products have been developed hand in hand with the tendency to draw inspiration from Asian cuisines.

Although the future of *eaux de vie* seems uncertain, the wine market appears to be on a firmer footing. Whereas the consumption of wine in producer countries is decreasing, in Denmark (the non-producing country with the highest *per capita* rate), consumption is on the increase. Since the fifties and sixties and the advent of mass tourism, contact with wine-producing countries has continued to grow, thus stimulating wine consumption at home. After tasting French, Italian, Spanish or German wines *in loco*, Danes began taking bottles of wine back north with them, to help them relive their pleasant holiday memories.

It is obviously hard for a Valpolicella – so perfect with a plate of spaghetti in a restaurant on Lake Garda – not to be disappointing when served with boiled potatoes and meat balls (fried in margarine) in white sauce. Danes however get to the bottom of their bottle, so to speak, and fortunately the increasing interest in wine is slowly bringing about a kind of new gastronomic tendency.

Bordeaux at Christmas

In some circumstances, however, no new trend has succeeded in holding sway. I refer here, for example, to the meal the Danes prize above all others both in terms of emotional value and quality: Christmas dinner. The main traditional dish is duck stuffed with apples and prunes, with side dishes of red cabbage stewed in honey and potatoes caramelized in sugar; a further meat dish might be roast pork with crackling.

This meal, which is usually eaten on the evening of December 24 (a devout part of Danish Christmas), is accompanied by the best bottles available. In the main Bordeaux wines are uncorked, since they accompany the fatty, slightly bitter duck meat well; however the elegant tannic characteristics of Bordeaux seem entirely out of place with the excessively sweet side dishes. It is better to opt for different sort of wines, possibly Spanish ones whose smoothness and sweet aromas of vanilla and cinnamon help overcome such difficulties.

Since they are newcomers to wine, the Danes apply themselves assiduously to finding out about it and understanding how it relates to food. Indeed, the advent of wine and other products, such as olive oil, in the sixties and seventies set Danish cuisine off to a new start, helping it to discover new ways of preparing classic raw ingredients.

Another classic ingredient of renewed interest is salmon, which was still plentiful in Danish rivers one hundred years ago (to the extent that workers refused to eat it more than four times a week). In the past this fish was eaten when cooked or even dried and accompanied by beer. Today it is preferred either raw or marinated in olive oil, accompanied by *eau de vie* or more often by white wine, such as a good Riesling or a young, light Chardonnay. This would have been inconceivable even thirty years ago. But this is not all: smoked salmon has long been a Baltic Sea speciality that is smoked on account of the fat it has accumulated before it is fished in the autumn. It cannot be likened to farmed salmon. In many cases its rather oily taste does not combine well with white wines and leaves a metallic taste in the mouth. On the other hand, with red wines, especially young ones preferably made with carbonic maceration (Beaujolais, Côtes-du Rhône and others), the oiliness is successfully dominated by the body of the wine; often the tastes of both the salmon and the wine are heightened.

It is often remarked in Denmark that Protestantism plays an important role in the way people relate to food, not insofar as cooking itself is concerned, but rather in regard to their perception of pleasure. Protestants traditionally see food as mere fuel for the human body, something that should be shorn of pleasure. This topic is the central theme of the film *Babette's Feast* (by Gabriel Axel: to be re-read or seen again!): two Norwegian sisters who spurn pleasure from habit are totally flummoxed by Babette, a cook-artist who spends all her money on preparing a splendid feast for them and their friends.

Protestantism may well play some part in this attitude. Yet the point remains that in the past the available products and gastronomic traditions were exceptionally poor. Despite the obstacles, in Denmark and other Scandinavian countries new traditions are now being developed in which wine plays an important role. We are witnessing a flowering of creativity that has possibly outstripped that of countries with more deep-rooted culinary cultures. Sometimes the lack of tradition can create the conditions for greater expressive freshness and freedom. It is certainly true that the marriages between food and wine celebrated in Nordic countries today imply a certain degree of promiscuity; yet it is precisely these happy and unfaithful marriages with new partners that sanction the good health and vitality of Scandinavian gastronomy.

Note

1 A tartine with a bread base and fish (soft, sweet-fleshed fish such as marinated herring, raw or smoked salmon) and cheese or sausage topping. The best are small and generously trimmed, decorated with dill, cucumber and radishes, among other things. They are delicious snacks that can be eaten at any time, day or night.

A LATTER-DAY RELIGION

Lesley Chamberlain

$\mathcal{V}$egetarianism is an acceptable religion in Britain today. No one asks any longer why you hold this particular belief. Even though followers of the vegetarian faith are still technically in a minority, they are nowadays treated to equal rights wherever they go. What really matters in an acceptable religion is that no one asks or cares whether its members are true believers. Only a few modern-day vegetarians presume they have the moral high ground, giving them the right to make themselves a social nuisance. In their case there is a faint tension about the land, in otherwise carnivorous restaurants and at similar dinner parties.

The television cameras recently went behind the scenes at one of Britain's largest hotels, the Adelphi in Liverpool, and it was amusing to watch the traditional-minded chef dealing with the vegetarian 'problem'. He was in the kitchen, preparing a banquet for 640 people, and the number of vegetarian reservations kept rising by the hour. The BBC bleeped out the besieged cook's comments as unsuitable for family viewing. His brief was originally 47 vegetarians, 8 vegans, and two people who don't eat food touched by other people. By the evening there seemed to be 'a few hundred' who 'had decided overnight or this afternoon' that they weren't going to eat meat. Had the chef been the owner of the restaurant, and able to afford a loss of business, he might have turned them away. In any case he suspected them of being somehow fake.

Well, vegans aren't fake. They don't eat meat, or fish, or any dairy produce, not even eggs, and if they're not careful they can leave their children malnourished. There have been some published cases. But some vegetarians eat fish, some not, and some even eat the occasional bacon sandwich. Plenty more people, less conceptually confused, describe themselves as 'mostly vegetarian'. The poor chef was right to feel there was something elusive about the opposition to his menu that night, but what he hadn't grasped was that purity of belief doesn't matter much to vegetarianism any more. Most people just want the option, without putting in a special advance order. And they expect to be able to do it in restaurants, if not at dinner parties.

The last time purity of belief mattered was before the war, when in the conventional British mind vegetarianism was definitely cranky and sectarian. The writer George Bernard Shaw epitomized it, though he was far too brilliant to be anything but his own man. The popular idea of a vegetarian was a man with a beard and sandals, and queer ideas and peculiar relationships. He was almost certainly a Socialist or an anarchist and possibly homosexual. The late Victorian dropout Edward Carpenter comes to mind. He abandoned a career as a Cambridge mathematician for a blissful Lawrentian life in the country with his male lover, a local labourer. Apart from eating only vegetables, he wrote books, sitting outside all year round. People used to drive out and look at him for something to do on a Sunday afternoon. Now, a hundred years on, both his vegetarianism and his homosexuality have become not only acceptable but fashionable. With the same word vegetarian we are talking about a quite different phenomenon, then and now.

If one were to take purity of modern vegetarian belief seriously, it would be quite difficult to isolate. When Beatle George Harrison discovered the Lord Krishna in the early 1970s, a vast public found a reason for joining him in not eating meat. It would be interesting to know just how many fans followed suit because it was Harrison. The Vedic wisdom is that any involvement with killing animals, including eating them, perpetuates bad karma and engenders violence in human beings. Vegetarianism, despite Hitler, has this aura of pacifism, which appealed to post-Vietnam hippies and always appeals to the young. But until recently vegetarianism was also a way of differing from your parents. Similarly, if the rich and beautiful give up meat, many us will copy them because we mainly want to be rich and beautiful too, not because we are converting to Buddhism.

According to Krishna

Perhaps you have to know the person well to detect real sincerity. I have one friend whose vegetarianism is so serious that, if I invite him to a culinary mixed dinner, I don't carve the meat in front of him. On the other hand I am deeply suspicious of vegetarians who proselytize their cause in the most aggressive and militant fashion: for instance, the author of an otherwise splendid 400-page *The Heretic's Feast A History of Vegetarianism* that was published in London a few years ago. Such people mostly want to feel righteous and to fight for a cause. The question remains whether any of these kinds of modern vegetarian can expect to be automatically catered for, privately or commercially. Publicly it is a matter for business. Privately, the etiquette is still uncertain. But my feeling, in terms of the dishes served, is no. Choose from what there is. There is always too much.

Part of Krishna's argument would logically compel many of us to be vegetarians, by the way. It is that if I eat meat, by implication I should be capable of killing the animal with my own hands. I agree. Anything else would be sheer bad faith. Except that, put to the test, I wouldn't kill the beast unless it were a matter of human life or death. In the end both this moral conundrum and the matter of vegetarian etiquette remind me that in a civilized world food and religion don't mix. Conviviality matters more than adhering to principles, whatever they are.

But, as I began by saying, probably the reason for the huge growth in pseudo- or quasi-vegetarianism in Britain in the last 20-30 years is that it hardly signifies a belief entailing moral commitments, and doesn't have to try too hard to be sociable. Nor is it gastronomic sacrifice, and thank God for that, for practical vegetarianism probably owes its spectacular growth in Britain to the superior supply of varied fresh vegetables we all now enjoy, and the coincidental decline in the general quality of meat.

There are health arguments against too much, or even any, red meat, which may or may not be valid. Avoiding meat may make us live longer and feel better. None of these factors make vegetarians essentially more moral than anyone else, nor certainly gastronomically more discriminating. After all, many of them buy pre-packaged and processed vegetarian foods, which is the usual fate of the mass of carnivores and herbivores alike.

Yet perhaps vegetarianism is not any old choice. Some years ago, when Russia first opened up to the West, I was struck by the pathos of middle-aged women envying their Western counterparts their slim figures. 'We would be vegetarian too, if only there were enough vegetables.' One of the innumerable ghastlinesses of the Communist world was that it shovelled meat at its citizens because that was the cheapest fodder, served in large quantities which kept them filled up for hours, so they didn't yearn for cafes and snackbars in their woefully inhospitable towns. There is a case for saying that all meat-eating was a hangover from a nineteenth-century view of what affluence consisted in, gastronomically speaking; and also that it was a continuing reaction to the deprivation of the war. But it struck me then that vegetarianism in the West was actually a beacon of the luxury the free world had managed to create for itself, three-quarters of the way through the 20th century. We don't really worship Krishna, but the freedom to feel good. In fact we worship choice, our present condition, which is not exactly heroic; a mere confirmation that we live in times of extreme affluence.

PAUL'S LUNCH

Laurence Ossipow

*S*eptember 1983. Two months have passed since I began my inquiry and tonight I'm going to see one of my proselytes: Paul, 30 or thereabouts . . .

I walk into an old building which towers above all the others in a busy street. In the vestibule I look for the letter box. I find it straight away; it stands out because it's covered by a piece of adhesive tape to stop people leaving advertising material. The door of the apartment opens onto a narrow corridor which leads to the various rooms and the kitchen. I am taken into the kitchen. Near the window, on the tiled floor, there's a cat basket. Beside the fridge is a sink under which lies a bottle of Ecovert (an ecological detergent for dishes). The cat must have knocked it over. Through the half-closed doors of a cupboard I catch a glimpse of pans and food. On a set of pale wooden shelves in the corner I see some books. 'It's my section of vegetarian and macrobiotic food and guru-mysticism,' explains Paul. On the top shelf, glass vases are filled with cereals, sea salt and algae. There are also a few tins of trace elements. Hanging on the wall are a poster of a South American Indian playing a flute, a calendar and sticker – 'food that respects ecology and the Third World'. Also hanging on the wall is a form with a diet compiled by a diviner.

'There's something not right about that diet. I can't understand how the guy expects me to eat marmalade and white bread for breakfast,' this proselyte tells me. On the large wooden table at the centre of the kitchen, a halo of candlelight surrounds a bunch of dry flowers and a freshly made mixed salad. The radio is tuned to Couleur 3, which is broadcasting light music. Careful to be elegant in every gesture, Paul is busy fixing lunch. He teaches me how to peel an avocado without wasting a scrap of pulp. He then cuts the fruit in two, opens it and removes the core. Next he cuts it into thin crescent-shaped slices. He offers me a choice of apple juice, white wine or beer. We both opt for the beer and we start our meal. The mixed salad (lettuce, carrots and various seed sprouts) is pleasantly crisp. My guest arranges the rest of the lunch on the plates: a ball of cooked corn accompanied by fennel stewed with raisins. To season the food, Paul passes me a jar of *gomasio* (toasted sesame seeds, sea salt and *tamari*, a sort of soy sauce). We talk through the meal. Later in the evening, instead of a pudding Paul suggests we share a joint. [Ossipow, 1997: 62][1]

This dinner at a convert's house in Geneva was one of my first 'field' experiences among vegetarians and followers of a macrobiotic[2] diet in French-speaking Switzerland. I believe it is still relevant vis-à-vis the relationship between vegetarians and food, their way of eating their meals and, more generally, the significance they attach to the concept of gastronomic pleasure.

Flavours rediscovered

To understand the pleasure vegetarians experience in food it's worth hearing what proselytes have to say about their shift from the old style eating (what they define as carnivorous) to the new style. Underlying this transition is a very complex set of causes and motivations (Ossipow 1997; 212-226), either triggered by a single event or reached over a long period of time. Still amazed by this change in their way of eating, the people I have spoken to never stop comparing their omnivorous past with their vegetarian present. They see the food of omnivores, the diet that includes meat, as not only 'lifeless' (in so far as it is the product of the slaughtering of animals) but also as 'tasteless' in so far as it is smothered in sauces and the like which hide the flavour of foods, themselves the product of myriad manipulations. They see vegetarian food, instead, as non-manipulated. My converts are adamant that, thanks to this type of diet, they have discovered (they often say 'rediscovered' as if theirs were the true 'original' diet) the 'real' taste of food. In their view genuine taste derives from the fact that organic vegetables, cereals and pulses are less adulterated and ripen more slowly. It's also worth adding that food is not camouflaged if you eat it raw or simply, without too many fats, spices, sauces and so on. Vegetarians don't snub softness, but they do show a clear preference for the crispy, the unrefined and the raw. These three characteristics are almost synonymous with true taste and texture. This is one of the most important dimensions of taste which vegetarians say they discover thanks to their new diet.

They compare the crunchiness of their cereals and vegetables to the soft, nervy or tough structure of meat. They also say that by removing meat from the centre of the meal they can concentrate far better on the flavours of ingredients once relegated to a bit part as side dishes. Meat and fish, they say, are 'corpses on the plate' which are toxic and impure, and thus likely to pollute all the other foods which accompany them. Leaving aside special holiday meals – for which many vegetarians delight in inventing a whole new gastronomy – the tendency is to split foods into groups which should be eaten separately one from another (fruit between meals, salads at midday, cereals in the evening). Vegetarian pleasure in food thus consists in separating rather than associating flavours. Finally, abstaining from alcohol and smoking cigarettes – by no means an absolute rule, as the dinner at Paul's proved – helps the palate regain its lost virginity and wonderment at the delight of flavours discovered anew.

Statements on the real taste of food give us an idea of how part of vegetarian pleasure manifests itself. They also introduce us to the insiders' rhetoric so often used by proselytes; this language also tends to widen the gap between the old life with its old food and the new practices. De facto, any thoughts about diet are at once a reconstruction of the past and present in an ethnological perspective, and an implicit or explicit desire to find arguments in favour of vegetarianism. During the past ten years, vegetarians have increasingly enjoyed the legitimization which dietetics has offered them. As they never fail to point out, what they have been preaching for ages corresponds exactly to the tips we read in the press or hear from nutritionists (see *Nouvel Observateur*, August 6 1998, for example): the focus should be on green vegetables and those rich in carotene, wholemeal cereals to increase the volume of food fibres, reductions in animal protein, different types of oil rather than butter and so on. In a crescendo of self-congratulation, they also point out that the great chefs are increasingly cooking non-meat dishes and introducing ingredients – flowers, shoots, sprouted seeds, soya-based products – that were once virtually the exclusive preserve of vegetarians and those devoted to a macrobiotic diet. The pleasure of food thus also derives from awareness that it is the 'right' food.

The 'apprenticeship' needed to become familiar with this 'right' food and the pleasure of its flavour is rarely a solitary experience. Vegetarians and especially devotees to macrobiotic food follow courses, read books and attend study groups during which lecturers highlight both the flavour to be discovered in food and its nutritional properties. A given food may, for example, be 'good' for the heart or liver or to counteract stress. The pleasure of eating is thus often reduced to the contemplation of health rather than taste.

A certain lightness
The light meal is the type vegetarians appreciate most of all. Raw food, simple preparation, texture and separation of flavours combine with a desire to eat small quantities of 'light' food. This includes cereals, which many 'normal' eaters consider 'heavy'. That raw vegetables are universally considered light foods

doesn't come as strange even to non-vegetarians. The lightness of the meal reflects a lightness of being sought by vegetarians both within and outside the realm of food. Many of them love sports in which they slide and fly (and indeed 'savour' speed). Some young people (the butt of criticism from 'oldie' vegetarians) use psychotropic substances which stimulate their individual growth and philosophical leanings. Others undertake different forms of fasting and bodily purification. Frugal meals, fasting, purification techniques: it all conjures up a sense of privation, mortification and desire for total self-control. Yet these experiences are not devoid of feelings of pleasure. As Caroline W. Bynum points out in *Holy Feast Holy Fast*, these practices are not only a matter of self-denial and self-punishment. For the women saints of the Middle Ages they were a way of merging with Christ. For the vegetarians of today they are a way of coming closer to themselves and to nature as they conceive of it, be this imbued with religious spirit or otherwise.

Table manners

You can't fix and eat a good meal just like that. Depending on whether its function is contemplative or convivial, it is accompanied by specific rituals or gestures. A number of proselytes (especially the macrobiotics among them) have shown me how the preparation of a meal has to be associated with gesture, which reveals not only the concentration and skill of the chef but also his respect for the form and nature of the food. This is why Paul taught me to cut the avocado into crescent-shaped slices which respected the form of the fruit. Other macrobiotics taught me to cut carrots lengthwise to conserve the memory of their original shape and a part of their ascendant energy. Lovers of raw vegetables advised me to arrange them on the plate in their original shapes.

Special attention is also devoted to the actual eating of the meal. The table has to be carefully laid. The colour of the candles, the tablecloth and the napkins, of the flowers (often the plant used to decorate the table is also served on the plate) should be in tune with the food that is served, particularly on special occasions. Macrobiotic practitioners also attach great importance to tableware and cutlery. This is why they often prefer to use wooden cutlery or chop sticks, which take them closer to the exotic roots of their eating principles, at the same time avoiding the sensation of bitterness or coldness produced by metal cutlery, be it stainless steel or silver. Vegetarians use fewer specific utensils but play with other elements to enhance the presentation of the meal. It's something they do for their own pleasure but also for that of guests, partly out of playfulness but also to promote vegetarianism. A young proselyte I know told me that on more than one occasion he staged 'all-vegetarian' lunches for his school mates. No plates, no cutlery, just a knife for the bread. Cabbage leaves for plates and sticks of celery and carrots for cutlery, and sliced bread not only to accompany the various dishes, but also to transfer them from the serving dishes to the plates.

Once at the table, some of the devotees I know start the meal with a moment of meditation, a sort of prayer, a song of thanks to the Creator or to the pleasure of partaking of food. It is a good rule to eat slowly, savouring every ingredient and, preferably, keeping the different tastes separate in the macrobiotic fashion. The daily meal resembles a moment of meditation. Vegetarians eat their meals calmly and slowly, and many normal eaters aspire to do the same. It's just that vegetarians make this part and parcel of their daily lives, in radical contrast to the stress of 'normal' eaters and the brutality of 'carnivores'!

Presenting food pleasantly and experimenting with new tastes are both geared to personal pleasure and to promoting convivial get-togethers with non-vegetarians. Ten years ago, it seemed absurd for vegetarians to serve guests totally meatless meals. Usually they ended up by organizing snacks that catered to a common sweet tooth; that way the vegetarians didn't feel too vulnerable to criticism for their eating habits. Today things have changed.

Pleasure and transgression

The (re)discovery of authentic flavours, respect for the chosen rules, the certainty of eating 'properly' and ritual behaviour at table combine together to define the pleasure of eating. Having said that, vegetarians are anything but saints! Just like 'normal' eaters, they infringe the rules they themselves have set. Transgression doesn't run to eating meat, but it manifests itself most of all in the structure of the meal, in the approach to sweet food and the consumption of alcoholic beverages and cigarettes.

Like anyone else, vegetarians are often in a hurry, and hence frequently fail to observe the rules which define a complete meal. They thus end up by contenting themselves with a 'condensed meal'[3] – rice or pasta with vegetables, soup or a vegetarian sandwich – or food to nibble at – yogurt, a chunk of bread and cheese, the odd peeled carrot, olives and biscuits. Such deviations from the habitual structure of the meal are more common among vegetarians (almost a form of positive sobriety) than among those who follow a macrobiotic diet, who are much more attentive to the *ying-yang* balance that is always generated by food.

Products containing white sugar are generally avoided since this type of sugar is regarded as toxic. While generally scorned in declarations on good eating habits, sugar is often quietly consumed in private. In collective eating events, sweet flavours come almost exclusively from 'approved' products: hence cane sugar, malt, solid fruit compotes and carob as opposed to chocolate. As a child, the creator of the 'vegetable' meal, educated to be a vegetarian, used to hide sweets behind the books in his bookshelf. One devotee lectured me on the horrors of sugar without bothering to hide his shopping bag full of bars of chocolate. One of my female informants confesses that she can't resist traditional cakes made of plain flour and refined sugar. The consumption of sweet products is thus criticized because it clashes with specific health principles, but is then adapted to the person to the extent that he or she continues to respect the ban on meat (cakes must not contain animal fats).

Sometimes young and not so young vegetarians indulge in veritable 'orgies', not unlike those of 'normal' eaters and drinkers. However, after an evening spent drinking and smoking, young vegetarians say they devote more attention than their omnivorous counterparts to recovering from the experience. They also reckon they are better informed on how to go about it: light meals, restorative diets of fresh vegetables and fruit and partial or total fasting are the secrets.

The alternation of strict observance and transgression varies from individual to individual and also varies in the course of life. Neophytes tend to stick closely to the rules, though they may slacken in the course of the years, and in some rare cases even return to a partially meat-based diet (see 'Those who become omnivores (again)' (Ossipow 1997; 299-301). Greater observance generally prevails in special moments in life – pregnancy, the birth and education of children, illness and so on; conversely, a slightly more lax attitude may accompany travel, meeting a non-vegetarian partner, conversion to a religion which does not explicitly demand vegetarianism.

Eternity

Pleasure is thus very much part of a cuisine that excludes some foods and, at the same time, introduces or (re)discovers others; it is also integral to a gastronomy which, more often than not, tends to separate tastes without ruling out the interplay of associations and blends. Moreover, pleasure of this sort is both personal and promotional. Yet followers of a vegetarian or a macrobiotic diet do not believe that there is no pleasure without risk. For vegetarians, carnivores who eat beef without worrying about the fact that it may have come from a cow infected by spongiform encephalitis are out of their minds. Meat they say is toxic *per se*, and in this case may even prove lethal. Those who risk catching salmonella or other infections by eating a Vacherin made of unpasteurized milk are considered less absurd, though vegetarians still struggle to understand how they are prepared to run such risks (or be totally unaware of them) just for the sake of taste. In the final analysis, apart from the different motivations and concepts that underpin it, the vegetarian option also implies a desire for control of the self and of the environment. Thus the pleasure of food should not be accompanied by risks: eating vegetarian also means rejecting the idea of illness and death and dreaming of eternity.

Notes

1 Ossipow, Laurence, *La cuisine du corps et de l'âme: approche ethnologique du végétarianisme, du crudivorisme et de la macrobiotique en Suisse*, Ed. de l'Institut d'ethnologie et de la Maison des sciences de l'homme, 1997 Neuchâtel, Paris.

2 University of California Press, 1987, Berkeley, Los Angeles.

3 On the question of structural change and processes of concentration or condensation of meals, see Claude Fischler, *L'homnivore*, Odile Jacob (Points), pp. 165-70, Paris 1993.

THE RIGOURS OF SNACKING

Sylvie Guichard-Anguis

*D*uring the course of the past century, Japanese cuisine has expanded and grown richer at an amazing rate. Despite such changes, however, various rules continue to hold rigid sway over the consumption of food. These rules establish particular groups of products and the binding relationships between such fare and the dishes in which they are served. To break these rules is more a symptom of freedom of spirit and originality than any desire to revolutionize the consumption of food. Thus artists, and in particular the myriad potters who make earthenware dishes in the Japanese archipelago, particularly enjoy underlining their individuality by departing from what could be conceived as a certain conformism. In order to give rein to their creativity, they opt for associations that would be inconceivable in other more formal spheres. It is generally women's magazines which showcase such displays, focusing predominantly on their aesthetic appeal.

The rules in question ensure a degree of continuity in how things are done, while the possibility of choice continues to grow each year. The rules make it possible to integrate all the innovations within pre-existing categories, so that the *corpus* of consolidated customs is not upset. In this way the tacit rules governing the combination of food and drink appear to persist despite the internationalization of Japanese cuisine.

Sake or wine

One of the fundamental rules recommends using food and drink from the same geographical area. Japanese dishes are accompanied by local alcoholic drinks. In other words, *sake* accompanies *sushi* and *sashimi*, whereas red and white wine are drunk with French and Italian recipes. Some restaurants have taken the lead from the non-conventional trend of women's magazines and now propose innovative combinations, such as white wine with raw fish dishes. However, efforts such as these are unlikely to make their way into ordinary everyday practice.

A second important rule holds that alcoholic drinks should be consumed with savoury dishes, and non-alcoholic drinks with desserts. As a result, in Japan alcoholic drinks, be they sweet or otherwise, are not drunk with local desserts or with those made following western recipes. When a diner asks for tea it signifies that he/she does not mean to carry on eating the predominantly savoury dishes laid out on the table in front of him/her. Granted, sugar is often a discreet ingredient of the soya sauce used in many fish-, meat- and vegetable-based recipes. Asking for tea also implies that no further alcohol will be drunk. At this point, fresh fruit may be served: indeed it is fruit, *kashi*, that provides the generic name for desserts. It should be noted in passing that indigenous Japanese cuisine has no recipes for fruit cooked in alcohol, whereas *sake* and *mirin* (a kind of sweet rice spirit) are used extensively in the preparation of savoury dishes. Only the *ume* plum has the privilege of making up one of the ingredients of a delicious sweet spirit.

When combined with the first rule, the second prescribes very rigid behaviour as far as eating desserts is concerned. Thus a red fermented tea from India or Ceylon may accompany cheese cake, whereas a green tea produced in Japan can accompany a Japanese *wagashi* dessert. Hot drinks are preferred with all kinds of dessert. Among these, tea holds sway above coffee and hot chocolate, which are usually drunk alone. Hot chocolate has been launched with great success on the Japanese market, and friends often ask us to join them for a cup, given its slimming properties! I should add that the hot chocolate served in Japan is a much lighter version of the dark, dense liquid that can be ordered in some renowned European premises. But to get back to tea, each type of green tea corresponds to a precise category of dessert. For the more refined desserts, such as those that are prepared for gatherings centred around the tea ceremony, the choice is between the best infusions, *gyokuro* or *sencha*, or powdered versions such as *matcha*.

Local variety

The choice of crockery is also dictated by rules. Local dishes are served in earthenware produced according to the traditions of the area, whereas foreign dishes are served on crockery from the region of provenance, or, at a stretch, on imitation crockery produced in Japan. In other words, it is not likely that *sashimi* or *sushi* will be served on 'Royal Copenhagen' china, or that a Japanese lacquer box will contain a slice of apple tart.

The extraordinary variety of restaurants in Japan is to some extent the result of these rules. The subdivision of the various types of savoury and sweet dishes, and the rule concerning drinks, ensures that diners move on to another restaurant once they have consumed the essential fare. Appeasing the desire for an excellent dessert, a cup of fermented tea or a good cup of coffee means leaving the typical Japanese restaurant which only serves fruit and occasionally sorbets and green tea. Diners move on to eateries specialized in these dishes. A large part of the attraction of some central districts, and their liveliness, is the profusion of specialized eateries and the crowds which migrate from one restaurant to the next.

The fact that the different stages of a meal can be broken up in this way means that it is always the right time to eat something, and a meal can never be considered completely over. Japan has institutionalized snacking as a national occupation. If you sit opposite someone on a Japanese train journey of a couple of hours you will understand what I'm on about. With a little luck, you will see your travelling companion extract little packets of all kinds of savoury and sweet foods from a bag and accompany them with the appropriate drink, possibly purchased on the train itself. This habit has led to the proliferation of kiosks and small vendors which also add to the liveliness of a town.

VENUS IN THE SUPERMARKET
Lesley Chamberlain

*W*hen Elizabeth David published a *Book of Mediterranean Food* in 1950, she transformed the British culinary landscape. A sometime resident of France, Italy, the Greek Islands and Egypt, Mrs David had done her shopping and collected her recipes first hand. She wrote: 'I hope to give some idea of the lovely cookery of those regions to people who do not already know them, and to stir the memories of those who have eaten this food on its native shores, and who would like sometimes to bring a flavour of those blessed lands of sun and sea and olive trees into their English kitchens.'

Touched by David's culinary genius and writing flair, the post-war British proceeded to develop a cosmopolitan range of gastronomic enthusiasm second in breadth to none in the world. In fact Mediterranean food is now a routine choice, alongside the dishes of the Indian subcontinent, expatriate Chinese cooking, and most recently the food and cooking of Southeast Asia. But to many palates the Mediterranean cuisines remain the most seductive.

Nepanthé

As with the fate of all pure ideas in the corrupt world, there is something ridiculous about the Mediterranean story. Mrs David's inspiration was Norman Douglas, the British-born traveller, diplomat and aesthete deeply out of fashion in today's egalitarian and supertechnical times. Douglas wrote an idiosyncratic cookery book (*Venus in the Kitchen*), but his Mediterranean masterpiece was the novel *South Wind* (1917). In that book the island of Capri is loosely disguised as Nepanthé, and he describes the curious, often hilarious lives of foreigners there, as the local mentality transforms their values. The foreigners are Anglo-American and either criminal refugees or such ardent devotees of the Classical World that they do not notice the loucheness of the present. But above all, through the authorial mouthpiece of Mr Keith, *South Wind* is a peon to the primacy of aesthetic values over the moral and the useful. Mediterranean civilization is static in its eternal beauty and mystery. Being quite incompatible with modern progress, Nepanthé is a last refuge for those tranquil men and women who prefer the beauty of a piece of sculpture called 'the Locri faun' to the alleged beauty of a motor car. It does not matter that the faun is, in some senses, a fake.

Douglas described an archetype. Anyone who has digested the social import of the Mediterranean in British life of the 1990s will recognize the continuing presence of enchantment, escape, self-discovery and self-abandon in the holidays we take, the second homes, and the films and books that reflect that spiritual exodus from the north.

I saw an excellent TV drama recently, in which an apparently well-heeled Englishman, dealing in property, had become, well frankly, a Mediterranean bore, all his personal inadequacy decked by a foreigner's enthusiasm for the local bread and wine. In the end his tyrannized family murdered him. There is a similar sort of 'justified' murder in *South Wind*. In life, of course, the Spanish Mediterranean thirty years ago became a haven for British criminals on the run, and only EC extradition laws have made it less attractive.

You can see this habit of migration from the law of one's native land as symbolic. There is, culturally speaking, something utterly fraudulent and self-indulgent about the British love of the Mediterranean. And yet the Mediterranean is also a true tonic for orderly, repressed, undemonstrative, modest Protestant natures. It is a genuine passion, to which the only known antidote is Scotland. As Douglas's hero Mr Keith put it: 'The meagre soil and parsimonious culture, the reasonable discourse of the people, their wholesome disputatiousness, acted as a kind of purge or tonic after all this Southern exuberance.'

Brand name

So where does this leave us *vis à vis* the *bouillabaisse* and the *paella*, the *skordalia* and the *hummus*, the *tarama* and the *tahina* which have done more to dent British patriotism and the domestic holiday trade than the political invention of Europe? (Though of course they are part of the same historical upheaval.) They fill our supermarket shelves and our subconscious desires for a better life. They dominate our conscious shaping of our leisure and lifestyle. If the Mediterranean always had appeal for those who went there or read about it, perhaps via an interest in the Classical world, food is the medium which has brought home the Mediterranean message to a less affluent and less well-read, but ever-growing public. The marketing people have moved in. Everyone knows about the Mediterranean through marketing, and especially through food marketing. 'Mediterranean' in Britain is now a brand name, along with all the other brand and supermarket names rapidly taking over our daily lives and our politics.

It is true that never in Britain have we had so much access to such good food in the way of olive oils, wines, charcuterie, fresh herbs and so on. I have met young men who claim they could not live without pesto sauce for their pasta. Even my septuagenarian father has come round to garlic and oregano. As with Norman Douglas's picture of Nepanthé/Capri, much of this shift in the food and leisure culture is genuine and to be celebrated. But it trails fraudulence and fakery in its wake, and is easily exploited and debased. The British food market is now full of modified 'Mediterranean' products, of the ready-made, quick, and 'useful' variety. An 'olive oil' spread trying for a share of the market which 'healthy' soft margarine long ago stole from butter employs every cliché in the book in an attempt to extend its market downwards. The advertisers of Olivio would have us believe (with the inclusion of some genuine Italian dialogue) that Italian peasants never die because they eat things like this spread: or that Mediterranean old-age pensioners are so well-preserved by their diet that they still play football and their women still want them for their bodies.

The Mediterranean promises the British better appetites all round, and a longer life in which to enjoy them. Even the British government has advised on the healthiness of a Mediterranean diet. In fact the Mediterranean as a cultural goal has become thoroughly vulgar. If I didn't like the sun, and wine and olive oil, I'd be off to Scotland.

WHAT A STATE
John Irving

$\mathcal{B}$efore World War I, the small city of Carlisle now in the county of Cumbria, in the north-west of England, boasted an astonishing number of inns and public houses; a register published in 1847 records more than 120 figure against an urban population of fewer than 50,000 inhabitants. The number of such establishments was cut drastically in the course of World War I, largely as a consequence of a series of events in nearby Gretna, just over the border in Scotland, a self-contained township founded in August 1915 with its own police force (male and female) fire service, power station, hospital, school, laundry, shops, offices, halls, clubs and other recreational facilities. The story began when the British government sponsored the building project in Gretna to house workers at an HM Munitions Factory in the area. At the time, Britain risked losing the war on account of lack of ammunition, and the London government decided to remedy the situation by calling in around 30,000 women and men from all around to make the so-called 'Devil's Porridge', an explosive paste, at the Scottish plant. Bringing so many different people together in such a confined environment inevitably triggered social consequences. Dissatisfied with their lot, on Saturday nights the munitions workers (mostly from Ireland) would catch the last train to Carlisle to spend their week's earnings on booze. The rowdiness, drunkenness and violence that ensued soon became intolerable, and, at one stage, the British government feared that, in the wake of the Easter Uprising in Dublin in 1916, unrest might also spread to the British mainland. Not that it was only the Irish who caused trouble. I have to confess that a story runs in the family that a great-great uncle of mine, a certain Armstrong, was sent before the magistrates on a charge of drunken and disorderly behaviour. 'Armstrong, you've gone through a fortune with your drinking', the chief justice thundered. 'No, my lord, the fortune went through me!' was Armstrong's reply.

David Lloyd George, the energetic but puritanical minister of munitions in Asquith's wartime government, decided to undertake what nowadays would be known as a 'social experiment', almost a foretaste of the Prohibition in America in the 'Roaring Twenties'. He ruled that, in order to restore law and order to

Carlisle city centre and its medieval lanes, the state would proceed to control the production, distribution and sale of alcoholic drinks. The government thus bought up all the city's pubs, shutting down many of them and replacing them with larger managed houses. A new strict code of rules was introduced to encourage punters to adopt more moderate, decorous behaviour. One of these was the banning of the sale of beer and other alcoholic beverages to under-eighteen-year-olds. The measure was subsequently extended to the rest of the UK and stands to this day. The 'social experiment' was given the name 'State Management Scheme' and continued for 55 years until 1971. It was supervised by a central control board (with 'se coercere' as its motto), which included a director of the Butler's brewery and Sydney Neville from Whitbread. The Board took over Carlisle's four breweries and closed down three of them. All beer was then brewed at the Carlisle & District State Management Scheme Old Brewery (originally opened in 1756) in the Caldewgate neighbourhood in the shadow of the city's Norman castle. Its award-winning ales and beers included Carlisle Extra Stout, Mild, Light Ale, Special Export and Nut Brown, which won the First Prize Silver Medal at the Brewers' Exhibition at Olympia, London, in 1960. Certain spirits and Guinness were also bottled under licence. Though it was cheaper than beer elsewhere, Carlisle's also managed to make consistent profits. Money was re-invested and, thanks largely to the designs of the London-based architect Harry Redfern, the city was graced with a number of architecturally attractive public houses (the Redfern Inn in Etterby was named after the architect himself). Redfern's buildings include the Cumberland Inn, built in 1929-30 in Botchergate, Carlisle's central thoroughfare, the White Inn (formerly The Crescent), in Warwick Road, The Farrier, in the popular Raffles district, and The Malt Shovel, in Rickergate, built in 1928 with a functional exterior concealing a bar, dining room, billiards room, landlord's quarters and a stable for eight horses. One of my favourites used to be the Turf Tavern, the sloping roof of which once served as the grandstand for the Swifts racecourse in Rickerby Park. With its basic, no-nonsense décor, fireplaces and games rooms, it conjured up an almost rustic atmosphere, even though it was only a stone's throw from the city centre. Other pubs – such as the Wrestlers' Arms Inn, the Earl Grey and the Saracen's Head – were more of the spit-and-sawdust type, but no one could argue that they did not possess character.

Over the years, people in Carlisle grew very fond of their State Management Scheme beer, unavailable anywhere else. The government's decision to sell off the whole caboodle – brewery, pubs and all – was met with outrage. Locals had grown proud of their unique pubs and beer, and viewed the prospect of drinking the mass-produced ales of big outside breweries with the utmost distaste. There was no looking back, however, and, eventually, in 1971 all the city's pubs were sold to national brewers, who proceeded to change many of their names, much to the disgust of the people of Carlisle.

Theakston's bought up the Carlisle Brewery in 1974, but the move proved unwise. 'It brought problems with it,' recalls Paul Theakston, managing director of the corporation, 'and one of the problems was that the amount of money needed for growth and development to actually fulfil the promise of the place was greater than the resource we had and the result of that was that we ended up bringing in outside shareholders for the first time, both individuals and ultimately an investment trust. And it was this fact that in the early 80s led to Theakston's losing its independence and going to another brewer.' As a result, in 1984, the brewery was taken over by Matthew Brown, who closed it down definitively in 1987. Thus, after a long and glorious history in the sector, the city of Carlisle now no longer produces beer commercially.

Just for the record, Carlisle now has a population of about 102,000 and roughly 60 pubs.

THE GREAT BRITISH TRIFLE
Sarah Freeman

*A*long with rice and Christmas pudding, trifle is the most famous of all traditional British sweets. Like the unfortunate rice pudding, however, it has been deeply unfashionable in recent years. Publisher Tom Jaine, who has just brought out a little book devoted to it, says that he attributes its fusty image to the demise of the restaurant sweet-trolley, although it is almost certainly also due to its association in many people's minds with packet custards and jellies, cheap jam, and those obstinate slices of stale cake which would otherwise be wasted. I have served my own version of it regularly over the years, stuck with toasted almonds and piled high in a huge, stemmed strawberry-patterned Wedgwood bowl. There has never been any question of its popularity: despite its size, the bowl is invariably scraped clean – yet, at least until now, I have never dared to include the recipe in a cookery book.

But fashion swings and tastes change. Now it seems that a trifle revival may be on hand. At St John, a trend-setting London restaurant near the City (strongly recommended to every *Slow* reader), 'Tom's Cherry Trifle' is served during the cherry season and features in the chef, Fergus Henderson's, cookery book. We are not told who Tom is, but he was evidently brought up to his mother's trifles: 'unlike my mother's, the fruit isn't set to a jelly but in a thick compote and so remains a little runny'. There is a recipe for trifle in one of the TV chef Nigella Lawson's cookery books, and it is served both at another celebrity chef's restaurant in Holland Park and at Cucina, a small restaurant cum cookshop in Hampstead (north London) which is notable for its imaginative English-style puddings. And in addition is the book from Tom Jaine, written and researched by Helen Saberi and Alan Davidson of *The Oxford Companion to Food* fame, who turned to trifle by way of light relief after the huge task of compiling the *Companion*.

The trifle as we know it, they tell us, is almost exactly 250 years old: the first recipes, so far as they could discover, were given in 1751 in a compendium called *The Lady's Companion* and the second edition of the famous *The Art of Cookery Made Plain and Easy* by Hannah Glasse. Earlier versions were flavoured creams or fruit fools, which continued to be served under the name of 'Trifle' for another

100 years – and very good they could be, as we discovered. Helen and Alan were not able to specify exactly where the idea of amalgamating the cream with alcohol-soaked cake or biscuits came from, but suggest that it might have evolved from a pudding called 'Floating Island', which consisted of pieces of bread or brioche and jelly floating in the cream.

The book also reveals that jelly is as traditional to trifle as cream, alcohol, and cake or biscuit (though one has to remember that until the twentieth century, the jelly would have been home-made with fresh fruit). Somehow, it had never occurred to me before that you might put jelly into a trifle, even though, as the book makes clear, there are no rules about what it should contain. Trifle-lovers, however, become as heated over the question as others in Britain about whether one should add the milk or tea first. Jelly to set the bottom will give a firmer result than if only soaked cake is used: with a thick custard and stiffly whipped cream, a trifle made with jelly does not necessarily need a bowl.

After reading the book, which includes over 90 recipes, I felt that I had no choice but to hold a trifle-tasting. Not all the members of my convivium, as yet unaware of the new trend, responded with the enthusiasm that the book generated in me, but twelve of us gathered round the dinner-table and, after a simple meal (roasted vegetable tart and gammon with caper sauce: very English!) were treated to the spectacle of four enormous bowls topped with whipped cream and decorated with raspberries, almonds, peel, and amaretti. A fifth, much smaller and plainer-looking, contained an example of flavoured cream – 'Swiss Cream or Trifle (*Very Good*)' from *Modern Cookery for Private Families* (1845) by Eliza Acton, who is rightly described by Helen and Alan as 'the finest cookery-writer in the English language'. Three of the four large bowls were modern interpretations, and, like Fergus Henderson's, featured fresh fruit; the fourth was the recipe given by Mrs Beeton, whose book, *Household Management* (1861), became far more famous than Miss Acton's and indeed is still regarded as almost synonymous with British traditional cookery. Despite being Mrs Beeton's biographer and having traced a large proportion of her recipes to Miss Acton, I am not sure where the one for her trifle came from, but it was rich, nutty, and delicious (Mrs Beeton, it should be explained, never claimed to be a cook, and invented only one out of the total of about 1,500 recipes that she published). When we had done as much justice as we could to the five confections, we unanimously voted Miss Acton's Swiss cream, which was pristine and delicate, as the best, with Mrs Beeton's contribution a runner-up: none of the modern ones, we all agreed, could touch them. It is possible that the Swiss cream had an advantage because, as it is not alcoholic, I advised trying it first – but I had tasted it, with my own and Mrs Beeton's, as I made them, and already had no doubt about my own opinion.

We shall give another tasting later in the year, with more members and different trifles: in the meanwhile, I give the recipe for the Swiss cream: 'Flavour pleasantly with lemon rind and cinnamon, a pint [600 ml] of rich cream, after having taken from it as much as will mix smoothly to a thin batter four teaspoonful of the finest flour; sweeten it with six ounces [175 g] of well-refined sugar in lumps; place it over a clear fire in a delicately clean saucepan, and when it boils stir in the flour, and simmer it for four or five minutes, stirring it gently without ceasing; then pour it out, and when it is quite cold mix with it by degrees the strained juice of two moderate-sized and very fresh lemons. Take a quarter of a pound [125 g] of macaroons, cover the bottom of a glass dish with a portion of them, pour in a part of the cream, lay the remainder of the macaroons upon it, add the rest of the cream, and ornament it with candied citron sliced thin. It should be made the day before it is wanted for table. The requisite flavour may be given to the dish by infusing in the cream the very thin rind of a lemon and part of a stick of cinnamon, slightly bruised, and then straining it before the flour is added; or, these and the sugar may be boiled together with two or three spoonsful of water, to a strongly flavoured syrup, which, after having been passed through a muslin strainer, may be stirred into the cream. Some cooks boil the cinnamon and the *grated* rind of a lemon with all the other ingredients, but the cream has then to be pressed through a sieve after it is made, a process which it is always desirable to avoid. It may be flavoured with vanilla and maraschino, or with orange blossoms at pleasure; but is *excellent* made as above.'

From *Trifle*, p 102, published by Prospect Books, Allaleigh House, Blackawton, Totnes, Devon TQ9 7DL.

THE POETS' LAKES

Laura Mason

I do not know of any tract of country in which, in so narrow a compass, may be found an equal variety in the influences of light and shadow upon the sublime and beautiful features of the landscape (William Wordsworth, *Guide to the Lakes*, 1810).

The Lake District was popularised by William Wordsworth and his friends, the 'Lake Poets'. Since the early 19th century, their writing has inspired people to visit the area. It became a national park in 1951. About 30 miles across, it contains the highest hills in England, several large lakes and many smaller ones. The valley sides are netted with stone walled enclosures, and scattered with traditional farm buildings.

The 2001 foot-and-mouth epidemic devastated the local rural economy, especially the Herdwick sheep. These, and other breeds including Swaledales, Leicesters and Teeswaters produce the open hill landscape by close grazing. Cattle are raised on lower ground: the once-popular beef shorthorn has disappeared, but the black Aberdeen Angus is sometimes seen. Dairying is unimportant, though an artisan cheesemaker works north of the area at Thornby Moor.

Kendal and Penrith are important centres. Their butcher's shops sell excellent local lamb and beef (the best meat remains in the area) and large coils of Cumberland sausage, a fresh pork sausage with a much lower rusk content than most English sausages. Rum butter, a traditional confection of butter, sugar, rum and nutmeg, is ubiquitous. A Kendal speciality is Kendal Mint Cake, thin brittle slabs of candied sugar with mint oil. In Penrith, the Toffee Shop makes traditional English toffee, and very good fudge, sugar boiled with butter and milk. Near Penrith, Wetheriggs pottery makes country slipware. Both towns have farmers markets – Penrith every week, Kendal once a month, and Low Sizergh Barn Shop (south of Kendal) stocks a wide range of food from the area.

Windermere is the largest and most accessible lake. Formerly it was noted for char (*Salvinus alpinus*), preserved by potting with sweet spices and butter. This fish is now a rarity, and the fishery is closed for 2002 due to low stocks. Although brown trout is found in the streams, it is rarely offered on menus, but wild salmon from the Solway Firth sometimes appears. Detour south to the Lyth valley for damson trees (*Prunus institia*). Planted in the mid-19th century, they provide pink blossom in spring and dark red fruit in September. Some are used in puddings or with meat. Call at the Masons Arms pub (Strawberry Bank) for damson beer, inspired by Belgian traditions.

Return north and visit Townend at Troutbeck to view a traditional Lake District farmhouse kitchen. Then visit Grasmere, a town which is a shrine to Wordsworth. It also contains the Grasmere Gingerbread Shop established by Sarah Nelson in the 1840s. The gingerbread is hard, spicy and very good. Another bakery speciality can sometimes be found in Hawkshead to the west of Windermere. This town continued to make 'wigs', a type of spiced, enriched white bread roll, after other places in England had stopped. Periodically teashops in the town revive the idea, so the visitor may be lucky and find an example. Nearby is Hill Top at Near Sawrey, once home to the writer Beatrix Potter, well known for the Peter Rabbit children's books. Her illustrations show cottage interiors in the early 20th century. She was also a sheep farmer, favouring Herdwicks.

From Sawrey, travel south down the shore of Coniston Water (also associated with children's stories, the 'Swallows and Amazons' series by Arthur Ransome) to Flookburgh, a centre for fishing on the wide sands of Morecambe Bay. Most important are shrimps (*Crangon crangon*) which are often potted for eating with toast at lunch or teatime. Then take the coast road west, skirting the Furness hills to Wabberthwaite, which lacks scenery but makes up for it in the Post Office, where the Woodall family have been making excellent hams, bacon and sausages since before the Second World War. A number of other butchers in the area cure bacon, and at least one, Shaws at Silloth, has returned to the tradition of rearing pigs in a woodland environment.

Nearby, in the Duddon Valley, farmers have established Cumbrian Wool, a co-operative which processes the wool from local sheep including Herdwicks. To see sheep farming at its toughest, take the road north-east to Wastwater, a bleak lake bounded one side with scree slopes, and locked in to the north by Great Gable and Scafell Pike. Back on the coast road again, continue north to Cockermouth, birthplace of Wordsworth and home to Jennings Bros, the major brewery in the area. From here, travel south-east down Lorton Vale for exceptionally pretty scenery around Buttermere, and the impressive Honister pass. Continue north to Keswick, a centre for tourism. It seems an unlikely place to find a pencil museum, but making these was a local industry as early as the 16th century.

Finish by travelling east to Ullswater, one of the more beautiful lakes. Its south shore is home to Sharrow Bay Hotel (the other great Lake District restaurant is Miller Howe on Windermere). Another centre of Herdwick wool production is Crookabeck Angoras at Patterdale, at the southern end of the lake.

More information on Cumbrian food producers and numerous craftsmen working in the area, can be obtained from:

Made in Cumbria, County Offices, Busher Walk, Kendal, Cumbria LA9 4RQ +44 (0) 1539 732736 or visit www.madeincumbria.co.uk

Herdwick sheep

Herdwicks are considered peculiar to the Lake District. They are slow-growing, hardy and 'heafed' – that is, they have a homing instinct which leads them to return to their native pastures when moved. They are also partially responsible for the bleak nature of some Lake District hills: like all sheep, they graze the grass very closely and inhibit the growth of tree cover. The lambs are born black and become paler with age; older adult sheep are white. A mixture of the wool from sheep of different ages produces a characteristic grey shade, once seen in locally produced cloth, and still produced in knitting yarn. The meat is lean and slightly gamey.

The breed's staunchest defender was Mrs Heelis, better known as Beatrix Potter. She maintained Herdwick sheep on her estates and left much land to the National Trust, on condition that Herdwicks be grazed on it. By the late 20th century the breed had become uncommon outside the Lake District. The foot-and-mouth epidemic of 2001 affected the Lake District badly and many flocks were culled, but they are recovering.

Cumbrian Wool, Pike Side Farm, Ulpha, Broughton in Furness, Cumbria LA20 6EY, UK

+44 (0) 229 885361 cumbrian.wool@virgin.net sell products made from the wool of Herwicks and other traditional breeds

Crookabeck Angoras, Patterdale, Penrith +44 (0) 17684 82456 www.herdwickwool.com sell spun Herdwick wool, knitted garments and wool from their own angora goats.

Rum butter is well recorded in local childbirth rituals in the 19th century. Large bowlfuls were prepared, and visitors were expected to partake and then leave a silver coin for the newborn in exchange. A little of this extremely sweet confection was also given to the child as its first taste of earthly food. It is now mostly eaten with hot plum pudding at Christmas.

Sugar and spices and rum are also combined as a filling for rum nicky: this is a large single-crust pie case filled with the mixture and decorated with an ornamental pastry lattice before baking. Another popular dish, available on most menus in the area is sticky toffee pudding, based on a sponge mixture with dates or raisins baked over a rich toffee sauce.

Restaurants and pubs

There are two grand restaurants in the area. Sharrow Bay (Ullswater) was founded in the late 1940s by the late Francis Coulson, and Miller Howe (Windermere) in the late 1960s by John Tovey (now retired). Both establishments live on in style, serving exquisite world-class cooking for those with deep pockets. Advance booking is essential. Best bargains are said to be afternoon tea at Sharrow Bay and lunch at Miller Howe. The Miller Howe Cafe in Windermere is run by a former chef of John Tovey's.

For less formal food in traditional surroundings, go to a pub. Several of these brew their own beer, and most of the others stock beers brewed by Jennings Bros at Cockermouth. Anyone who wishes to make a serious exploration should buy *The Good Pub Guide*. Consistent favourites over the years include the Punchbowl at Crosthwaite (near Kendal) and the Queen's Head at Troutbeck. There are at least another twenty pubs in the area worth visiting for historical interest, beer, food or all three, and the picture changes constantly. Changes in ownership can make a once-dull pub into one to watch, as is currently happening with the Greyhound at Shap.

The eclectic influence known as 'modern British' has reached the Lake District. Simple dishes of Lakeland farmhouse cookery such as the 'tatie pot' (potatoes, lamb and black pudding) have more or less vanished. However, a move towards including more local produce on menus is visible. This seems likely to accelerate in the aftermath of foot and mouth, and a co-operative supplies locally produced meat to many establishments. Portions are devised for people who have walked fifteen miles on a cold day, and tend to be large.

The Good Pub Guide 2003 is edited by Alisdair Aird and published by Ebury Press, London.

THE NEW IRELAND
Roz Crowley

*I*reland has always had a tradition of warm, open hospitality. The country's financial wealth has been realized only in the last ten years. As a poor nation, Ireland's hospitality until quite recently evolved around the home, where the poorest of families provided the warmest of welcomes. A cup of tea in your hand (as opposed to the formality of on a saucer), a ball of malt (a glass of whiskey) with a generous plate of hairy bacon and floury potatoes topped with rich salted butter were standard fare for those lucky enough to have meat to offer. With most dining done at home and most drinking done in pubs, the exception was the seasonal fairs at which animals were bought and sold, and where food and drink coupled with music and dancing, followed the selling of beasts around the country. Any excuse for a party and the Irish will open a bottle of whiskey or stout, no matter what the wealth of the household, and in some cases this has been translated today in the small hotels, bed and breakfasts and restaurants nation-wide.

'Low restauration' is not a term used in Ireland. There are expensive restaurants, many of them of excellent quality, and cheap restaurants, influenced by American fast food outlets and interpretations of European, Mexican and Eastern food. It is not unusual to find a pasta dish with a side serving of American French fries topped with curry sauce! The worst of this style of dining out has taken a foothold in the cities' main streets, as they have world-wide, and there is also the influence of prebaked, prepackaged, prepared foods for restaurants which have sacrificed individuality for convenience in catering for large numbers.

In contrast, a dedicated band of food lovers has sought to re-introduce and celebrate the use of farm produce, with many restaurateurs supporting organic farmers in their efforts to fight global blandness and chemical intervention. These restaurateurs, who range from the owner chefs of big country houses serving their own meat and vegetables, to tiny sidestreet cafés serving traditional scones, butter and jams made from local fruit, are fighting a battle for taste. Produce is best when it comes from the dedicated farmers who use their pastures diligently and take pride in their animals and garden produce. Sensing the demise of these

183

treasured producers, some consumers have begun to realize that they must defend the right to keep taste in Irish food.

Fusion or confusion?

Probably one of the strongest traditions in Ireland since recorded time has been that of bread and cake making. Scones and oatcakes, soft maize soda bread, wheaten loaves and a range of white yeast breads have been the preserve of the farmer's wife who handed down her skills to her daughters. With modern trends, this tradition is dying but having survived the scourge of the sliced pan (the sliced yeast bread all too readily embraced by toast and sandwich makers), alternatives can be found in restaurants where chefs wear their skills as a badge of honour. With them, a band of new breadmakers supply an ever increasing number of dynamic farmers' markets and small restaurants with old fashioned soda breads, yeast breads and a range of adopted traditional breads of Italy (though Ireland did make its own range of flat breads for centuries), with Middle Eastern countries adding a further variety. Organic restaurants and juice bars serve wraps, innovative salads and smoothies, and pubs serve anything from excellent fresh food to prepackaged, overseasoned chicken wings and processed cheese sandwiches. Ireland's restauration is going through a restoration, or a further fusion of influences, some say more of a confusion!

Cheesemakers have done much for Ireland's restaurant trade, generating a pride in local produce. Chefs create simple dishes and compile interesting selections of cheeses which have their own local characteristics, mainly marked by a richness from the full fat milk of cows and to a lesser extent goats. Once a means of using excess milk and preserving it with salt for leaner months, butter making on farms is largely a thing of the past, with large dairies supplying butter used for cooking and baking. At the same time, farmers' wives are making cheese as a means of rendering their quota-ridden farms viable.

Sunday lunch is a popular tradition at home in rural areas and in hotels and restaurants where mothers with traditionally large families (at least two or three) and now fathers who share parenting responsibilities, treat themselves to a meal with their children and extended family. It is here you will find traditional roast lamb and beef dishes with floury roast potatoes crisped with the fat of the meat. Bacon and cabbage and corned beef (salted and pickled in saltpetre), are still popular, accompanied by a creamy mixture of mashed potatoes with shredded cabbage or kale, when it is known as 'colcannon' or, when mixed with spring onions, scallions or leeks, as 'champ'. Fashionable restaurants serve this from time to time, along with roast duck, venison and roast pork accompanied by apple sauce. There is also dramatic fusion food, pretentious at times, but also an exciting amalgam of fashionable leaves and fungi, noodles and grains. Smoked fish like eel and trout are popular with smoked salmon in demand, despite the anticipated demise of the wild variety. Main courses are followed by light iced desserts but also by rich fruit tarts, apple still being the most popular, lightened by blackberry and blackcurrant seasonal additions. Served with lightly whipped full cream, these dishes underline the traditional style of restauration in Ireland, one of plenty and rich with cream, butter and starchy foods. The substitution of butter with olive oil, and creamy sauces with reduction emulsions, has happened yet in the majority of restaurants, the heartier options are still more popular, except with the youngest of diners who favour the lighter influences of Thai and Chinese cuisine.

Natural and traditional

Potatoes are still to be found on every menu, in all its plain and fanciful disguises and the plight of over a million labourers in 1845 has done little to alter this passion for the humble spud. In fact, the potato, if anything, is enjoying a resurgence of interest, despite the reduction of strains. Seed savers and those interested in keeping Ireland's cuisine as varied as possible, encourage the propagation of varieties in danger of extinction, and modern Irish chefs specify potato varieties to enhance their menus.

The Irish have taken a long time to recover from the Catholic religion's view of fish as penitential, when it was seen as a means of fasting and penance to eschew meat on a Friday and instead consume fish. So disliked was it that eggs were preferable to the sea's bounty and even in famine times was not seen as an alternative to starvation. However, remnants of Middle Stone Age culinary activities, in the form of waste shell deposits found on the south coast, indicate a tradition of shellfish consumption which is now reflected in the keen interest of restaurateurs and consumers in fish from rivers and seas. Fish appears on most menus at all levels of restauration. Much of it is fresh and wild but with declining river stocks, fresh wild fish is not always easy to find. Fish farming has become an industry and the seas are overfished, not just by the Irish.

Organic farmers and chemical-free gardeners are showing their larger commercial counterparts that organic vegetable farming is viable in Ireland but large supermarket chains are making their work difficult with central buying a precondition of contracts. In some ways, this demand makes fresh farm produce more available to conscientious restaurateurs who appreciate their superior taste and quality. Listing their suppliers on menus, restaurateurs give credit to the farmers who care about their produce. This quality does not come cheap in Ireland and so if Low Restauration means Cheap Restauration, then it does not exist. If it means natural food, with a nod to traditional dishes, but embracing the nuances of their European neighbours and Eastern traditions, then the New Irish Cuisine is Low Restauration, and seeking out the best will bring rewards to those who appreciate good food from its provenance to its taste.

SALT, FAT AND SMOKE
Regina Sexton

*T*he traditional Irish palate has always relished the taste of salt, fat and smoke – and still does, in some quarters. These three indulgences come together deliciously in smoked bacon and ham which, unsurprisingly, were once special festive and celebratory foods. Unfortunately, good quality bacon and ham are increasingly difficult to source, as the Irish commercial pig industry is growing to gargantuan proportions. In recent years, the upsurge in salmon farming stands as a haunting portent of the large-scale domestication of a wild species, mirroring the intensification of commercial pig farming. Given this current crisis, fish producers who champion the wild salmon are themselves to be championed.

Slow Food has created a presidium to safeguard the livelihood of those who continue to produce traditional smoked salmon the old-fashioned way: taking the wild fish at the peak of its season, curing it lightly, then smoking it mildly and tenderly to produce an exquisite Irish wild smoked salmon.

Significantly, three of the four producers of presidium smoked salmon are based in County Cork, Ireland's largest county. Cork is the most southerly point of the island, looking onto the north Atlantic. The county has a strong maritime tradition. Salmon fishing and fisheries serving the domestic and foreign markets have a very long history. During the boom time for the industry in the 14th, 15th and 16th centuries, certain families, like the O'Driscolls, were legendary for their fishing prowess. Nowadays, Frank Hederman, Sally Barnes and Anthony Creswell are celebrated for their smoked salmon from the Cork area. All are small-scale producers, employing no more than two people at a time, and their business space is also the family home. A fourth producer, Peter Dunn, is based in Dublin.

Frank Hederman lives and works in Cobh in East Cork. He has been dealing in fish and working with boats since he was 13. Even today, he is still but a stone's throw from the coast. Boats and the smell of the sea have always been part of his life. In the early 1980s, Frank recognized a gap in the market and decided to produce high quality smoked salmon. He admits that, at the time, it was a bit of a gamble simply because smoked salmon was not widely known and appreciated. Anecdotal evidence, for example, confirms that until relatively recently, the Irish palate was not trained, ready or open to enjoy the taste and texture of this exceptional product. Understandably, unfamiliarity with the modern version, together with a strong tradition of heavily smoked and salted fish, bred a little suspicion. This was compounded by a certain confusion as to how the delicate wild smoked salmon should be handled and cut. Frank sources his fish from the Dunmore East fisheries that operate just east of his home base. His fish is dry salted and smoked with beech chips. When he began production in 1982, he sourced wood for burning in the nearby Midleton Distillery, famous as the producer of some of the best Irish whiskeys. Frank carried home the used oak barrels, chopped them up and made chips for smoking. After years of hands-on experience, and with a desire to constantly refine, define and improve the product, Frank moved to beechwood smoking. He is adamant that beech produces the best flavour, one that is mild and low in tannins and acidity.

Both Anthony Creswell, of Ummera Smoked Products, and Sally Barnes, of the Woodcock Smokery, are based on the coast of west Cork, an area of unrivalled scenic beauty. The Gulf Stream courts the coast at this point, mellowing the surf. I'm reminded of this as I drive to meet Anthony and Sally at the Ummera Smokehouse on a sunny May afternoon. The village of Timoleague, where Anthony is based, sits in the valley of the river Argideen, renowned for its runs of migratory fish, sea trout in particular. The valley is lush green, now broken only by mischievous May flowers: bluebells, white ramsons, yellow celandine and wood anemones that look like fried eggs on stalks. The Argideen flows into the sea at Timoleague and a 13th-century Franciscan friary marks the site.

The Creswells have been smoking wild salmon here since 1971. Before that, Anthony's father, a keen fisherman, smoked his own and his friends' catches for their private use. Through trial and error, he perfected his salmon smoking technique, creating a product deserving of a wider audience. In the late 1970s and early 1980s, Creswell's smoked wild salmon came to the market. Anthony joined the business on a full-time basis in the mid 1980s after 20 years working in the wine trade. The methods developed by Anthony's father are those that are still employed today. Wild salmon is cured in a brine of pure sea salt and organic raw sugar cane, then oak smoked. Anthony, following his years of experience in the wine trade, says that 'as they mature the finest wines in oak casks, why not smoke the finest salmon in oak!' Why not indeed, as oak is also a native tree in Ireland.

Sally Barnes lives a little further west in the 17th-century town of Castletownsend, which is best known as the home of the novelists, Somerville and Ross. The town runs downhill towards the sea and, after a few hours here, you'll come home with a salty, sea-sprayed face. Sally is Scottish by birth so you could say that her skill in handling salmon is instinctive, even genetic. A schoolteacher by training, Sally decided to come to Ireland with her fisherman husband after an uneventful and unrewarding spell of teaching in London. She started by hot-smoking fish in a tea chest with a hole bored in the bottom. In 1983, she moved up a gear, establishing the Woodcock Smokery and unleashing her cold-smoked wild salmon on an unsuspecting market. Her success rests in the simple treatment of the fresh fish. First, she dry cures in salt and smokes with oak or beech shavings or a combination of both, depending on what's on hand.

A step northwards and eastward towards Dublin brings you to Dunn's Smokery. In 1822, John Dunn turned his pub in Moore Street, in the heart of Dublin City, into a fish shop. The retail shop moved to D'Olier Street in 1895 and, in a basement smokehouse in this location, the Dunns started smoking wild salmon in the late 1930s. In 1966, the present owner, Peter Dunn, moved again and established a wholesaling business in Manor Street in the City. Here he installed four smoking kilns. Today, the Dunns dry salt their wild salmon and mildly smoke it with oak.

The four Irish smokers in this presidium use only wild salmon from local inshore and in-harbour fisheries, caught by men licensed to operate no more than six miles from the shore in small boats. They purchase fish only from fishermen who practise traditional, skilled methods of salmon fishing with drift and draft nets.

The presidium links the present fishing industry with the salmon fisheries of past generations, and also supports the local economy, local livelihoods and local pride. In addition, consumers of this smoked salmon enjoy a pure product made from wild fish, instead of their farmed, captive counterparts. The wild salmon choose their own feeding grounds, and swim themselves into pure muscle – they are far superior to their flabby meal-fed and caged counterparts. Finally, the Irish wild salmon smokers have taken a traditional product using traditional ingredients, simply salt and wood smoke and, in modifying a traditional curing technique, they have achieved a modern classic of unsurpassed elegance that remains true to its historical pedigree.

CONTRIBUTORS' LIST

Françoise Aubaile-Sallenave (Spices and Aromas), *France*, researcher.

Enrique Bellver (En Sevilla), *Spain*, food and wine journalist, executive – Slow Food Seville.

Hocine Benkheira (Either Milk or Fish), *Algeria-France*, lecturer at University of Algiers.

François Bonal (The Origins of Champagne), *France*, wine historian.

Stephen Brook (The Enviable Profession), *Great Britain*, travel and wine writer.

Raymond Buren (The Banquet), *Belgium*, honorary magistrate.

Lesley Chamberlain (Ale Movement, Bar-Restaurant-Bazaar, Venus in the Supermarket), *Great Britain*, author of books on philosophy, travel and cooking.

Daniel Chavarria (The Devil's Avocado), *Cuba*, writer.

Vic Cherikoff (More from Less), *Australia*, scientist, founder of Bush Tucker Supply Australia.

Elisabeth Clift (Pickles), *Great Britain*, cook and innkeeper.

Roz Crowley (The New Ireland), *Ireland*, journalist.

Carlos Delgado (Remember Spain, Without a Tablecloth), *Spain*, vice-president of the Slow Food Movement, editor-in-chief of *Vino y gastronomi*, wine and food writer for *El País*.

Davide Faggioli (Belgian Paradise), *Italy*, researcher.

Wendy Fogarty (Slow Food UK), *Great Britain*, co-ordinator Slow Food UK.

Roger Feuilly (The French Selection), *France*, wine and food writer and executive of Slow Food France.

Sarah Freeman (The Great British Trifle), *Great Britain*, journalist.

Misette Godard (Vinegar and Provence), *France*, journalist, food history academic.

Sylvie Guichard-Anguis (Kindling the Japanese Flame), *France*, expert in Japanese culture and society, freelancer for the Centre National de la Recherche Scientifique.

Sophie Herron (Slow Food Australia), *Australia*, journalist and Slow Food website contributor.

Annie Hubert (Sunday Morning in Limogne, Khao Soy and other Noodles, The Convict's Diet), *France*, director of the Centre National de la Recherche Scientifique, Bordeaux.

John Irving (What a State), *Great Britain*, editor of Slow Food International website and the English edition of Slow magazine.

Michael Jackson (The Post-Industrial Pint), *Great Britain*, journalist, consummate beer and whisky expert.

Julian Jeffs (Sherry), *Great Britain*, journalist and wine writer.

Hugh Johnson (The Queen Bee), *Great Britain*, wine critic, writer and historian.

Radha Kapoor-Sharma (Chutneys), *India, France*, lecturer in comparative and French literature at the University of Delhi.

Manfred Kreiner (5000 Varieties), *Germany*, journalist, expert in consumer and environmental issues, contributor to *Der Spiegel*.

Nelly Krowolski (Shopkeepers and Peddlers), *France*, expert in Asian culture, researcher at the Centre National de la Recherche Scientifique.

Laura Mason (The Poets' Lakes), *Great Britain*, historian of British food.

Clodagh McKenna (Slow Food Ireland), *Ireland*, co-ordinator Slow Food Ireland.

Jørgen Mønster Pedersen (Herring Countries), *Denmark*, teacher.

Laurence Ossipow (Paul's Lunch), *Switzerland*, Neuchâtel University, writer/researcher.

Carlo Petrini (Foreword), *Italy*, founder and president of the Slow Food Movement.

Marco Riva (Mapping What We Eat), *Italy*, professor of food technology at Milan University.

Piero Sardo (Vermouth), *Italy*, wine and food critic, executive – Slow Food Italy.

Regina Sexton (Salt, Fat and Smoke), *Ireland*, food and wine journalist.

Philip Sinsheimer (Falafel), *France*, research fellow at the Ecole des Hautes Etudes en Sciences Sociales in Paris.

Michel Smith (Nursery Slopes, The Revival Route), *France*, wine and food writer.

Grazia Solazzi (Holland, Pilsner and the Others), *Italy*, journalist.

Pier Lorenzo Tasselli (Frozen Fast Food), *Italy*, physicist, executive of Slow Food Italy.

Vito Teti (Chilli Pepper), *Italy*, professor of ethnology at the University of Calabria.

Giorgio Triani (Balsamic Vinegar), *Italy*, sociologist.
Manuel Vázquez Montalbán (A Lifestyle), *Spain*, journalist, essayist and
  novelist.

SLOW FOOD INTERNATIONAL

Slow Food is an international movement which came into being in Paris in
1989. Its head office is in Bra, in Piedmont, in the north of Italy. National
associations have been established in the USA, Italy, Germany and
Switzerland. Slow food has members in 47 countries organized into 620
local Convivia, or Chapters.

A Convivium is a local Slow Food group of members. It stages local events
like taste workshops on food and drink, visits to food producers and
thematic dinners. The Convivia form a lively international network of
knowledge, taste and enjoyment.

You can join Slow Food by contacting the head office (phone: +39 0172
419611 or email: international@slowfood.com) or one of the national
offices:

Italy	+ 39 0172 419 630	info@slowfood.it
Germany	+ 49 (0)251 793 368	info@slowfood.de
Switzerland	+ 41 (0)1 380 3949	info@slowfood.ch
France	+ 33 (0)1 455 19044	info@slowfoodfrance.com
Spain	+ 34 93 3473893	iberica@slowfood.com

Free-Phone numbers:

UK	0800 91 71 232
Austria	0800 28 11 41
Belgium	0800 79 329
Netherlands	0800 022 77 94

Fully paid up membership entitles you to:
• a personal membership card
• five issues of the magazine *Slow*
• the right to attend all events organized by your local convivium and Slow
Food events around the world